Dear mum,

Happy Birthday! Don't try ↄ
drink these all at once ...

Love, Raↄ

◌ **Collins**

SUPER
PLONK

ABOUT THE AUTHOR

Malcolm Gluck is wine correspondent of the *Guardian*. His major hobbies are quaffing, spitting, scribbling and cycling. He follows these pursuits daily.

Collins

MALCOLM GLUCK

SUPER PLONK 2005

THE TOP 1000

First published in 2004 by
Collins, an imprint of
HarperCollins *Publishers*
77–85 Fulham Palace Road
Hammersmith
London W6 8JB

The Collins website address is www.collins.co.uk

09	08	07	06	05	04
6	5	4	3	2	1

Editor: Susan Fleming
Design: Bob Vickers
Indexer: Hilary Bird

A catalogue record for this book is available from the British Library

ISBN 0-00-716041-0

Printed and bound in Great Britain by Clays Ltd, St Ives plc.

To
JAVIER MARIAS,
for writing like wine flows.

. . . a man cannot make him laugh; but that's no
marvel, he drinks no wine.

Falstaff, *Henry IV*, Part II

CONTENTS

ACKNOWLEDGEMENTS

I rely upon my own individual judgement where wine is concerned, but everything else requires a team. I am, then, grateful to publishing director Denise Bates and my editor Susan Fleming. I thank Jane Rose who directs the marketing, Jane Hollyman who manages it, Louise Lawson who organises publicity and my book-signing tour, Nick Ford who runs the sales team, and Bob Vickers who has made such a bold move with the design. My literary agent, Felicity Rubinstein, is also to be thanked. And my debt to my two Sues, Gluck and Bolton, who manage all the data, is enormous.

INTRODUCTION

Those readers who complained that last year's book was too snooty have touched my heart. Although this 2005 edition of the book is still built around the top 1,000 16-point-and-plus superplonks, I also include all the wines from the major retailers which scored 14, 14.5, 15 and 15.5 points (all those below those ratings can be accessed via superplonk.com).

I am very grateful to all those readers who wrote and e-mailed me on this topic, and indeed many others, and to whom I have individually replied. I am also grateful to all those readers who turn out on chilly autumn nights to hear me speak and watch me slurp at bookshops. In this regard, it appears I lead a charmed and lucky life. Not for me (so far) the level of torture, indignity and abuse suffered by the confessing authors in *Mortification*, the splendid collection of horrors edited by Robin Robertson and published by 4th Estate last year. In this book 70 writers, several on book-signing tours (similar to the extensive one I embark on every autumn around the UK), reveal their most embarrassing moments. I am not worthy, I am glad to say, to mingle in such company. My embarrassing moments – certainly any worthy of public revelation – must all be in the future.

However, this is not to say I don't come close to screaming at times or that my path is forever smooth. My book tour of 2003 took me to the giant Borders in

London's sleaziest street (Oxford), Ottakars in Maidenhead, Haywards Heath and Stafford, Waterstones in Leeds, Borders in York, Ottakars Truro, then Borders in Bristol, Swindon and Bournemouth and, phew, Ottakars in Abergavenny (where, touchingly, they said I was the first author who'd ever shown up in town).

What, of course, makes my book signings different from any author's in *Mortification* is that lots of bottles are opened (donated by different, generous retailers to whom I acknowledge a debt). Readers are encouraged to try three whites and three reds. I try to maintain fluency and sobriety as I'm talking, and slobbering, for two hours. So, in a possible reversal of the usual procedure, it is not the author who is tipsy by the end of the evening but the assembled readers. Tipsy readers, in my experience, are always kind to sober authors. Well, judge for yourself.

8th October BORDERS, OXFORD STREET

The tasting/book signing, due to start at 7pm, lacks proper wine glasses (only plastic monstrosities are available), and just twelve bottles of wine have arrived from the sponsoring retailer. It is now just after six, and since hanging around the shop seemed futile I have beaten a retreat to All Saints church in Margaret Street.

I am also surprised to find no tickets have been sold because none were issued.

'No,' had said Ruth, the shop's events organiser when I arrived, 'we don't sell tickets. We never sell tickets for authors' events.'

She was answering my question.

'So how many people do you expect?' I asked.

'Well, we've been tannoying the event all day...'

'So. You don't know.'

In his spectacular All Saints Church, William Butterfield designed, for the cost of a small Victorian African war, north Soho's most congenial retreat. It is a wonderful church contriving in its tiled interior an Arts and Crafts feel but as far as I know unbelievers rarely form 25 per cent of a congregation. But this unbeliever is 25 per cent of a congregation now. Four of us! Is it a portent for the book signing to come? Will my 2003 tour get off to the worst possible start?

I creep as silently as I can out of the church as the service hits a lull, feeling chastened and doom-laden. A table has been set up on my return to Borders, and a couple of assistants are unpacking the plastic tumblers. The bottles of wine are from Sainsbury's and Waitrose. A couple of people wander in. The revolting muzak is turned down but can still be heard on the floors above and below (muzak in a bookshop! these people would play muzak in cemeteries).

A dozen people wander in over the next hour and a half. We sell six books and I sign them with seasonal good will. The hits amongst the wines are Sainsbury's Reserve South African Shiraz and Labeye Viognier/Chardonnay from Waitrose. The Tautavel from Waitrose was sulphuric – 'tom-catty' said one perceptive customer (of both bottles of the same wine).

Overall, the book signing was saved from utter pointlessness by Chi's cheerfulness and Debbie's vivacity. Chi was the Borders assistant who opened the bottles and harried customers. Debbie was a *Guardian* reader from Chiswick: bright, single, cat-loving, vegetarian. I could have kissed her when she bought copies of the book.

9th October OTTAKARS, MAIDENHEAD

I arrive at Paddington Station to chaos. No trains. Hundreds of starved-looking passengers thronging the concourse. This is how the Russian Revolution started, wasn't it? I am told there are signalling problems at Reading.

After five minutes of forlorn hopes becoming forlorner, and my expectation of reaching my destination zero, there is sudden movement towards a single locomotive and from the shouts of exultation I gather that this train, the only one capable of movement so it appears, will actually call at Maidenhead.

The tasting when I finally get there, yet again against my wishes (and instructions), has not been ticketed. This presents us with the reason why a wine author signing must be ticketed: with so much free wine on offer, unless attendees have to fork out for tickets, scores of students and odd layabouts turn up, don't buy the book, drink lots of the wine, and spend all their time nattering to one another about how blessèd life is.

Highlights amongst the Majestic wines were Château d'Acquéria Lirac, Les Fontanelles Syrah, Santa Carolina Chardonnay, a magnificent Casa Lapostolle Cuvée Alexandre Merlot 2000, and a terrific Vasse Felix Margaret River Chardonnay from Western Australia. One of the students remarks that this last wine reminds him of tinned sweetcorn. The most challenging questions concern tasting technique and how important it is to get the whole of the wine to touch all the tastebuds (which why it is vital to swill the wine as if gargling).

I take supper on Maidenhead Station, waiting for the 9.57 (which is several minutes late). It consists of a single chunk of date cake purchased from a surly Indian who insists I give him the right change as he is officially closed. The cost of this splendid repast will, as always, go on my expenses, and thus my publisher is out of pocket to the tune of £1.

The culinary delights of which the book-tour author can avail himself will continue to astonish the reader as this diary progresses and the publisher's generosity grows.

14th October OTTAKARS, HAYWARDS HEATH

The taxi driver who takes me from the station to the town centre refuses to give me a receipt. 'I have no paper. And I need those cards for the evening trade,' he says angrily when I suggest I take one and he scribble on it. I retort then in that case I cannot pay. He finally agrees to fill in a page torn out from my notebook. I wish him a busy evening filled with happy drunks full of bilious curry.

A customer at the bookshop tells me he has written *The Knight of the Whistle*, a biography of a local 93-year old football referee. The author is a local newspaperman. He enjoys drinking the Villa Maria Riesling 2002 with its screwcap. The other wines are Porcupine Ridge Sauvignon Blanc 2003, Catena Chardonnay 2001, Fairview Goats do Roam 2001/2, Southern Right Pinotage 2001/2, and Radford Dale Shiraz 2002. All New World, note; one Kiwi, an Argentine, and four South Africans.

There is wine to spare. The shop has sold 40 tickets (eureka! they sold tickets!).

11th November WATERSTONES, LEEDS

The Leeds signing turns out to be the best yet. It's always like this at this Waterstones: terrific staff make the difference and the manager and his mates are old hands. The wines – the list of which I have unaccountably lost or had stolen from me by a jealous rival (I admit the former theory is too fantastic to hold water) – inspire lots of questions from a lively and informed crowd. I learned something too: which is that women see more shades of colour as well as sensing more flavours (and smelling more nuances of aroma) than men do.

Did I not say this was a cultured and civilised bookshop? Having, prior to the tasting, discovered a newly published book in the history section – *The Culture of Defeat* by Wolfgang Schivelbusch – they present me with a copy as a thank-you present for such a successful evening (and those wines helped! and I have lost the list...I mean had it filched). It has been translated from the German; and a reading of the first chapter, before being called to perform, inspires the thought, I am sure borrowed from somewhere, that a translation is like a lover – when it is handsome it is not faithful (and if it is faithful it is ugly).

For dinner I am expected at Simply Heathcote's. This proves to be a triumphant marriage of British cooking and Chilean wine. My dish of local black pudding and duck with a bottle of Errazuriz Reserve Cabernet Franc turns out to be pretty nigh perfect.

12th November BORDERS, YORK

I introduce myself to Valerie Gourdin, who is organising the event, but she fails to understand my French. Once she has grasped that the man standing before her is not trying to pick her up but her author she is charming. A thirsty crowd has gathered, and I run through the wines, talk about the book, and answer questions on everything from cosmic strings to marriage guidance (it pays to be versatile when one is a wine writer). The wines? They were Las Colinas Reserve Cabernet/Carmenere 2001, Radcliffes

Corbières Mont Tauch 2002, Sainsbury's Reserve
Selection South African Shiraz 2001, Villa Wolf Pinot
Gris 2002, Argento Reserve Chardonnay 2001, and
Oyster Bay Sauvignon Blanc 2002, the screwcap of
which causes some measure of interest (as does the
wine itself, for it is clearly the most sensual of the
evening).

Two ladies, one of whom I discover is a sex
therapist, invite me to join them across the road for a
drink when we finish, but I am late for my dinner
appointment at Melton's in Scarcroft Road.

18th November OTTAKARS, TRURO

Lunch on the train is courtesy of the Sainsbury's
Metro store at Paddington Station. Why could not a
first-class buffet be so generous and interesting? I eat
dates, Emmental cheese and an apple. *The Times*
crossword is annoyingly easy and we arrive at Truro
half-an-hour later than scheduled.

I have a few hours before the book signing and
so I take in the stained-glass windows of Truro's busy
and workmanlike cathedral. The windows, though
they depict the usual saints and sinners, also include
representations of Dante, Handel, Isaac Newton,
Queen Victoria and even Savonarola and Alfred the
Great. One window commemorates the martydom of
St Pancras, who was a 14-year-old Phrygian (killed by
order of Diocletian in 304 AD). I wonder how many
commuters realise that St Pancras is named after a 14
year old?

The signing at Ottakars is lively and well attended and many of the questions thoughtful and provocative. What is complexity? How can an alcoholic liquid be truly complex?

My definition, and use, of the term implies that the wine does not take a direct passage from nose to throat but meanders, takes by-ways, shows us glimpses of other routes (via strands of aroma, flavour and, above all, texture).

For dinner I have been invited to be a guest of a restaurant called Sevens, fifty yards up the street from the hotel. Its owner, David White, is a *Guardian* reader (and a professional musician), and he is keen to see me fed and watered (though he has an engagement that night with one of the symphony orchestras).

19th November BORDERS, BRISTOL

The taxi to Truro station, extremely antique, is driven by a charming pixie chauffeuse (complete with bobbled hat). Her get-up is in aid of a children's charity and she donates my tip to it.

The train I board stops at St Austell, Par, Lostwithiel, Bodmin, Liskeard, Menheniot, St Germans, Saltash, Devonport, Plymouth, Ivybridge, Totnes, Newton Abbott, Teignmouth, Dawlish, Exeter St Davids, Taunton, Bridgwater, Highbridge, Weston-Super-Mare, Worle, Yatton, Nailsea and Backwell, arriving at Bristol Temple Meads after four hours and five minutes.

One of humankind's tenderest conceits is that one's train has commenced its journey at the station of embarkation. This kind of journey inspires reflections like that.

Borders is opposite the site where Friese-Green, the inventor of the moving picture camera, served his apprenticeship (between 1869-1875) as a photographer. I daresay nowadays you could go from 'prentice to pro in six months.

The book signing gets under way and a lively session ensues in which some 70 souls and I drink our way through several Sainsbury's bottles plus a special sweetie from Great Western Wines. The Sainsbury's wines are Graham Beck Chardonnay 2002 £5.99, Réserve St Marc Sauvignon Blanc, Vin de Pays d'Oc 2002 £4.03, Kendermanns Pinot Grigio 2002 £4.03, Prahova Valley Reserve Pinot Noir 2000 £3.99, Concha y Toro Casillero del Diablo Shiraz 2001 £4.99, and the own-label Reserve Selection South African Shiraz 2001£5.49. The special sweet wine is Las Casas de Toqui Late Harvest Sémillon 1999, but of the six half-bottles supplied one is corked and so 70 of us do not get much in our glasses but what little we do get does stun us as this Chilean dessert wine is magnificent (rating 18 points).

After the tasting I walk to Fishworks in Whiteladies Road; for a city with a sizeable Caribbean-derived population and, one assumes, town councillors, it is gratifying that politically correct bureaucrats have not changed it to Allpersons Avenue or some such. I have a glass of Assodi Fiore Chamay

Longhe du Braida Rochetta Tamorro (get your tongue round that, duckie!) with some winkles and cockles. This is followed by prawns and then several frighteningly huge razor clams of sufficient girth and concavity as to suggest they were detached from the fronts of bulldozers. With them I drink Il Baciale Monferrato Rosso Braida. Both wines, note, from the same winery, Braida in Piedmont. Before he died Giacomo Bologna, the proprietor, made a great reputation for himself and his wines (which I have been unable to confirm until now).

20th November BORDERS, SWINDON

Plan to spend the day in Bristol and catch afternoon train to Swindon. At the docks I visit the dry-dock rehabilitation of the SS Great Britain, the Concorde of its day. Designed by Brunel in the earlier part of Victoria's reign it was, so they say, the 'World's First Great Ocean Liner' and has been gradually restored since 1970 when it was towed, at the expense of a billionaire called Hayward, to Bristol's western docks from the Falkland Islands. The islanders had towed it out to some offshore rocks and sunk it (some years previously) as it was cluttering up their marine views. Hayward's money, along with public subscription and now lavish lottery funding, will see the ship, a magnificent piece of history as important as any complete dinosaur fossil, one day fully restored though not, one presumes, sea-worthy. The engine, designed by Brunel's dad, is a massive masterpiece and must have been awesome in its day (well, it is pretty awesome now with its arrangement of pistons and rods and brooding sense of deadly mechanical intent).

The train to Swindon takes no time. It is raining and the taxi seems to take ages to reach the out-of-town complex which accommodates Borders, a large electrical retailer, a sports shop, a Boots and a Wal-Mart/Asda. I buy some cheap tennis balls at Wal-Mart (proper ones, Slazenger, but a third less expensive than any pro-shop).

The signing at Borders takes some time to get going, not helped by wines which, according to the Asda wine advisor who comes with them, his manager had insisted on sending us instead of choosing high pointers from the book. Thus we get a pink Zinfandel which no-one will admit to liking (I loathe the wine) and other bottles which this manager, presumably against his wine advisor's advice, simply wanted to get shot of. One or two of the wines aren't bad, though, and we manage to have a good laugh together, the customers and me. A fair few copies of the book are signed and I get a train to Paddington with a smile on my face.

25th November BORDERS, BOURNEMOUTH

Arrive at the Miramar Hotel, on East Cliff Road. A player piano is belting out sweet custardy music. A vast bevy of geriatric ladies, exquisitely turned out, are finishing lunch in a side room.

There is a rack of Oxfam style clothes behind the reception desk. An old lady up a metal ladder is pinning up Christmas decorations. The receptionist cannot find my reservation. I hear another receptionist tell someone on the phone 'a sea-view room is ten pounds'. My reservation is found. Room 105. I go up. Surely that receptionist meant '*another* ten pounds'?

I stroll down to the bookshop from the hotel. Thresher has supplied the wines: Château La Clotte-Fontane Cremailh, Coteaux du Languedoc 2001, Errazuriz Merlot 2001, River Route Merlot Cabernet Sauvignon 2001, Kendermann's Organic White, Villa Maria Sauvignon Blanc 2002 and Torres Viña Esmeralda 2002 – these last two being deliciously screwcapped. Two bottles of the La Clotte-Fontane, having ascertained their corks had caused no spoilage, are poured into a jug to await further developments.

And so the evening commences. I offer a glass of the Kendermann's Organic White to someone and she says 'Oh, I don't drink. I'm diabetic.' A man wanders in shouting and begins to listen to music behind me on headphones provided. The cd department is adjacent. He quietens down after a while and when he tries to grab some booze he is hustled away.

After we have gone through the wines, I produce the jug of La Clotte-Fontane. Everyone has drunk it from the bottle and I ask how they like it now it's had a few hours to take in air. There is general astonishment that two hours of total breathing has produced an even more dramatic, aromatic, sensual, exciting red wine. The questions begin to flow along with the wine and I sign a pile of books.

A woman wishing to deal in wine hands me a bottle from Wurttenburg. What do I think? I open the wine for everyone. I can hardly carry a bottle around with me (as she seems to expect). I ask for views of the wine. 'Rubbish,' shouts a punter. The woman looks awkward. I tell her I really cannot comment in depth on this wine, which is drinkable but very far from being Wurttenburg's finest (which are almost never exported from Germany anyway), as I am a wine writer and not a consultant.

Two students enquire 'Any wine?' 'If you buy a book,' I reply. They wander off. I slip them a half-empty bottle before I leave.

A man from a local organisation says to me, as I depart, 'More people have come to see you tonight, on a rainy evening, than came to see the town's Christmas lights we switched on last Sunday – and we had fireworks.' Humbled by this, I beat a retreat and go to my dinner.

26th November A BOURNEMOUTH MORNING

Kipper with the *Guardian*. Both are an acquired taste and bones must be spat out from both. I can now appreciate why a sea-view room is only ten quid. Only three people seem to be staying at the hotel which probably boasts 50 rooms (unless everyone else has breakfast in their rooms or kips in until the lunch gong goes).

There is an entertaining old couple at the next table. The waitress comes up and wishes the pair good morning for the second time (having already done it once as they entered the dining room).

'Bonjour,' says the man, wearily.

The wife looks irritated, then sympathetic, then resigned. They order tea. The waitress promises to return soon.

'Eggs. Poached. I think,' says the wife dreamily, consulting the card.

'Oeufs pochés,' mutters the man.

The wife sighs. Tea arrives. The waitress strikes a heroic pose to take their order.

'Poached eggs and bacon please,' says the woman.

'Fried eggs for me, and sausage and bacon.'

These things arrive in a twinkle. Next time I lift up my head from the crossword and my kipper debris, the pair of them are tucking in.

'Can we have brown toast? And butter?' calls the woman.

'Beurre,' mutters the man.

The wife takes a deep breath. It is a tribute to the mildness of the climate this does not kill her immediately. Outside, the sun makes a brave, very British stab at shining.

The bloke was still practising his French when I left.

27th November OTTAKARS, ABERGAVENNY

The taxi from Abergavenny station takes me to the
wrong hotel. It is the Clytha Arms I want. I am not
charged for the mistake. The driver has a literary turn
of mind. He has, he tells me, read Mickey Spillane.

The signing/tasting at Ottakar's turns out to be
a splendid affair, one of the most satisfying. Waitrose
has supplied some splendid bottles and the crowd is
combative, intelligent and rewardingly inquisitive. I
cover a lot of ground on wine and health, cork
problems, wine and food. We taste our way through
Norton Reserve Malbec 2000, Concha y Toro Merlot
2002, Da Luca Primitivo/Merlot Tarantino 2002
(a 17-pointer at £3.99), Trincaria Inzolia/Cataratto
2002, Gracia Reserva Chardonnay 2001, and
Basserman-Jordan Riesling 2002. The first and the
last of these wines both, after the tasting from bottles,
being presented in jugs and, as on other occasions,
both wines are hugely improved after a few hours of
breathing.

The other experiment we try is the same wine
from a normal pub glass, the so-called Paris goblet,
and then from a large so-called Burgundy glass. The
difference is dramatic. One woman, tasting the
Norton, says 'The wine in the little glass tasted crap.
In this glass it's wonderful.'

We also find one of the wines has been spoiled
by its cork and a useful debate ensues about cork taint
and, for the first time, many of those present begin
the grasp the vicious subtlety of the problem.

Delightfully, among the crowd is the landlord and landlady of the Clytha Arms, Andrew and Bev, and they tell me that their daughter is cooking up a storm for my dinner later.

This is enjoyed, in the cosy dining room of the place, after I have tasted Felinfoel bitter beer to give me a liquid bridge between the wines at the bookshop and those I want to experience on the pub's wine list. These latter are a white wine from Monmouth, 1999 Monnow Valley White with my first course of mussels with garlic and pine nuts, and Domaine Rocher Cairanne 2000 with rabbit and wild mushrooms with herb dumplings. (My daughter, in her carry-cot, received her first smell of roast garlic, truffles and wild mushrooms under the tables at Monsieur Rocher's London restaurant when he had one years ago. His Cairanne, from his own vineyard where he now lives, is wonderfully rich and herby and finely textured.)

Afterwards, a sucker for more work, I try the new Nerola wines from Miguel Torres in the bar with Andrew and Bev's family. Nice bunch (the family, not so much the wines).

28th November BACK TO HOME

At Abergavenny station as I await the train to Newport, some youngsters are smoking cigarettes on the opposite platform. The announcer gives us verbal laverbread over the tannoy and workmen hammer away at refurbishing the bogs. So this is rural life.

Voice on train tannoy: 'Sorry to say we've run out of hot water for hot drinks. But we have just telephoned for a new tank.' To greet us at Didcot Parkway? To run over any passengers who alight? These fellows running the railways are full of ideas to crush passengers.

The crossword has a comforting, and possibly portentous, clue: 'Little Malcolm might be made to stop talking' (4, 2). The answer, of course, is 'clam up'.

And so I shall. At least until my next UK tour comes around.

HOW THIS BOOK WORKS

Last year, I revised my whole approach to this book, except in one crucial aspect: value for money is still the essential criterion for any wine's inclusion.

I am still the only wine writer who rates wines on this humane basis and I suspect I always will be. For me, there is no romance in expensive wine unless the liquid in the bottle is sublime.

The usual suspects are to be found here. The supermarkets are Aldi, Asda, Booths, Budgens, the Co-op, Marks & Spencer, Morrison's, Safeway, Sainsbury's, Somerfield, Tesco and Waitrose. The wine shops are Majestic, Oddbins and the 1st Quench Group (which includes Thresher), but you will also note e-tailers, smaller merchants and such important regional merchants as Yapp Bros.

You will note also that I have done away with describing all wines under 16 points. The wines rating 14, 14.5, 15, 15.5 points are listed only. The website, superplonk.com, carries details and ratings of all the wines I taste, but the book concentrates on the top raters.

Nothing could be simpler. But immediately you ask: how does this rating system work? This is how.

HOW I RATE A WINE. WHAT MAKES A SUPERPLONK A SUPERPLONK

It is worth repeating: value for money is my single unwavering focus. I drink with my readers' pockets in my mouth. I do not see the necessity of paying a lot for a bottle of everyday drinking wine and only rarely do I consider it worth paying a high price for, say, a wine for a special occasion or because you want to experience what a so-called 'grand' wine may be like.

I do taste expensive wines regularly. I do not, regularly, find them worth the money. That said, there are some pricey bottles in these pages. They are here because the wines are genuinely worth every penny (which is what the definition of a superplonk is). A wine of magnificent complexity, thrilling fruit, superb aroma, great depth and finesse is worth drinking. Such a wine challenges the intellect as much as the palate and its value lies, like a great theatrical performance or outstanding novel, in its unforgettableness. I will rate it highly. Even though it costs a lot, the lot it costs is justified.

20 points Life rarely throws up perfection. Indeed, some aesthetes regard true beauty as always revealing a small flaw. I do not. There is no flaw in a 20-point wine. It has perfect balance, finesse, flavour and finish – dull terms to describe the sum of an unforgettable experience. A perfect wine is also perfectly affordable. That is not to say (necessarily) £2.99 or even £4.99, but a sum related to common sense. Even if such a wine costs £100 it is still worth 20 points and the possible pain of acquisition. I exclude from this auction-antiques which cost thousands of pounds, for these are the perverted passions of wine collectors and the prices paid rarely bear any relation to the quality of the liquid in the bottles. No wine is truly worth thousands of pounds and no civilised individual would pay it.

19 points What's a point between friends? Or between one wine and another? 19 points represents a superb wine of towering individuality and impact. Almost perfect and well worth the expense (even if it is an expensive bottle), such a wine will flood the senses with myriad smells, tastes and flavours and provide a tantalising glimpse, whilst it lasts, of the sheer textured genius of great wine. Such a wine is individual, rich, subtle yet potent, and overwhelmingly delicious. It can start, and finish, a conversation.

18 points This is an excellent wine but lacking that ineffable sublimity of richness and complexity to achieve the very highest rating. Such a wine offers superb drinking and thundering good value and it must exhibit a remarkably well-textured richness. True, I do emphasise texture above other aspects of complexity (like all those fruits some tasters are determined to find in a wine), and here the texture is so well married to the acids and sugars that it is all of a piece. Such a wine is remarkable, immensely drinkable, complex and compelling.

17 points An exciting, well-made wine, almost invariably hugely affordable, which offers real glimpses of multi-layered richness. It will demonstrate individuality and incisiveness and it will offer a seductive mouthfeel and sense of luxury. It may be a more immediate wine than those rating higher, but it will still linger in the memory the day after it is drunk – for it will have given a delightful and impressive performance.

16 points This is a very good wine indeed. Good enough for any dinner party and any level of drinker (with the possible exception of those most toffee-nosed of snobs for whom pleasure usually comes associated with a fat price-tag). Not necessarily an expensive wine is implied here but it will be a terrifically drinkable, satisfying and multi-dimensional one. It will be properly balanced and often be excellent with particular kinds of dishes (which it enhances).

ALDI

Aldi Stores Ltd,
Holly Lane,
Atherstone,
Warwickshire cv9 2sq

Tel: (01827) 711800
Fax: (01827) 710899
Customer help-line: (08705) 134 262

Website: www.aldi.com

For Aldi wines 14 points and under visit
www.superplonk.com

16.5

RED £2.99

Casa Alvares Cabernet Sauvignon NV　ITALY
Chunky, very open-hearted, even buxom fruit with
classy tannins which plummily linger.

16.5

RED £4.99

Ile La Forge Cabernet Sauvignon,　FRANCE
Vin de Pays d'Oc 2003
Very lengthy tannins here, of serious demeanour. Has
succulence yet real dry tannic firmness. A lovely,
serene, confident, caressing Cabernet.

16.5

RED £4.99

Ile La Forge Syrah, Vin de Pays d'Oc 2003　FRANCE
Complex, rich, multi-layered and hence serious, but
also delightfully playful and soft to quaff. The berries
are genteel yet firm, with a charred undertone plus
licorice. A truly terrific liquid.

16.5

RED £4.99

La Forge Estate Merlot, Domaines Paul Mas,　FRANCE
Languedoc 2002
Smoky intensity, hint of cracked leather.

16.5

RED £4.99

La Forge Estate Cabernet Sauvignon,　FRANCE
Domaines Paul Mas, Languedoc 2002
Tangy blackberries, hint of grilled raspberry, firm
touch on the tannic finish.

16   RED £8.99

Château Mérissac, St-Emilion 2000   FRANCE
Classy richness, savoury berries with a touch of black
cherry. Excellent lift the wine gets from its roasted
tannins and a hint of herbiness.

16   RED £4.99

Ile La Forge Merlot, Vin de Pays d'Oc 2003   FRANCE
Interesting clash of styles in the same liquid. Offers a

There is something happening at the edges of the world of wine
retailing which I could never have predicted: the transformation of
the wine buyer into nothing more than a glorified fag buyer. The
individual who buys cigarettes for a retailer needs know nothing of
the history of Monsieur Nicotin, the difference between Turkish
and Virginia, and may even believe that a filter tip is something
the jockey passes down to the punter. The fag buyer hardly needs
to even travel or even smoke. Why? Because all cigarettes are
brands. The professional buyer of them merely follows fashion and
stocks what is demanded by the customers or can be promoted.
The shock (to me) is the realisation that we are in danger with
some retailers of approaching a similar situation with wine. The
UK's first tee-total wine buyer is probably being interviewed for the
very job right now. For who needs to drink wine to buy the brands
which are rapidly becoming so prominent on certain wine retailers'
shelves? No wonder so many wine writers are facing extinction
when their jobs have become otiose; when did you last meet the
tobacco correspondent of a newspaper?

brusque tannic side and a very fresh, juicy, soft-berried dimension.

16

WHITE SPARKLING £2.79

Moscato Spumante NV   ITALY

A brilliant torrid-weather aperitif of low alcohol (7%) but high sensuality and perfumed deliciousness. Really grapey, touch sweet, but in the right circumstances, a glass or two is sheer pleasure.

16

WHITE £2.79

Montepulciano d'Abruzzo 2003   ITALY

Astonishingly good value for money and absolutely spot on: there's even a hint of tobacco to the fruit which is earthy yet generous.

16

RED £3.99

Naoussa (100% Xynomavro) 2002   GREECE

Excellent backbone of smoky tannin to rich, nicely tanned berries. Has texture and class and a suggestion of chocolate on the finish.

16

FORTIFIED £6.99

Souza LBV Port 1998   PORTUGAL

A real quaffing port at a bargain price. It has sweet berries, hints of ripe damsons and blackberries, but there is an over-toning of tannins which give it real class. True, it's hardly in the class of great vintage port, but for £6.99 this is a terrific LBV.

OTHER WINES 15.5 AND UNDER

15.5

RED £3.99
Charles de Monteney Merlot, Bordeaux 2003   FRANCE

RED £3.99
Goumenissa 2002 (70% Xynomavro,30% Negoska) GREECE

RED £3.99
Hacienda San José Malbec 2002   ARGENTINA

WHITE £3.99
Hacienda San José Sauvignon Blanc 2003   ARGENTINA

RED £8.99
La Closerie de Malescasse, Haut-Médoc,   FRANCE
Bordeaux 2001

15

RED £3.49
African Rock Pinotage 2003   SOUTH AFRICA

WHITE £2.99
Badgers Creek Australian White Wine   AUSTRALIA

WHITE £2.49
Budavar Chardonnay 2002   HUNGARY
Screwcap.

RED £2.49
Budavar Merlot 2003   ROMANIA

RED £3.99
Evolution Old Vine Shiraz NV   AUSTRALIA

RED   £4.99

Morgon Domaine des Montillets 2001   FRANCE

WHITE   £3.49

Mayrah Estates Chardonnay NV   AUSTRALIA

WHITE SPARKLING   £5.49

Philippe Michel Crémant de Jura Brut NV   FRANCE

14.5

WHITE   £2.79

Cape Spring Chenin Blanc 2003   FRANCE

RED   £2.99

Château Selection Claret Bordeaux 2001   FRANCE
Screwcap.

RED   £3.49

Mayrah Estates Cabernet Sauvignon NV   AUSTRALIA

WHITE   £2.29

Solitus Bella Viña NV   SPAIN

RED   £8.99

Siran de Margaux 2001   FRANCE

WHITE   £3.99

Monteney Gascogne 2003   FRANCE

14

RED   £3.49

African Rock Cabernet Sauvignon 2003   SOUTH AFRICA

RED   £2.99

Badgers Creek Australian Red Wine   AUSTRALIA

RED (25cl) £1.99
Cabernet Sauvignon 2003   CHILE
Screwcap.

RED £3.99
Hacienda San José Malbec 2001   ARGENTINA

WHITE £3.99
Mondiale Sauvignon Blanc NV   SOUTH AFRICA

RED (25cl) £1.99
Merlot 2003   CHILE
Screwcap.

WHITE £2.49
Niersteiner Gates Domtal Spätlese 2002   GERMANY

RED £3.99
Nemea 2001 (100% Agiorgitiko)   GREECE

WHITE £3.99
Pinot Grigio Villa Malizia 2003   ITALY

RED (25cl) £1.99
Shiraz 2002   AUSTRALIA
Screwcap.

ASDA

Head Office:
Asda House,
Southbank,
Great Wilson Street,
Leeds LS11 5AD

Tel: (0500) 100055 (230 branches nationwide)
Fax: (0113) 2417732

Website: www.asda.co.uk

For Asda wines of 14 points and under visit
www.superplonk.com

17

Alsace Gewürztraminer,   FRANCE
Réserve du Baron de Turckheim 2002
Staggeringly delicious smoky lemon/pear/lychee
spiciness, very controlled and fresh (not smoky). A
superb example of Alsace genius. A unique white
wine.

17

Drylands Riesling 2002   NEW ZEALAND
Superbly oily pear, pineapple, lychee and grapefruit to
finish. Wonderful now – perfectly mature and
sensual.

17

Peter Lehmann Shiraz 2001   AUSTRALIA
One of Australia's most excitingly perfumed and
brilliantly textured Shirazes under seven quid.

17

Villa Maria Private Bin Chardonnay 2002   NEW ZEALAND
Screwcap. Has such beautiful footwork as it dances on
the tongue with subtlety, leafy melon and lemon. So
calm, so insouciant, so classy.
Also at Oddbins, Waitrose.

17

Villa Maria Private Bin Gewürztraminer 2003   NEW ZEALAND
Screwcap. One of the most delicately delicious
Gewürzes I have tasted. Such precocity! Such wit!

17

Red £5.47

Concha y Toro Casillero del Diablo CHILE
Cabernet Sauvignon 2003
Massively chewy berries of huge charm, concentration
and class. One of South America's most agreeably dry
yet tongue-tingling Cabs.
Also at Budgens, Tesco.

16.5

WHITE £5.52

Booarra Chenin Blanc 2002 AUSTRALIA
Superb Chenin of great class and textured clout.
Offers a delicious chalky sub-text to its novel
pineapple, smoky pear fruit.

16.5

WHITE £4.99

Domaine Caude Val Sauvignon Blanc, FRANCE
Domaines Paul Mas, Languedoc 2003
Screwcap. Delicious concentrated gooseberry, slightly
chewy.

16.5

RED £4.99

Fat Bastard Syrah, Fat Bastard Wine Company, FRANCE
Languedoc 2002
Superb texture with hints of chocolate to the tannins.

16.5

WHITE £4.94

Forresters Petit Chenin 2003 SOUTH AFRICA
An utterly superbly well-balanced, smoky citrus and
concentrated, gooseberry/pineapple white wine.
Hugely classy, deeply delicious.

16.5   WHITE £7.98

Grant Burge Zerk Sémillon 2002   AUSTRALIA
18 points in 2007. Classic Aussie Sémillon offering
more appeal and class than many a white Burgundy at
five times the price. Gently vegetal citrus and apricot
(very subtle) with superb texture.

16.5   RED £6.98

Graham Beck Coastal Shiraz 2002   SOUTH AFRICA
So gloriously thick and rich, calm, firm and hugely
classy. Controlled spice, herbs, chocolate and wholly
well berried up to its neck.

16.5   RED £7.97

Hardy's Oomoo Shiraz 2001   AUSTRALIA
The label alone is worth the money and the liquid
doubles that. This is a startlingly vivid Shiraz of deep
smoky berries, herbs, chocolate and fine tannins.

16.5   WHITE £4.48

Lindemans Bin 65 Chardonnay 2003   AUSTRALIA
Always one of Oz's finest under-a-fiver Chardonnays,
in this vintage it has some added finesse.
Also at Tesco.

16.5   WHITE £4.98

La Chasse du Pape Chardonnay/Viognier 2003   FRANCE
A beautifully conceived artefact of apricot, dry melon,
citrus and a touch of tannin to keep it dry and very
prim (yet flavoursome). Remarkably elegant yet rich in
personality.

16.5
FRANCE

**Paul Mas Viognier, Domaines Paul Mas,
Languedoc 2003**
Very crisp, but beautiful cellar-worthy specimen.
Lime/apricot.

16.5
WHITE £8.98
AUSTRALIA

Rosemount 'Hill of Gold' Chardonnay 2001
Delicious class in a glass here. The liquid offers an
oily underlay to the thick pile carpeting of pear, melon
and citrus peel and is triumphantly sure of itself.

16.5
WHITE £6.99
SOUTH AFRICA

Sauvignon Blanc 2003
Superbly textured gooseberry and under-ripe melon
acidity.

On corks and corkscrews (No. 1)

There is an exquisite torture involved in wine. It recalls the Arctic
British winters of years ago, before the electronic starter motor
was invented. Families would clamber aboard the old Austin and
in their hearts would fester the dread that this would be one of
those times when the starting handle would be unable to budge
the ice-cold engine and so it would refuse to start. I feel like this
every time I order a bottle of wine in a restaurant. Will the wine be
healthy? Will it be tainted by its cork? Or will it just have been
rendered dull by that one and a quarter inches of tree bark? Will I
have to send it back? Will the wine waiter be a prat and
unsympathetic?

16.5   WHITE £6.01
Serafino Chardonnay 2003   AUSTRALIA
Scott Robinson, who makes this wine, is a sexy beast
with knobby knees. His Chardonnay is much more
refined.

16.5   RED £8.98
Serafino Shiraz Reserve 2001   AUSTRALIA
Intense savoury ripeness of great depth and spicy
insistence. It really is a marvellously vivacious,
sensual, rich, deep all-embracing red wine.

16.5   WHITE £7.95
Tabali Special Reserva Chardonnay 2003   CHILE
Remarkably affable fruit of rich Ogen melon, creamy
pear and a touch of faraway spice. Quite superbly
lissome and lithe.

16.5   RED £5.52
Trio Merlot 2001   CHILE
Superbly chewy, slightly leathery plums with tanned
berries of litheness and concentration.

16.5   WHITE £4.99
Argento Chardonnay 2003   ARGENTINA
Superbly textured, oily fruit with that high-class, high-
wine act being fruity, dry, tangy and complex all at the
same time.
Also at Budgens, Majestic, Somerfield, Tesco.

16.5

WHITE £4.97
CHILE

**Concha y Toro Casillero del Diablo
Chardonnay 2003**
So deliciously creamy and taste-bud caressing.
Also at Budgens, Majestic.

16.5

RED £8.58
CHILE

Errazuriz Max Reserva Cabernet Sauvignon 2000
Very jammy but immensely lengthy tannins give it
backbone and oomph. Has a candied cherry opening
which becomes dark and spicy.
Also at Budgens.

16.5

RED £5.96
SOUTH AFRICA

The Wolf Trap 2002
Wonderful chocolate-edged berries and cherries with
complex acids and tannins. Superbly complete, deep,
well roasted fruit.
Also at Somerfield.

16.5

RED £8.94
CHILE

Coyam 2001
A superb blend of 34% Cabernet Sauvignon, 30%
Merlot, 22% Carmenere, 12% Syrah, 3% Mourvèdre. It
has great fruit yet it's not overdone or crude. The
tannins are firm and elegant. The berries are very
expansive. (Hawk-eyed readers will note the
percentages given to the grape varieties add up to 101%,
nevertheless this is what the wine claims. It must be
part of the Asda/Wal-Mart added-value mentality.)
Also at The Wine Society.

16

WHITE £4.48

Asda Australian Chardonnay Reserve 2003   AUSTRALIA
Unites firm melony richness with a citrussy freshness
and the result is a stunning level of class for the
money.

16

WHITE £3.74

Asda South African Chardonnay 2003   SOUTH AFRICA
Terrific value for money here – with lovely dry melon,
a hint of citrus, a touch of pear.

16

WHITE £9.57

Asda Chablis 1er Cru 2002   FRANCE
First-class white Burgundy. Has a wonderful chalky
(mineral) richness and demure dryness of real class.

16

DESSERT WHITE £3.28

Asda Moscatel de Valencia NV   SPAIN
Screwcap. Has a hint of bitter/sweet marmalade to the
sweet honey.

16

WHITE £4.01

Andrew Peace Mighty Murray Chardonnay 2003   AUSTRALIA
Has some real creamy class to it.

16

WHITE £4.96

Anakena Chardonnay 2002   CHILE
Classily dry and stately Chardonnay of charm and
concentration. Crisp finish to lovely, subtle
melon/lemon with a vague smoky undertone.

16

RED £5.98

Anakena Cabernet Sauvignon Reserve 2002 CHILE
Plummy ripeness with a touch of tobacco. Ripe
tannins, dry and fulfilled.

16

WHITE £9.98

Bonterra Rousanne 2002 USA
Delicious muted peach and apricot with a hint of
raspberry. For all that, it's refreshingly different and a
treat of a glugger.

16

RED £8.98

Bonterra Zinfandel 2001 USA
Superb textured, smoky berries of great exuberance
and vivacity. Stylish, rich, food-eager, this is a bustling
red of charm and warmth.

16

WHITE £5.02

Brown Brothers Chenin Blanc 2003 AUSTRALIA
What a delicious pineappley and soft pear wine.

16

WHITE £5.00

Booarra Sémillon 2003 AUSTRALIA
Screwcap. Tangy, ripe, fresh, gooseberry and citrus
spicy, fish dish wine.

On corks and corkscrews (No. 2)
The corkscrew's obituary is being written. It is entitled: Fed-Up
With Being Screwed By Duff Corks, Drinkers Got Screwcapped.

16

RED £5.98

Booarra Grenache 2002   AUSTRALIA

Screwcap. Interesting sour cherry and plum fruit,
juicy but a miracle of dryness on the finish.

16

WHITE £5.97

Concha y Toro Trio Sauvignon Blanc 2003   CHILE

Dry, very dry under-ripe gooseberry.
Also at Booths.

16

RED £6.97

Columbia Crest Two Vines Shiraz 2001   USA

A big juicy, chocolate-drenched, plump, buxom red of
great form to drink with casserole-type food.

16

WHITE DESSERT (half bottle) £4.02

Cranswick Botrytis Sémillon 2002   AUSTRALIA

18.5 points in 2012. Superb honey with hint of spicy
peach and pineapple. Wonderful with ice-cream.

16

RED £2.97

Asda Chilean Cabernet Sauvignon 2003   CHILE

Delicious tannins bring an exciting display to a
resounding climax and the berries all sing in unison.

16

WHITE £4.44

Asda Sauvignon Blanc Reserve 2003   CHILE

Terrific Thai food wine. Great citric finish.

16

RED £4.98

Asda Cabernet Sauvignon Reserva 2002   CHILE

Very chocolate-drenched, yet dry.

16   RED £7.76

Château Prieuré-Les-Tours Graves 2000   FRANCE

A deliciously classy claret with superbly well-grilled
berries with bustling tannins.

16   RED £5.47

Concho y Toro Casillero del Diablo Shiraz 2003   CHILE

Earthy herbs are submerged under richly berried fruit
with a good tannic backbone.

16   WHITE £4.92

Douglas Green Sauvignon Blanc 2003   SOUTH AFRICA

Remarkably toothsome, making some concessions to
Sauvignon's austerity but saving them by a finish of
plumply subtle melon/gooseberry.

16   WHITE £5.98

Danie de Wet Chardonnay 2002   SOUTH AFRICA

Superb unwooded fruit of great class, bite, tanginess
and sheer silky style.
Also at Somerfield.

16   RED £5.96

Errazuriz Carmenere 2002   CHILE

You see, it has a mark of good wine; sweet fruit with dry
tannins so the final effect is classy.

16   RED £5.56

Errazuriz Cabernet Sauvignon 2002   CHILE

Superbly chewy berries: chocolate and hint of spice.
Also at Somerfield.

16

RED £5.48
CHILE

Errazuriz Cabernet Sauvignon Estate 2001
Delicious dry spice and roasted raisins.

16

RED £9.98
USA

Gallo Coastal Cabernet Sauvignon 2001
On this showing Gallo's best under a tenner. Real
class to the textured berries, sensual tannins, herby
undertone, even a hint of licorice.

16

RED £6.48
FRANCE

Gerard Bertrand Coteaux du Languedoc,
Les Terrasses Quartenaires 2001
Intense grilled chocolate on the finish. Leading this
finale, the berries express themselves dryly and very
characterfully.

16

WHITE £4.02
AUSTRALIA

Lindemans Cawarra Colombard/
Chardonnay 2003
Remarkably firm, delicious, dry yet layered and lithe.

16

RED £4.82
AUSTRALIA

Lindemans Bin 55 Shiraz/Cabernet 2002
Real length of flavour in the mouth. Performs finely
and flavoursomely with roasted berries and gripping
tannins with a hint of chocolate.

16

RED £5.12
AUSTRALIA

Lindemans Cawarra Shiraz/Cabernet 2003
Lovely spicy richness with burned berries and warm
tannins.
Also at Tesco.

16

WHITE £9.98

Matua Valley Paretai Sauvignon Blanc 2003   NEW ZEALAND
Screwcap. Good with small fry though not as small as
the diet of the leviathan on the label (a whale). It has
courageous fruit of sprightly gooseberry, the
regulation metaphor where this grape is concerned,
but with unusually high-class texture.

16

RED £5.97

Misiónes de Rengo Reserva   CHILE
Cabernet Sauvignon/Syrah 2003
Brilliant curry red of sweet plum fruit opens up, then
a raw steak red intrudes, and finally the two sides to
the wine coalesce and produce a wine perfect with
chicken.

16

WHITE £6.61

Nepenthe Tryst White 2003   AUSTRALIA
Superb extracted citrus richness. Truly delicious, has
finesse yet flavour.

16

RED   (3 litre box) £15.98 (75cl) £4.98

No. 2 Merlot NV   FRANCE
A really classy, tannicly emphatic Merlot of mildly
leathery, spicy berries with real length, breadth and
depth.

16

RED £8.98

Penfolds Thomas Hyland Shiraz 2001   AUSTRALIA
Terrific.

16   WHITE £8.98

Penfolds Thomas Hyland Chardonnay 2003   AUSTRALIA
Classy follow on from the 2003, which it resembles in
fruit but not in acid structure. It may, though, cellar
better over 18 months.
Also at Thresher.

16   WHITE £4.37

Penfolds Rawsons Retreat Sémillon/   AUSTRALIA
Chardonnay 2002
A terrific blend of dryness yet witty flavoursomeness.
Also at Tesco.

16   WHITE £5.97

Peter Lehmann Sémillon 2002   AUSTRALIA
Screwcap. 18 in 2008–2009. Deliciously oily,
gooseberry/grapefruit flavoured. Will improve, thanks
to its screwcap, dramatically over half a decade (and
beyond). Utterly superb thirst-quencher.
Also at Booths, Oddbins, Tesco.

16   RED £6.98

Porcupine Ridge Cabernet Sauvignon 2002 SOUTH AFRICA
Brightly approachable berries, good burned undertone
with tannins of tenacity and savoury depth.

16   RED £6.98

Ravenswood Vintners Blend Zinfandel 2001   USA
Chunky berries with cool tannins, a hint of spice, a
touch of savourily grilled plum.
Also at Booths, Majestic, Somerfield, Waitrose.

ASDA

16

RED £6.11
AUSTRALIA

Serafino Shiraz 2000
Sheer velvet luxury here. You sink into this wine
rather than drink it and as it slowly engulfs the
tastebuds with savoury berries and gently grilled
tannins, you lose all track of time.

16

RED £5.53
SPAIN

Torres Coronas Tempranillo 2001
Hint of dry chocolate to the warm berries.

16

RED £5.98
AUSTRALIA

**Talking Tree Cabernet
Sauvignon/Cabernet Franc 2000**
More northern Italian in feel than Aussie. But it's
terrific! Real firm spice, dry cocoa tannins, and terrific
texture.

16

WHITE £7.98
NEW ZEALAND

Villa Maria Sauvignon Blanc 2003
Screwcap. Classic Kiwi richness of ripe gooseberry
with citrus.

16

WHITE £4.44
AUSTRALIA

Wolf Blass Eaglehawk Chardonnay 2003
Delightfully creamy, melony and yet fresh to finish.
Also at Sainsbury's.

16

FORTIFED £11.82
PORTUGAL

Warres Bottle Matured LBV 1992
An excellent alternative to vintage port with its

savoury tannins, underpinning the sweet fruit. Great
with blue cheese.

16

WHITE £4.99
FRANCE

Les Jamelles Viognier 2003
Superb dry apricot and lemon, dry and crisp, which
goes faintly peachy as it dries in the throat.

16

WHITE £4.47
CHILE

Misiónes de Rengo Chardonnay 2003
Dry, incisive, very pert citrus with under-ripe
gooseberry and a vague hint of peach. Superb with
grilled fish. Very classily styled.
Also at Somerfield.

16

WHITE £5.12

Porcupine Ridge Sauvignon Blanc 2003   SOUTH AFRICA
Screwcap. Delicious gooseberry and citrus. Ripe but
delicate.
Also at Somerfield, Waitrose.

16

WHITE £3.79
HUNGARY

Pinot Grigio, Akos Kamocsay 2003
Superbly tangy-to-finish. Smoky apricot.
Also at Marks & Spencer.

16

WHITE DESSERT (half bottle) £5.47
Brown Brothers Orange and Muscat Flora 2002   AUSTRALIA
Sweet honey and pineapple/peach fruit. Superb with
Greek pastries. 17.5 points in 2008.
Also at Budgens.

16

<table>
<tr><td></td><td align="right">WHITE £4.97</td></tr>
<tr><td>Concho y Toro Casillero del Diablo</td><td align="right">CHILE</td></tr>
</table>

Concho y Toro Casillero del Diablo Sauvignon Blanc 2003
Spirited, tangy, lemonic – and brilliant with shellfish. Also at Tesco.

OTHER WINES 15.5 AND UNDER

15.5

	RED £4.68
Asda Argentinian Malbec Reserve 2002	ARGENTINA

	WHITE £4.44
Asda Chilean Sauvignon Blanc Reserve 2003	CHILE

	WHITE £2.98
Asda Chilean Sauvignon Blanc 2003	CHILE

	WHITE £2.97
Asda Chilean Chardonnay 2003	CHILE

	RED £2.81
Asda Chilean Red NV	CHILE

	RED £3.00
Asda Chilean Merlot 2003	CHILE

	RED £7.98
Asda Château La Rose Larmande, St-Emilion 2001	FRANCE

	RED £8.44
Brown Brothers Graciano 2000	AUSTRALIA

	WHITE £5.02
Brown Brothers Muscat 2003	AUSTRALIA

RED £4.88
Concha y Toro Casillero del Diablo CHILE
Lot 59 Merlot 2003

WHITE £3.98
Danie de Wet Chardonnay 2003 SOUTH AFRICA

WHITE £6.96
Da Chardonnay, Limoux 2002 FRANCE

RED £4.92
Douglas Green Shiraz 2003 SOUTH AFRICA

RED £3.31
Created for Curry Red NV CHILE

RED £5.02
Graham Beck Railroad Cabernet/ SOUTH AFRICA
Shiraz 2002

WHITE £4.48
Hardy's Stamp Sémillon/Chardonnay 2003 AUSTRALIA
Also at Somerfield.

WHITE £5.56
Jacob's Creek Dry Riesling 2002 AUSTRALIA
Also at Tesco.

WHITE £4.88
Kumala Organic Colombard/ SOUTH AFRICA
Chardonnay 2003
Also at Booths, Sainsbury's.

RED £6.02
Lindemans Merlot Reserve 2002 AUSTRALIA

WHITE £4.87
Lindemans Bin 77 Sémillon/Chardonnay 2002 AUSTRALIA

RED £4.17
Prahova Valley Pinot Noir 2000 ROMANIA

WHITE £3.99
Riverview Gewürztraminer, Akos Kamocsay 2003 HUNGARY
Also at Safeway, Sainsbury's, Waitrose.

RED £5.98
Riebeck Wine Cellars Shiraz Reserve 2003 SOUTH AFRICA

RED £4.02
35 South Cabernet Sauvignon 2003 CHILE

WHITE £4.38
Torres Viña Sol 2003 SPAIN
Screwcap. Also at Majestic, Thresher.

RED £9.99
Xanadu Shiraz 2001 AUSTRALIA

15

WHITE £3.48
Asda Californian Chardonnay 2002 USA

RED £3.78
Asda Australian Cabernet/Shiraz NV AUSTRALIA

RED £6.98
Asda Marqués del Norte Rioja Reserva 1998 SPAIN

FORTIFIED £6.57

Asda LBV Port 1997   PORTUGAL

FORTIFIED   (70cl) £3.71

Asda Amontillado   SPAIN

WHITE £3.51

Andrew Peace Mighty Murray White 2003   AUSTRALIA

WHITE £4.99

Blason de Bourgogne Macon-Villages 2002   FRANCE

RED £9.01

Estancia Pinot Noir 2000   USA

RED £7.01

Fetzer Eagle Peak Merlot 2002   USA

RED £4.94

Forresters Petit Pinotage 2003   SOUTH AFRICA

WHITE £5.98

Grans Fassian Trittenheimer   GERMANY
Altarchen Riesling Kabinett 2002

RED £4.44

Hardy's VR Shiraz 2003   AUSTRALIA
Also at Somerfield.

WHITE SPARKLING £6.48

Hardy's Stamp Chardonnay/Pinot Noir NV   AUSTRALIA

RED £5.94

Ironstone Vineyards Petite Sirah 2002   USA

RED £5.76
Jacob's Creek Merlot 2002 AUSTRALIA
Also at Tesco.

WHITE £7.97
Jacob's Creek Reserve Chardonnay 2002 AUSTRALIA

RED £8.48
Jacob's Creek Reserve Shiraz 2001 AUSTRALIA

WHITE £7.94
Ken Forrester Family Reserve SOUTH AFRICA
Sauvignon Blanc 2002

RED £4.99
La Chasse du Pape Réserve Rouge, FRANCE
Gabriel Meffre, Rhône 2002
Also at Co-op, Morrison's, Safeway, Sainsbury's.

WHITE £5.56
Montana Chardonnay 2002 NEW ZEALAND

WHITE (3 litre box) £15.98 (75cl) £4.98
No. 4 Chardonnay, Vin de Pays d'Oc NV FRANCE

RED £5.94
Novas Carmenere/Cabernet Sauvignon 2002 CHILE

RED £6.56
Penfolds Koonunga Hill Shiraz/Cabernet 2001 AUSTRALIA
Also at Somerfield, Tesco.

ASDA

WHITE £4.98
Paul Mas Sauvignon Blanc,   FRANCE
Domaines Paul Mas, Languedoc 2003
Screwcap.

RED £5.98
35 South Cabernet Sauvignon Reserva 2001   CHILE

RED £5.02
35 South Cabernet Sauvignon Reserva 2002   CHILE

RED £3.64
35 South Cabernet/Merlot 2003   CHILE

WHITE £5.98
Slanghoek Sémillon 2003   SOUTH AFRICA

RED £4.98
Sirocco Cabernet/Syrah 2000   TUNISIA

RED £4.44
Shamwari Shiraz 2003   SOUTH AFRICA

RED £5.58
Viña Albali Cabernet Sauvignon Reserva 1998   SPAIN

RED £4.94
Wontanella Sangiovese/Petit Verdot 2003   AUSTRALIA
Screwcap.

WHITE £7.98
Zilzie Viognier 2003   AUSTRALIA

Pacific Bay Chardonnay/Pinot Grigio 2003
Also at Booths.

WHITE £4.94
USA

Nepenthe Tryst Red 2003
Screwcap. Also at Oddbins, Waitrose.

RED £6.61
AUSTRALIA

Hardy's Stamp Shiraz/Cabernet 2002
Also at Somerfield.

RED £3.93
AUSTRALIA

14.5

Asda Argentinian White NV

WHITE £2.59
ARGENTINA

Asda Argentinian Red NV

RED £2.56
ARGENTINA

Asda South African Sauvignon Blanc 2003

WHITE £3.27
SOUTH AFRICA

Asda Chablis 2003

WHITE £6.87
FRANCE

Asda French Cabernet Sauvignon NV

RED (3 litre box) £10.98
FRANCE

Asda Cava NV

WHITE SPARKLING £3.82
SPAIN

Asda South African White NV

WHITE (3 litre box) £10.88
SOUTH AFRICA

Asda Valpolicella Classico DOC 2002	RED £4.98	ITALY
Asda Chianti Classico DOCG 2002	RED £4.98	ITALY
Asda Marqués del Norte Rioja NV	RED £3.35	SPAIN
Asda Soave Classico 2003	WHITE £3.68	ITALY
Asda Californian Chardonnay Reserve 2002	WHITE £4.98	USA
Angove's Bear Crossing Sémillon/ Chardonnay 2003	WHITE £4.01	AUSTRALIA
Brown Brothers Sauvignon Blanc 2003	WHITE £5.98	AUSTRALIA
Buckingham Estate Shiraz 2002	RED £3.97	AUSTRALIA
Concho y Toro Casillero del Diablo Gewürztraminer 2003	WHITE £4.97	CHILE
Château Sirène, St Julien 2001	RED £10.86	FRANCE
Dumisani Pinotage/Shiraz 2002	RED £3.64	SOUTH AFRICA
Dumisani Chenin/Chardonnay 2003	WHITE £3.64	SOUTH AFRICA

Denis Marchais Vouvray 2003	WHITE DESSERT	£4.98
		FRANCE

Teuzzo Chianti Classico DOCG 2001	RED	£7.98
		ITALY

Wolf Blass Eaglehawk Cabernet Sauvignon 2002	RED	£5.02
		AUSTRALIA

Xanadu Secession Sémillon/Sauvignon 2002	WHITE	£5.98
		AUSTRALIA

Yellow Tail Chardonnay 2003	WHITE	£4.81
		AUSTRALIA

Kumala Organic Pinotage/Shiraz 2003	RED	£5.28
Also at Sainsbury's.		SOUTH AFRICA

14

Andrew Peace Mighty Murray Rosé NV	ROSÉ	£3.72
		AUSTRALIA

Asda South African Red NV	RED	£2.84
		SOUTH AFRICA

Asda Argentinian Malbec 2002	RED	£3.74
		ARGENTINA

Asda Australian Reserve Shiraz 2002	RED	£4.98
		AUSTRALIA

Asda Pinot Grigio del Venezia 2003	WHITE	£4.00
		ITALY

WHITE £4.98
Asda Pinot Grigio del Trentino DOC 2003 ITALY

WHITE £2.81
Asda Hungarian Dry Chardonnay 2003 HUNGARY

RED £3.00
Asda Tempranillo NV SPAIN

RED £4.18
Asda Marqués del Norte Classico Rioja NV SPAIN

ROSÉ SPARKLING £3.82
Asda Cava Rosado NV SPAIN

WHITE £3.58
Asda Vin de Pays Sauvignon Blanc NV FRANCE

WHITE £3.32
Asda Vin de Pays Chenin Blanc NV FRANCE

WHITE (3 litre box) £9.88
Asda Soave NV ITALY

FORTIFIED £4.82
Asda Ruby Port PORTUGAL

FORTIFIED £4.91
Asda Tawny Port PORTUGAL

FORTIFIED (70cl) £4.44
Asda Manzanilla SPAIN

FORTIFIED (70cl) £4.44
Asda Fino SPAIN

	RED £3.64
Banrock Station Red 2003	AUSTRALIA

	WHITE (3 litre box) £14.97
Banrock Station Colombard/Chardonnay NV	AUSTRALIA

	RED (3 litre box) £14.07
Banrock Station Shiraz/Mataro NV	AUSTRALIA

	RED £5.56
Barton et Guestier Côtes du Rhône 2002	FRANCE

	WHITE £5.78
Blason de Bourgogne 2002	FRANCE

	WHITE £9.98
Blason de Bourgogne Fuissé 2003	FRANCE

	RED £5.98
Château La Domèque Corbières 2002	FRANCE

	RED £6.82
Dourthe No. 1 Bordeaux Rouge 2002	FRANCE

	WHITE £5.93
Dourthe No. 1 Sauvignon Blanc 2003	FRANCE

	WHITE £4.99
Fat Bastard Chardonnay, Fat Bastard Wine Company, Languedoc 2003	FRANCE

Also at Safeway.

	RED £4.02
Hearty Red NV	PORTUGAL

	WHITE £7.48
Hogue Pinot Grigio 2003	USA

WHITE £7.48
Hogue Gewürztraminer 2003   USA

RED £5.56
Jacob's Creek Shiraz 2002   AUSTRALIA

WHITE SPARKLING £6.81
Jacob's Creek Chardonnay/Pinot Noir NV   AUSTRALIA

WHITE £5.42
Laroche Bourgogne Chardonnay 2002   FRANCE

WHITE £7.97
Laroche Chablis 2003   FRANCE

WHITE £7.52
Montana Sauvignon Blanc Reserve 2003   NEW ZEALAND

WHITE £6.98
Matua Valley Sauvignon Blanc 2004   NEW ZEALAND

WHITE £5.97
Misiónes de Rengo Reserva Chardonnay 2003   CHILE

RED £10.12
Neil Ellis Cabernet Sauvignon 2001   SOUTH AFRICA

RED £5.02
Rutherglen Estates Sangiovese 2003   AUSTRALIA

RED £5.92
Rock Red Shiraz/Grenache/Pinot Noir 2002   AUSTRALIA

ROSÉ £4.98
Roquemartin Côtes de Provence Rosé 2003   FRANCE

RED £5.98
Ruvello Cabernet Sauvignon Barda 2000   ITALY

ASDA

Rhone Ranger Côtes du Rhône 2002	RED £5.48	FRANCE
Redneck Old Vine Red Malbec/Shiraz 2003	RED £5.97	SOUTH AFRICA
Rosemount Melon Creek Verdelho/ Chardonnay/Sauvignon Blanc 2003	WHITE £4.98	AUSTRALIA
Spier Collection Sauvignon Blanc 2003	WHITE £10.20	SOUTH AFRICA
Spier Private Collection Pinotage 2000	RED £10.11	SOUTH AFRICA
Solaz Tempranillo/Cabernet 2001	RED £4.52	SPAIN
35 South Chardonnay 2002	WHITE £3.98	CHILE
Tabali Merlot Reserva 2002	RED £6.94	CHILE
Villa Regia Douro 2000	RED £4.28	PORTUGAL
Wolf Blass Yellow Label Cabernet Sauvignon 2002 Also at Tesco.	RED £7.52	AUSTRALIA

BOOTHS

4–6 Fishergate,
Preston,
Lancashire PR1 3LJ

Tel: (01772) 251701
Fax: (01772) 255642

E-mail: admin@booths-supermarkets.co.uk
Website: www.everywine.co.uk

For Booths' wines 14 points and under visit
www.superplonk.com

17.5   RED   £12.99
Casa Lapostolle Cuvée Alexandre Merlot 2000   CHILE
Hint of tobacco to the ripe berries and cherries.
The tannins hold it together. Drink now until spring
2005.
Also at Majestic, Safeway.

17.5   WHITE   £7.49
Wither Hills Sauvignon Blanc 2003   NEW ZEALAND
Screwcap. Unusual complexities here offering lime,
pear, pineapple and a hint of spice. More perfume,
friskier minerals and chewiness of texture. Simply one
of the Kiwis' sassiest Sauvignons.
Also at Oddbins, The Wine Society.

17   WHITE   £6.49
Casa Lapostolle Chardonnay 2002   CHILE
It achieves that linguistic contradictory miracle:
dryness with extreme liquidity. How can a wine be so
elegant, so full of finesse yet offer so refreshing an
experience?

17   WHITE   £4.99
Inycon Fiano Bianco di Sicilia 2003   ITALY
Superb, crisp Italian white. Wonderful.

17

WHITE £7.50

AUSTRALIA

**D'Arenberg Hermit Crab Marsanne/
Viognier 2002**
Screwcap. Superb dry apricot, pineapple and pear.
Wonderfully well textured.
Also at Small Merchants (Magnum).

17

WHITE £7.99

AUSTRALIA

**D'Arenberg Hermit Crab Marsanne/
Viognier 2003**
Screwcap. 18 points in 3 years (if cellared).
Wonderfully eccentric dryness to the fruit, an oily
textured apricot and lime (with a hint of herb), and
the finish is very elegant. Superbly classy.
Also at Oddbins.

16.5

WHITE £5.99

AUSTRALIA

**Brown Brothers Late Harvested
Muscat Blanc 2003**
Beautifully Muscat grape, dryly spicy aperitif.
Absolutely wonderful in torrid gardens or by winter
firesides.

16.5

WHITE £6.49

CHILE

Casa Lapostolle Sauvignon Blanc 2003
Super dry, under-ripe fruit yet this subtlety is
amazingly emphatic and suggestive of richness rather
than achieving it full on. A classic Sauvignon Blanc.
Also at London Stores (Selfridges), Small Merchants
(Partridges), E-tailers (Everywine, Barrels and Bottles).

16.5   RED £5.99

Château Pierrail Bordeaux Supérieur 2001   FRANCE
Sheer Merlot magic. Terrific energy from the burned
berries and plums and wonderfully warm tannins.
Stunning claret for the money.

16.5   WHITE SPARKLING £12.99

Champagne Baron-Fuente NV   FRANCE
Superbly elegant and dry with a superb after-tang of
dry wild raspberry.

16.5   RED £5.49

Chinon Cuvée de Pacques,   FRANCE
Domaine de la Roche Honneur 2003
Drink chilled to appreciate the extreme individuality
of its raspberry richness and slate-edged tannins.

16.5   WHITE £7.95

Springfield Estate Life from Stone   SOUTH AFRICA
Sauvignon Blanc 2003
Stunningly classy and chewy. Tight minerals and fine
extended gooseberry. In this vintage it has an
appealing vegetality.
Also at Small Merchants (SWIG, Palmers, Rex Norris,
Bin Two, Charles Stevenson, Magnum).

16.5   WHITE £8.99

La Voglie Verdicchio dei Castelli di Jesi Classico,   ITALY
Azienda Santa Barbara 2003
Superb! What a lovely combination of peach, apricot,
nuts and citrus. Real vigour and class here.

16.5

RED £5.99

Mas Collet Celler Capcanes Montsant 2001 SPAIN
A blend of Garnacha, Tempranillo, Carinena and
Cabernet Sauvignon which gushes with flavour
and depth, juicily edgy, without berries being OTT.
Fine tannins to the finish. Richly unguent and
gripping. Offers real excitement and complex
concentration.
Also at Waitrose.

16.5

RED £9.30

Springfield Estate Whole Berry SOUTH AFRICA
Cabernet Sauvignon 2001
Startlingly ripe and ready yet complex and serious. Its
appeal lies in its paradox of texture, tannins, and
tenacity with such vivid immediacy. Total plummy
pleasure. Fine tannins, hint of jam and chocolate.
Also at Small Merchants (SWIG, Rex Norris).

16.5

RED £6.29

Torres Santa Digna Cabernet Sauvignon 2002 CHILE
Intense berries which hold a very calm, assured centre
of mild cassis. But as the wine opens up in the glass a
tanginess develops – of some kind of fresher berry.
This is the young acidic side of the wine asserting
itself and it betokens great compatibility with rich
food. After 20 hours of breathing the wine shows dark
milk chocolate with nuts – very chewy.
Also at Small Merchants (Noel Young Wines, Tanners
Wine Merchants, Wimbledon Wine Cellars).

16.5
RED £8.50

The Custodian Grenache 2000 AUSTRALIA
Strawberries and blackberries, hint of prune. Firm
tannins, hint of earthiness.
Also at The Wine Society.

16.5
RED £9.99

The Futures Shiraz Peter Lehmann 2001 AUSTRALIA
So soft and stealing-up-on-the-palate fruity, it offers an
utterly original aspect of Aussie Shiraz: sheer poetry.

16
WHITE £3.89

Bellefontaine Chardonnay, FRANCE
Vin de Pays d'Oc 2002
Deliciously subtle opulence and cunning ripeness
mitigated by fine citrus.

16
WHITE £7.49

Bleasdale Verdelho 2002 AUSTRALIA
Screwcap. Warm, almost spicy fruit, hint of custard to
peach and lemon. Great wine for oriental food.

16
RED £4.99

Coteaux de Languedoc, FRANCE
Les Ruffes La Sauvageonne 2002
Dry chocolate, tobacco and charred raspberryish
plums.

16
RED £6.99

Peter Lehmann Clancy's Red 2002 AUSTRALIA
Juicy richness coloured by well-toned tannins.

16

RED £8.99

Château Jupille No Dash Carillon AC, FRANCE
St-Emilion 1999
Delightfully plump yet dry (and wry). Chewy tannins
complete a fine soft claret of distinction.

16

RED £2.99

Casa Morena Bodega Felix Solis, SPAIN
Vino de la Tierra NV
Very ripe and intensely eager berries but the creamy
(yet slightly burned) finish is appealing. It is not the
confected rubbish you would expect for the price.

16

RED £8.99

Château Maris Cru La Livinière AC, FRANCE
Minervois 2000
Soft, eiderdown-plump fruit with cherry/raspberry
under-toned tannins.

16

WHITE £3.99

Château de Béranger Picpoul de Pinet, FRANCE
Cave Co-op de Pomerols 2003
What a delightful change this makes (from
Chardonnay, Tony Blair, Match of the Day). It offers
crispness and fruit of elegance and bite.

16

RED £6.99

Casa Lapostolle Cabernet Sauvignon 2001 CHILE
Sheer class in a glass: rich yet delicate, firm yet
yielding, lingering yet welcome to stay forever. The
fruit is calmly berried, positively tannic and generous.

16   RED £4.99
Chateau Cuzan AC, Bordeaux 2001   FRANCE
Real classic claret. And for under a fiver a miracle of
grouchy dryness.

16   WHITE DESSERT   (half bottle) £9.99
Château Filhout Sauternes,   FRANCE
2ème Grand Cru Classé 1999
Deliciously waxy texture to honey and sweet peach.
Superb pudding wine.

16   RED £4.99
Domaine La Bastide Syrah, Vieilles Vignes,   FRANCE
Vin de Pays de l'Hautérive 2001
Bargain opulence here. Yet hang on, how does it
achieve such rich fruit with tobacco, yet finish so
searingly dry? Search me.

16   RED £7.99
Domaine Chaume-Arnaud,   FRANCE
Côtes du Rhône-Villages 2001
Hint of tobacco to the cherry/plum fruit. Has a
lingering, chewy finish of some style.

The major irony of my vinous career is that I am slowly working
my way out of a job – like one of those colonial governors whose
work eventually brings independence to the colony. One day every
wine drinker in the country who has ever read Malcolm Gluck will
say 'I don't need him any more. I make up my own mind now.'
Amen to that. Amen to the wine writer.

16

RED £4.99

Escobera Jumilla 2002   SPAIN

Definite cheroot overtones to the ripe berries.

16

WHITE £5.35

Springfield Estate Firefinch   SOUTH AFRICA
Colombard/Chardonnay 2003

'A nice summer wine,' says its maker – which damns
it with faint praise, for it has lovely refreshing
peach/lemon fruit.
Also at Small Merchants (Magnum).

16

RED £6.75

Springfield Estate Firefinch   SOUTH AFRICA
What the Birds Left Ripe Red 2002

A blend of 50% Merlot, 30% Ruby Cabernet, 20%
Cabernet Sauvignon, which manages to be jammily
ripe yet dry to finish with a touch of spice.
Also at Small Merchants (Bin Two, Rex Norris).

16

RED £8.49

D'Arenberg High Trellis Cabernet Sauvignon   AUSTRALIA
2001

Shows the superiority of the McLaren Vale berry.
Sweet hedgerow cosiness with seriously strict tannins.
Also at Oddbins.

16

WHITE £11.99

Iona Sauvignon Blanc 2003   SOUTH AFRICA

Intensely individual interpretation of the grape.
Offers extreme dryness with little buttering of
gooseberry, pineapple and lemon. Very subtle.

16

WHITE £8.49

Jordan Estate Chardonnay 2003 SOUTH AFRICA
Simply a classic of creamy lemon, lime, peach and
melon.
Also at Sainsbury's.

16

RED £2.99

Louis Chatel, Rouge Listel, FRANCE
Vin de Pays d'Oc 2002
What a bargain blend of Cabernet Sauvignon and
Merlot. It offers raspberry and plums and attentive
tannins. Mild rusticity, highly quaffable and food
friendly.

16

WHITE £7.99

La Segreta Bianco Planeta, Sicilia 2003 ITALY
What class in this blend of Grecanico, Chardonnay,
Sauvignon Blanc and Viognier. It has such dry
stylishness and aplomb from nose to throat.

16

ROSÉ SPARKLING £4.99

Palau Cava Rosado NV SPAIN
Delightfully dry and raspberry-edged.

16

WHITE £5.49

Peter Lehmann Sémillon 2002 AUSTRALIA
Screwcap. 18 in 2008-2009. Deliciously oily, gooseberry/
grapefruit flavoured. Will improve, thanks to its
screwcap, dramatically over half a decade (and beyond).
Utterly superb thirst-quencher.
Also at Asda, Oddbins, Tesco.

16

RED £8.99

Quinta de la Rosa Douro Tinto 2001   PORTUGAL
Smashing jammy stuff. Really enticingly perfumed
and fruited.

16

RED £6.99

Ravenswood Vintners Blend Zinfandel 2001   USA
Full and ripe yet with very lovely tannins coating the
lively tannins.
Also at Asda, Majestic, Somerfield, Waitrose.

16

WHITE £5.99

Sauvignon Blanc, Marlborough 2003   NEW ZEALAND
Very lengthy experience from gentle gooseberry to
chalky tanginess of pineapple on the finish.
Also at Thresher, Oddbins, Tesco, Safeway,
Somerfield, Sainsbury's, Co-op, Morrison's, Small
Merchants (Unwins, Londis).

16

RED £3.99

Sierra Grande Merlot 2003   CHILE
Superbly mouth-filling hedgerow berries, gently burned.

16

RED £3.99

Viña Sardasol Merlot, Bodega Virgen Blanca 2002   SPAIN
Now here the rustic richness has character and vigour.
Superb with cheese dishes, this wine.

16

RED £13.99

Wither Hills Pinot Noir 2002   NEW ZEALAND
Screwcap. One of the most convincing Kiwi Pinots.

Has a gaminess, feral berried richness and aromatic
intensity, and finishes well.
Also at Oddbins, Small Merchants (Jeroboams, Thos
Peatling, Ballantynes of Cowbridge), Waitrose, The
Wine Society.

16   WHITE £6.99
Yalumba Y Series Viognier 2003   AUSTRALIA
One of the loveliest expressions of the Viognier grape
around: delicacy with emphatic dry apricot and citrus.

16   WHITE £5.99
Concha y Toro Trio Sauvignon Blanc 2003   CHILE
Also at Asda.

OTHER WINES 15.5 AND UNDER

15.5   WHITE £8.99
Albarino Pazo de Senorans 2003   SPAIN

                                          ROSÉ £5.49
Bardolino Chiaretto Azienda   ITALY
Agricola Cavalchina 2003

                                           RED £3.49
Barocco Rosso del Salento 2002   ITALY

                                          WHITE £3.99
Castillo de Almansa Colección Blanco,   SPAIN
Bodegas Piqueras 2002

                                           RED £5.99
Chain of Ponds Novello Nero 2002   AUSTRALIA

Jackson Estate Sauvignon Blanc 2003
Screwcap.

WHITE £8.49
NEW ZEALAND

Palacio de Bornos Rueda 2003

WHITE £4.99
SPAIN

Poema Sauvignon Blanc Vino de la Tierra,
Castilla y Leon 2003

WHITE £5.49
SPAIN

Kumala Organic Colombard/
Chardonnay 2003
Also at Asda, Sainsbury's.

WHITE £4.99
SOUTH AFRICA

15

Albarino Pazo de Senorans 2002

WHITE £8.99
SPAIN

Bardolino Azienda Agricola Cavalchina 2003

RED £5.99
ITALY

Concerto Lambrusco Reggiano DOC,
Medici Ermete 2002

RED SPARKLING £6.49
ITALY

Château Lamôthe-Vincent AC,
Bordeaux Rosé 2003

ROSÉ £4.49
FRANCE

Domaine St Laurent AC, St-Chinian 2002

RED £3.99
FRANCE

RED £4.99
Eden Collection Organic Merlot,   FRANCE
Jacques Frélin 2002
Also at Waitrose.

WHITE £5.99
Falasco Garganega Vendemmia Tardiva,   ITALY
Cantina Valpantena 2002

WHITE £5.99
Flambeau d'Alsace Hugel 2002   FRANCE

RED £7.99
La Segreta Rosso Planeta, Sicilia 2003   ITALY

RED £5.59
Merloblu Castello di Luzzano, Vino da Tavola 2002 ITALY

WHITE £3.69
Nagyrede Estate Pinot Grigio 2003   HUNGARY

WHITE £4.99
Pacific Bay Chardonnay/Pinot Grigio 2003   USA
Also at Asda.

RED £6.99
Rasteau Rouge,   FRANCE
Domaine des Coteaux de Travers 2002

RED £7.99
Rosso di Montepulciano, Azienda Agricola   ITALY
Poliziano 2002

RED £4.29
Syrah Domaine du Petit Roubie,   FRANCE
Vin de Pays de l'Hérault Organic 2002

14.5

RED £3.79
Booths Claret Bordeaux NV FRANCE

ROSÉ SPARKLING £13.99
Champagne Baron-Fuente Rosé Dolores NV FRANCE

WHITE SPARKLING £18.99
Champagne Fleury Brut Biodynamic NV FRANCE

RED £5.99
Carmen Merlot 2002 CHILE

WHITE £8.59
Kim Crawford Riesling 2003 NEW ZEALAND
Screwcap.

WHITE £8.49
Pouilly Fumé Les Cornets, FRANCE
Domaine Cailbourdin 2002

WHITE £9.99
Skillogalee Riesling 2003 AUSTRALIA
16 points in 2008.

WHITE £7.49
Vassiliou Amberlones 2003 GREECE

14

ROSÉ £3.99
Bellefontaine Syrah Rosé, Vin de Pays d'Oc 2003 FRANCE

RED £6.49
Blue Rock Merlot/Malbec 2003 SOUTH AFRICA

RED £6.99
Bleasdale Shiraz/Cabernet 2002 AUSTRALIA

Castillo de Maluenda Blanco 2003

WHITE £3.29
SPAIN

Château Lamôthe-Vincent AC, Bordeaux Sec 2003

WHITE £3.99
FRANCE

Chapel Hill Winemaker Selection Pinot
Noir 2003

RED £3.89
HUNGARY

Chorey Les Beaune Beaumonts, Nicolas Potel 2000

RED £12.99
FRANCE

Crozes-Hermitage Blanc, Cave de Tain 2003

WHITE £6.99
FRANCE

Domaine Biblia Chora 2003

WHITE £8.49
GREECE

Inurrieta Tinto Norte, Bodega Inurreta Navarra 2002

RED £5.99
SPAIN

Jardin des Anges Organic Touraine,
Confrérie de Oisly et Thesee 2003

RED £4.99
FRANCE

La Remonta Malbec 2002

RED £5.99
ARGENTINA

Leitz Rudsheimer Magdalenenkreuz
Riesling Spätlese 2002
17 points in 2010.

WHITE £9.99
GERMANY

Mas de Daumas Gassac Blanc 2003

WHITE £13.99
FRANCE

WHITE £8.59
Ninth Island Chardonnay 2003   AUSTRALIA

WHITE £3.99
Peaks View Sauvignon Blanc 2003   SOUTH AFRICA

WHITE £6.99
Quincy Philippe Portier 2003   FRANCE

WHITE £4.99
Selva d'Oro Falchini Bianco di Toscano 2003   ITALY

RED £7.99
Sablet Côtes du Rhône-Villages,   FRANCE
Château de Trignon 2001

BUDGENS

Stonefield Way,
Ruislip, Middlesex HA4 0JR

Tel: (020) 8422 9511
Fax: (020) 8864 2800

E-mail: info@budgens.co.uk
Website: www.budgens.com

For Budgens' wines of 14 points and under visit
www.superplonk.com

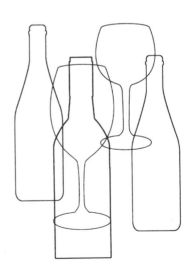

17   RED £5.49

Concho y Toro Casillero del Diablo   CHILE
Cabernet Sauvignon 2003
Massively chewy berries of huge charm, concentration
and class. One of South America's most agreeably dry
yet tongue-tingling Cabs.
Also at Asda, Tesco.

16.5   WHITE £4.99

Argento Chardonnay 2003   AUSTRALIA
One of the UK's classiest Chardonnays under a fiver.
Lovely cozy fruit of charm yet character.
Also at Asda, Majestic, Somerfield, Tesco.

16.5   WHITE £5.49

Concho y Toro Casillero del Diablo   CHILE
Chardonnay 2003
Delicious layers of fruit including baked pineapple,
spicy citrus and smoky melon.
Also at Asda, Majestic.

16.5   RED £8.99

Errazuriz Max Reserva Cabernet Sauvignon 2000   CHILE
Very classy, luxuriously appointed Cab with all mod cons
– including leather upholstery – and it motors
smoothly from nose to throat with élan and style.
Also at Asda.

16.5   RED £5.99

Errazuriz Merlot 2003   CHILE
Terrifically deep and molar caressing yet never gets
OTT or too familiar. Really crunchy tannins help.

16.5

WHITE £7.99

Riddoch Coonawarra Chardonnay 2001   AUSTRALIA

The best white wine in the store? Could be. The liquid
is a treat for the nose, a creamy thrill for the palate,
and a dry excitement for the throat.

16

WHITE DESSERT   (half bottle) £4.99

Brown Brothers Orange and   AUSTRALIA
Muscat Flora 2002

Sweet honey and pineapple/peach fruit. Superb with
Greek pastries. 17.5 points in 2008.
Also at Asda.

Many words apply to dessert wine. My *Guardian* editor headed a
brief to me last year 'Sweet & Sumptuous'. Of course many sweet
wines go better with blue cheeses than desserts as, equally, many
wines we might characterise as more sweet than dry (German
Rieslings of Spätlese categorisation, say) go splendidly with oriental
food. But 'sumptuous' does take us, it seems to me (and I am a
slave to my briefs), into the world of truly rich, honied white wines
and plump ports, and with such liquids myriad adjectival
opportunities occur: ambrosial, luscious, nectareous, mellifluous (or
should that be melliferous?), luxurious, honied, sybaritic, hedonistic.
Why should sweet wines occasion some of these
metaphors but not dry wines? A dry wine can be every bit as
luxurious and hedonistic, if not more so, than a sweet one but
somehow we associate sweetness with indolence, luxury,
indulgence. Sweet things, perhaps, make more impact than dry as
descriptors, there is more opportunity for rich embroidery, and as a
result we can picture the results more vividly.

16   WHITE **£4.99**

Cono Sur Viognier 2004   CHILE

Wonderful chewy apricot and lime richness. Superb
quaffing. Also great with oriental fish dishes.

16   RED **£4.99**

Cono Sur Pinot Noir 2003   CHILE

Terrific. Very firm and compressed. Very baby bouncy.
Cellar for 2–3 years to achieve 18 points.
Also at Majestic, Morrison's, Somerfield, Tesco,
Waitrose.

16   WHITE **£8.99**

Domaine Fouassier Sancerre Les Chasseignes 2003   FRANCE

One of the best of 2003s from Sancerre under a
tenner. Has tannins to it, rich yet elegant gooseberry
richness.

16   WHITE **£5.99**

Errazuriz Chardonnay 2003   CHILE

It's the texture of the wine which is so highly classy.
It allows all the nuances of the fruit, lemon, lime,
apricot and paw-paw to shine through.
Also at Tesco.

16   RED **£5.99**

Errazuriz Syrah 2001   CHILE

Yes, it's juicy. True, it has chutzpah. Admittedly, it's
immediate and does not conceal its charms. But, for
all that, its class is sheer and telling.
Also at Threshers, Waitrose.

16

WHITE £4.99
La Baume Sauvignon Blanc, Vin de Pays d'Oc 2003 FRANCE
Screwcap. Tangy gooseberry with a hint of grapefruit.
Superb with Thai food.
Also at Sainsbury's.

16

RED £4.99
La Baume Merlot, Vin de Pays d'Oc 2003 FRANCE
Screwcap. Delicious chewy plums, gently leathery and
very faintly wrinkled.
Also at Sainsbury's.

16

WHITE SPARKLING £6.99
Lindemans Bin 25 Sparkling Brut 2002 AUSTRALIA
Light, dry, classy – better than a hundred thousand
champagnes (at three times the price of this bubbly).

16

RED £4.49
Lazy Lizard Syrah, Vin de Pays d'Oc 2002 FRANCE
Most attractive layers of faintly burned cherry/berry
fruit with mild but charming tannins.

16

RED £4.79
Mezzomondo Montepulciano d'Abruzzo 2003 ITALY
In 2002 it had 13.5 points. The 2003 vintage is
delicious, vivacious, plums full of spicy, almost
opulent fruit, and the tannins are spot on.

16

RED £4.99
Osborne Solaz 2001 SPAIN
Superb Tempranillo/Cabernet blend of fine plums and
gracious tannins.

16   RED £4.49

Sunrise Merlot, Concha y Toro 2003   CHILE
Joyously living up to its solar billing, this is a bright,
bursting-with-energy red. Yet it finishes dryly and not
inelegantly.

16   WHITE £6.99

Villa Maria Private Bin Riesling 2003   NEW ZEALAND
Screwcap. Superb level of fruit, melon and a hint of
gooseberry, with fine citrus. 19 points in 3–10 years.
Also at Waitrose.

16   RED £4.99

Argento Malbec 2003   ARGENTINA
Superbly well-textured berries with a chocolate
undertone. Marvellously biteable fruit.
Also at Majestic, Somerfield, Tesco.

16   RED £6.99

Durius Tempranillo 2002   SPAIN
One of the best of Spain's under-six-quid
Tempranillos.
Also at Morrison's.

16   RED £8.29

Marqués de Griñon Reserva Rioja 1999   SPAIN
Grand, mouth-filling chocolate and blackberry
richness – thick coagulated tannins.
Also at Tesco.

OTHER WINES 15.5 AND UNDER

15.5

Peter Lehmann Clancy's Shiraz/Cabernet
Sauvignon/Merlot/Cabernet Franc 2002

RED £6.99
AUSTRALIA

Riverview Cabernet Sauvignon,
Akos Kamocsay 2003

RED £3.99
HUNGARY

15

Da Luca Primitivo Merlot 2002
Also at Waitrose.

RED £4.99
ITALY

Lindemans Bin 40 Merlot 2003

RED £5.99
AUSTRALIA

Lazy Lizard Chardonnay, Vin de
Pays d'Oc 2002

WHITE £4.49
FRANCE

Louis Jadot Macon-Blanc Villages 2003

WHITE £6.99
FRANCE

Nagyrede Cabernet Rosé 2003

ROSÉ £3.99
HUNGARY

Peter Lehmann Wild Card Chardonnay 2003

WHITE £4.99
AUSTRALIA

Palacio de la Vega Crianza 1999

RED £5.99
SPAIN

WHITE DESSERT £7.49
Quady Elysium Black Muscat 2002   USA

WHITE £4.99
Oxford Landing Sauvignon Blanc 2003   AUSTRALIA
Screwcap. Also at Morrison's, Somerfield, Tesco.

14.5

RED £5.49
Bonterra Shiraz/Carignan/Sangiovese 2002   USA

RED £5.29
Herrick Syrah, Vin de Pays d'Oc 2002   FRANCE

RED £5.99
Fetzer Zinfandel/Shiraz 2002   USA
Also at Safeway.

14

WHITE £5.99
Babich Unoaked Chardonnay 2002   NEW ZEALAND
Screwcap.

WHITE £6.99
Babich Sauvignon Blanc 2003   NEW ZEALAND

WHITE £6.99
Bonterra Chardonnay/Sauvignon/Muscat 2002   AUSTRALIA

WHITE £5.49
Deakin Estate Sauvignon Blanc 2003   AUSTRALIA

RED £5.99
Deakin Estate Shiraz 2002   AUSTRALIA

	RED £3.49
La Mura Nero d'Avola di Sicilia 2002	ITALY

	RED £5.79
Oxford Landing Cabernet/Shiraz 2002	AUSTRALIA

	RED £4.29
Prahova Valley Reserve Cabernet Sauvignon 2000	ROMANIA

CO-OP

Co-operative Wholesale Society Limited,
PO Box 53,
New Century House,
Manchester M60 4ES

Tel: (0161) 834 1212
Fax: (0161) 827 5117

Website: www.co-opdrinks2u.com

For Co-op wines 14 points and under visit
www.superplonk.com.

16.5
WHITE £4.99

Angove's Bear Crossing Chardonnay 2002   AUSTRALIA
Wonderfully oily fruit, comprising touches of pear,
lemon, pineapple and peach.

16.5
RED £4.99

Atlantique Cabernet Franc 2003   FRANCE
Screwcap. A superb modern example of this grape, its
best vintage in the Loire for at least half a decade, and
its screwcap will hold all its complex tannins together.
It is highly classy, rich, finely knitted and hugely
joyous.

16.5
WHITE £5.99

Co-op Côtes du Rhône Reserve White 2003   FRANCE
Classic Rhône white of good class, ineffable
Frenchness and great confidence. The tannins are
firmly in place, rare in a white, and the fruit is so
beautifully cut and elegant.

16.5
WHITE £5.99

Trio Chardonnay/Pinot Grigio/Pinot Blanc 2003   CHILE
Superbly fresh apricot and keen pineapple.

16.5
WHITE £5.99

Wolf Blass Sémillon/Chardonnay 2003   AUSTRALIA
Lovely! Wolf Blass's most perfect stab at this blend.
Offers rich melon Chardonnay with tongue-tingling
Sémillon citrussiness.
Superstores only.

16

RED £4.99

Argento Malbec 2002   ARGENTINA

It's a huge mouthful of baked plum fruit with, as the
tannins coalesce in the throat, burned blackberry and
raspberries.

16

WHITE £3.79

Co-op Argentine Torrontes Chardonnay 2003   ARGENTINA

A simply delicious, dry, grapey aperitif. It really does
whet the whistle.

16

WHITE £4.49

Co-op Argentine Old Vines Sangiovese 2003   ARGENTINA

Terrific vivacity here, which stays the course from
nose to throat dryly, wryly and seriously deliciously.

16

WHITE £4.29

Co-op Australian Lime Tree Chardonnay 2003   AUSTRALIA

And lime tree is very apt, for the fruit has a citric
intensity relieved by a leafy richness.

16

WHITE £4.49

Co-op Chilean Gewürztraminer 2003   CHILE

Very lemony, lychee-edged freshness with a hint of
passionfruit.

16

RED £6.99

Luis Felipe Edwards Malbec Terraced 2002   CHILE

18 points in 18 months' time. Wonderfully rich,
complex, layered berries, chocolate, spice and tannins.

16

WHITE   £7.99
Las Brisas Chardonnay Reserve 2002   CHILE
Delightful touch of wood to rich melon and lime.

16

WHITE   £4.99
Les Jamelles Viognier 2003   FRANCE
Superb dry apricot and lemon, dry and crisp, which
goes faintly peachy as it dries in the throat.

16

WHITE   £3.99
Kingston Estate Chardonnay/Verdelho 2003   AUSTRALIA
Screwcap. Very forward apricot, peach and dry paw-
paw fruit. Classy yet exuberant.

On corks and corkscrews (No. 3)

When Peter Gordon opened the famous Sugar Club restaurant in
Notting Hill's All Saint's Road, some time in the last millennium, I
went three times in the first three weeks of its opening and each
time I had to send the first bottle of New Zealand white wine back
because it was ruined by its cork. Even I was embarrassed, and
not a little upset, by the third time but at least by then the
manager knew the score. We'd discussed it before. He instantly
brought a second bottle and we tasted them side by side and, as
on the first two occasions, he expressed his astonishment yet
complete agreement. 'There's no doubt that the second bottle is
fresher and crisper, more pleasantly aromatic, than the first. I
wonder how many of my customers, though, would have accepted
the first bottle as the way the wine was supposed to be?' Yes, and,
sadly, never bought the wine again because it was so darned dull.

16

RED £5.99

Misiónes Cabernet Franc Reserve 2003   CHILE
Jam layers, spice layers and roasted berry layers.

16

WHITE £5.29

Oxford Landing Sauvignon Blanc 2004   AUSTRALIA
Screwcap. Delightfully gooseberry fruit of tang and
taste.

16

RED £5.99

Trio Merlot/Carmenere/Sauvignon 2002   CHILE
Sheer exuberant blackberries with spicy grilled plums.
Hint of chocolate to the tannins. Lovely chewy
ripeness and classiness.

16

WHITE £5.99

Sauvignon Blanc, Marlborough 2003   NEW ZEALAND
Very lengthy experience from gentle gooseberry to
chalky tanginess of pineapple on the finish.
Also at Thresher, Oddbins, Tesco, Safeway,
Somerfield, Sainsbury's, Booths, Morrison's, Small
Merchants (Unwins, Londis).

16

WHITE £7.49

Oyster Bay Sauvignon Blanc 2003   NEW ZEALAND
Screwcap. Deliciously refreshing yet less immediate
than that suggests. It has real tangy richness.
Also at Majestic.

OTHER WINES 15.5 AND UNDER

15.5   RED £9.99
Bethany Cabernet Merlot 2001   AUSTRALIA

                                          RED £4.79
Co-op Australian Lime Tree Merlot 2003   AUSTRALIA

                                          WHITE £4.49
Co-op Fair Trade Chilean Sémillon 2003   CHILE

                                          RED £4.99
Co-op Fair Trade Chilean Carmenere 2002   CHILE

                                          WHITE £3.79
Co-op Long Slim Chardonnay/Sémillon 2003   CHILE

                                          RED £5.49
Co-op Chilean Cabernet Sauvignon Reserve 2001 CHILE

                                          RED £5.99
Gracia Cabernet Sauvignon Reserva 2002   CHILE

                                          WHITE £4.99
Orchid Vale Chardonnay/Grenache,   FRANCE
Languedoc 2002

                                          WHITE £5.99
Thandi Chardonnay 2003   SOUTH AFRICA
Also at Tesco.

15   RED £3.99
Co-op Chilean Cabernet Sauvignon 2003   CHILE

	WHITE	£3.99
Co-op Vin de Pays d'Oc Chardonnay 2003		FRANCE
	WHITE	£4.49
Chileño Sauvignon Blanc 2003		CHILE
	RED	£5.99
Gracia Carmenere Reserva Especial 2003		CHILE
	WHITE	£3.99
Jon Josh Estate Chardonnay 2002		HUNGARY
	RED	£3.99
Kingston Estate Cabernet Sauvignon/ Petit Verdot 2003 Screwcap.		AUSTRALIA
	RED	£8.99
Las Brisas Pinot Noir Reserve 2003		CHILE
	WHITE	£7.99
Las Brisas Chardonnay 2002		CHILE
	RED	£4.59
Co-op Mountain Vines Cabernet Reserve 2001		CYPRUS
	WHITE	£5.49
Starlight Coast Chardonnay 2002		USA
	WHITE	£5.49
The Boulders Pinot Grigio 2002		USA
	RED	£5.49
The Boulders Shiraz Reserve 2002 Screwcap.		USA

14.5

WHITE £4.49

Co-op Fair Trade Chilean Oaked Sémillon 2003   CHILE

RED £4.99

Co-op Fair Trade Cabernet Sauvignon 2003   SOUTH AFRICA

RED £4.99

Co-op Australian Lime Tree Cabernet   AUSTRALIA
Sauvignon 2003

RED £3.99

Co-op Chilean Merlot 2003   CHILE

RED £4.69

Gracia Merlot Curioso 2003   CHILE

WHITE £4.29

Lily White Côtes de Gascogne 2003   FRANCE

WHITE £6.99

Château du Bluizard Beaujolais Blanc 2002   FRANCE

ROSÉ £4.49

Masterpeace Rosé 2003   AUSTRALIA

WHITE SPARKLING £23.99

Piper Heidsieck Cuvée Sublime Demi-Sec NV   FRANCE

14

RED £4.99

Co-op Fair Trade Cape Cabernet   SOUTH AFRICA
Sauvignon 2003
At selected branches.

RED £4.99

Co-op Fair Trade Chilean Carmenere 2003   CHILE

	RED	£4.29
Co-op Jacaranda Hill Shiraz 2003		AUSTRALIA
	RED	£3.79
Co-op Long Slim Cabernet/Merlot 2003		CHILE
	WHITE	£4.29
Co-op Mountain Vines Sémillon 2002		CYPRUS
	WHITE	£4.29
Château Pierrousselle Blanc 2003		FRANCE
	RED	£5.99
Palandri Boundary Road Shiraz 2002		AUSTRALIA
	WHITE	£5.99
Rosemount GTR 2003		AUSTRALIA
	RED	£5.99
Wolf Blass Shiraz/Grenache 2002		AUSTRALIA

E-TAILERS

BARRELS AND BOTTLES

E-mail: sales@barrelsandbottles.co.uk
Website: www.barrelsandbottles.co.uk

Tel: (0114) 2556611
Fax: (0114) 2551010

EVERYWINE

E-mail: admin@everywine.co.uk
Website: www.everywine.co.uk

Tel: (01772) 329700
Fax: (01772) 329709

LAITHWAITES

E-mail: orders@laithwaites.co.uk
Website: www.laithwaites.co.uk

Tel: (0870) 4448383
Fax: (0970) 4448282

VINTAGE ROOTS (ORGANIC WINES)

E-mail: info@vintageroots.co.uk
Website: www.vintageroots.co.uk

Tel: (0118) 976 1999
Fax: (0118) 976 1998

VIRGIN WINES

E-mail: help@virginwines.com
Website: www.virginwines.com

Tel: (0870)1642034
Fax: (01603) 619277

For all E-tailers' wines 14 points and under visit
www.superplonk.com

17
WHITE £11.99
NEW ZEALAND

Montana 'P' Patutahi Estate Gewürztraminer 2002
Everywine
Simply mouth-watering delights of vague Turkish delight and lime and lychee.

16.5
WHITE £5.99
SPAIN

Lignum Blanco, Albet I Noya Penedes 2002
Vintage Roots
Superb, dry, woody Ogen melon, pear and fine citrus. Has tannins and great tension. Finer than many Meursaults.

16.5
WHITE £11.99
NEW ZEALAND

Te Muna Road Vineyard Sauvignon Blanc 2003
Virgin Wines
Screwcap. Very elegant and strikingly well textured. Also at The Wine Society.

16.5
WHITE £5.50
SPAIN

Xarello Classic, Albet I Noya Penedes 2003
Vintage Roots
Superb tangy gooseberry and citrus. Drink by summer 2004 for maximum sensuality.

16.5
WHITE £6.49
CHILE

Casa Lapostolle Sauvignon Blanc 2003
Everywine, Barrels and Bottles
Super dry, under-ripe fruit yet this subtlety is

amazingly emphatic and suggestive of richness
rather than achieving it full on. A classic Sauvignon
Blanc.
Also at Booths, London Stores (Selfridges), Small
Merchants (Partridges).

16

RED £5.50

Azul Y Garanza Navarra Tempranillo/Cabernet 2003 SPAIN
Vintage Roots
Very firm, ripe fruit, lovely roasted plum and
raspberry with fine tannins.

Arborfield is a village in Berkshire on the river Loddon. It has a
history which includes the ruins of the old parish church, circa
1256, in the grounds of Arborfield Hall. It is in this backwater
(which may have changed since my 1899 gazetteer apprised me of
the above facts) that, wholly appropriately, one of the country's
most old-fashioned wine merchants is to be found: Vintage Roots,
which concerns itself solely with organic and bio-dynamic
products where the use of chemicals is shunned. And not just
with wines. One of its Armagnac producers sent me a sample out
of the blue, confusing me with a spirits critic I guess, and it may
interest you to know that Bas Armagnac, Domaine de Saoubis is
an utter elixir. It reveals the actual suggestion of grapes (my life!)
along with a nuttiness and that beautiful oiliness of the best
brandies. Its complexity is suave and subtle and of the order of the
most accomplished single malts and Cognacs (and some
Calvados). It costs £25 and I rated it 18.5 points out of 20.

16

WHITE £4.50

SPAIN

Can Vendrell, Albet I Noya Penedes 2003
Vintage Roots
Very rich yet not inelegant. Thickly knitted,
citrus/melon fruit with a tangy finish.

16

RED £5.99

CHILE

Monos Locos Merlot 2003
Virgin Wines
Very polished, smooth, ripe unguent.

16

WHITE £8.00

SPAIN

Maturana Blanco Viña Ijalba Rioja 2002
Vintage Roots
Very unusual fish/spice wine! Creamy, rich, citrus
with smoky melon.

16

ROSÉ £7.99

SPAIN

**Pinot Noir/Merlot Rosé, Albet I Noya
Penedes 2003**
Vintage Roots
Delicious chewy cassis. Has light tannins, fresh and
frisky.

16

RED £5.75

SPAIN

Tempranillo Classic, Albet I Noya Penedes 2003
Vintage Roots
Lovely ripe plum and blackberry with finely textured,
warm tannins.

16

RED £6.75
CHILE

**Vinedos Organicos Emiliana 'Novas'
Cabernet Sauvignon/Merlot 2002**
Vintage Roots
Rich chocolate and black cherries.

OTHER WINES 15.5 AND UNDER

15.5

WHITE £5.99
MOLDOVA

Albastrele Sauvignon Blanc 2003
Laithwaites

WHITE £5.99
CHILE

La Vigubor 'Ventura' Sauvignon Blanc 2003
Vintage Roots

WHITE £5.99
CHILE

Monos Locos Sauvignon Blanc 2003
Virgin Wines

RED £5.50
CHILE

Touchstone Merlot 2002
Vintage Roots

WHITE £9.00
NEW ZEALAND

Vidal Estate Chardonnay 2003
Everywine

RED £5.50
CHILE

Touchstone Cabernet Sauvignon 2003
Vintage Roots

15

WHITE £7.99

Capel Vale Sauvignon Blanc/Sémillon 2002 AUSTRALIA
Everywine

RED £12.79

Goldwater Estate Wood's Hill NEW ZEALAND
Cabernet Sauvignon/Merlot 2000
Everywine

WHITE £5.99

Monos Locos Chardonnay 2003 CHILE
Virgin Wines

WHITE £6.99

Monos Locos Viognier 2003 CHILE
Virgin Wines

RED £6.99

Monos Locos Cabernet Sauvignon 2001 CHILE
Virgin Wines

RED £4.25

Organic Fruity Red NV SPAIN
Vintage Roots

WHITE £6.75

Vinedos Organicos Emiliana 'Novas' CHILE
Chardonnay 2003
Vintage Roots

14.5

WHITE £7.99

De Martino Legado Sauvignon Blanc Reserva 2003 CHILE
Virgin Wines

14

WHITE £7.99

De Martino Legado Chardonnay Reserva 2002 CHILE
Virgin Wines

RED £9.99

De Martino Single Vineyard Pinot Noir 2002 CHILE
Virgin Wines

WHITE £9.99

The Crossings Catherine's Run NEW ZEALAND
Sauvignon Blanc 2001
Everywine

LONDON STORES

FORTNUM & MASON

181 Piccadilly,
London WIA IER

Tel: (020) 7734 8040
Fax: (020) 7437 3278

E-mail: info@fortnumandmason.co.uk
Website: www.fortnumandmason.com

HARRODS

Brompton Road,
Knightsbridge,
London SWIX 7XL

Tel: (020) 7730 1234
Fax: (020) 7225 5823

E-mail: food.halls@harrods.com
Website: www.harrods.com

HARVEY NICHOLS

125 Knightsbridge,
London SWIX 7RJ

Tel: (020) 7201 8537
Fax: (020) 7 245 6561

E-mail: wineshop@harveynichols.com
Website: www.harveynichols.com

SELFRIDGES

400 Oxford Street,
London WIA IAB

Tel: (020) 7318 3730
Fax: (020) 7318 3730

E-mail: wine.club@selfridges.co.uk
Website: www.selfridges.co.uk

For London Stores' wines 15.5 points and under visit
www.superplonk.com

18.5

RED £16.49
CHILE

Torres Manso de Velasco 2000
Harrods
This is one of those masterpieces every bit as
satisfying as a Mozart piano sonata: effortless, tuneful,
silky, surprisingly elongated and very, very restful.
The wine is composed of smooth berries and tannins
as svelte as taffeta with a very soft (sotto voce?)
suggestion of creamy coffee. Yet in spite of these
delicate nuances I enjoyed it, and the wine showed all
its sides with a simple slab of real mature Cheddar.
Cellar it? If you enjoy greater vegetality, yes. But how
can this wine improve? It is magnificent now.
Also at Small Merchants (Thos Peatling, Portland
Wine Company).

17.5

WHITE £15.00
NEW ZEALAND

Reserve Chardonnay Marlborough 2001
Selfridges
Finesse, flavour, fabulous technique. The genteel
touches of charred hay and melon are wonderful.
Also at Small Merchants (Philglas & Swiggot,
Wimbledon Wine Cellars).

17

RED £37.50
CHILE

Casa Lapostolle Clos Apalta 2001
Selfridges, Harrods
A blend of Carmenere, Merlot and Cabernet which
deliciously sears the palate as one of the world's most
majestic reds should: imperiously yet sympathetically,
richly yet with finesse, boldly yet with layers of
complex berries and tannins.

16.5

WHITE £15.29

Goldwater Estate Zell Chardonnay 2002   NEW ZEALAND

Harrods

One of the most elegant yet subtly impactful of North Island Chardonnays.

16.5

WHITE £9.99

Knappstein Lenswood Vineyards   AUSTRALIA
Sauvignon Blanc 2003

Harrods

Screwcap. Simply light years fresher and tangier than any Sancerre.

Also at Small Merchants (Handfords).

16.5

WHITE £6.49

Casa Lapostolle Sauvignon Blanc 2003   CHILE

Selfridges

Super dry, under-ripe fruit yet this subtlety is amazingly emphatic and suggestive of richness rather than achieving it full on. A classic Sauvignon Blanc.

Also at Booths, Small Merchants (Partridges), E-tailers (Everywine, Barrels and Bottles).

16

WHITE £9.99

Knappstein Lenswood Vineyards   AUSTRALIA
Sémillon 2000

Harrods

Hints of many things and the sum of those delicate subtleties is sheer pleasure-giving liquid.

Also at Small Merchants (The Wine Library, Wine Importers of Edinburgh).

MAJESTIC

Head Office:
Majestic House,
Otterspool Way,
Watford, Hertfordshire WD25 8WW

Tel:(01923) 298200
Fax:(01923) 819105

E-mail: info@majestic.co.uk
Website: www.majestic.co.uk

For all Majestic wines of 14 points and under visit
www.superplonk.com

17.5

RED £4.99

Château Guiot, Costières de Nîmes 2003   FRANCE

Quite wonderful how this Grenache/Syrah blend goes
from plums and berries to silken chocolate and
roasted nuts.

17.5

RED £12.99

Casa Lapostolle Cuvée Alexandre Merlot 2000   CHILE

Simply wonderful ripe leather, spice, roasted berried
richness and fine tannins.
Also at Booths, Safeway.

17.5

WHITE £9.99

Montes Alpha Chardonnay 2002   CHILE

Superbly well-textured and classy, offering multiple
diversions for the palate, including smoky apricot and
lemon, peach and a delicious hint of grilled melon (if
such a thing is possible).

17.5

RED £15.99

Santa Rita Triple C 1999   CHILE

Magnificently sleek (yet muscled) rich (yet full of
subtleties). Wonderful liquid.

17

WHITE £4.69

Argento Pinot Grigio 2003   ARGENTINA

Wonderful lime-edged peach fruit which expands on
the tastebuds gloriously. Utterly delicious, classy,
elegant.

17

RED £8.99

FRANCE

**Château de Gaudou Cuvée Renaissance,
Cahors 2001**

Pure rustic heaven. Offers herbs, nuts, raunchy berries
and lengthy tannins. Brilliant with roast meats.

17

RED £7.99

FRANCE

**Domaine de Tourtourel, Pic St Loup,
Languedoc 2001**

Effortlessly proceeds to tease with roasted berries,
herbs and chocolate. The texture is pure taffeta.
Remarkably classy.

17

WHITE £17.99

GERMANY

**Gewürztraminer Grand Cru, Sonnenglanz,
Bott-Geyl 2001**

Lovely lime-edged grapefruit and rich peach fruit.
Will gain extra intensity within hours of decanting
and can be cellared to advantage for up to 8, maybe
10 years and maybe 20 to 30.

On corks and corkscrews (No. 4)

It makes me feel a bloody show-off sending wine back, all the
brouhaha involved in calling the waiter over and complaining. I hate
it. I've even had to do it at official wine dinners and lunches as well,
where the wine has been declared 'fit' by a so-called 'expert' let
alone considered OK by the sommelier serving the wine(s). Yet I'm
supposed to be a pro. So if I feel uncomfortable about this sort of
thing – not least because I dislike the thought that my companions
might think I'm just doing it for effect – how about anyone else?

17   RED £8.99

Pirramimma Petit Verdot 2001   AUSTRALIA

Seizes hold of the tastebuds with sensual berries,
spices and tannins and then, many seconds later,
releases to reveal cocoa.

17   WHITE £16.99

Pinot Gris Grand Cru, Sonnenglanz,   GERMANY
Bott-Geyl 2001

Wonderful apricot richness which develops
agonisingly slowly to also reveal spicy paw-paw. Open
and full decant up to 12 hours beforehand.

17   RED £10.75

Single Vineyard Cabernet Franc 2001   CHILE

Gorgeous hints of smoky berries and spice. Fine
tannins.

17   RED £14.99

The Ridge Syrah 2001   SOUTH AFRICA

Lovely coffee-toned tannins and deep-berried richness.

16.5   WHITE £8.49

Amberley Estate Sauvignon Blanc 2003   AUSTRALIA

A good rich edge, well rounded to apricot/gooseberry
fruit. Superb with Thai food.

16.5   RED £6.99

Bellingham Shiraz 2002   SOUTH AFRICA

Sheer heavenly chocolate and berried treasures here.

16.5

WHITE £10.99

Cape Mentelle   AUSTRALIA
Sémillon/Sauvignon 2002

The texture is amazingly gripping, showing white
tannins, under-ripe peach/pear/citrus and a vegetal
grassy undertone.

16.5

WHITE £3.79

Coldridge Estate Chardonnay 2002   AUSTRALIA

Developed superbly in bottle this 2002, and the price
is ridiculous considering the polished unguence of
liquid and its generous dollops of peach, citrus and
pear.

16.5

RED £5.49

Château La Selette, Minervois 2002   FRANCE

Terrific pace across the palate revealing grilled berries
and a touch of chocolate to the tannins.

16.5

WHITE £4.99

Cono Sur Viognier 2002   CHILE

It starts out crisp and fresh and then the apricot really
bites.

16.5

WHITE SPARKLING £13.75

Cloudy Bay Pelorus 1999   NEW ZEALAND

Superb, elegant, fruity (yet possessing great finesse),
this outshines all grande marque champagnes for the
money.

16.5

WHITE £5.49
CHILE

**Concha y Toro Casillero del Diablo
Sauvignon Blanc 2002**

So elegant, demure, full of itself yet not showy. Fine
citrus with overtones of apricot and pineapple.

16.5

WHITE £6.49

De Wetshof Estate Lesca Chardonnay 2003   SOUTH AFRICA

Superbly elegant where an abundance of subtle layers –
creamy, citric peachy, smoky by turns – tease the palate.

16.5

WHITE £6.99

**Fairleigh Estate Single Vineyard
Sauvignon Blanc 2003**   NEW ZEALAND

Screwcap. Superb tropicality without soppiness.
Teasingly rich yet finely wrought, it makes great glugging
and is perfect to enjoy with spicy poultry dishes.

16.5

RED £6.99

Goats do Roam in Villages 2002   SOUTH AFRICA

This is a treat for every sense from the deep garnet
colour through the savoury aroma to the finish of
roasted plums and cherries in the throat. It is sheer
hedonism. Stunning tannins, hint of cardamom.
Also at Somerfield, Tesco.

16.5

WHITE £5.99

Goats do Roam in Villages 2003   SOUTH AFRICA

A superb, dry, orange peel/citrus and dry pear.
Genteel plumpness, graciously textured, beautifully
complete.

16.5

WHITE £7.99

Kangarilla Road Chardonnay 2003 AUSTRALIA

Begins with citrus/peach, ends with mango and lime.
Quite a performance.

16.5

WHITE £5.99

Montes Reserve CHILE
Sauvignon Blanc 2003

Superb layers of smoky pear and brisk pineapple.
Brilliant wine for complex, creamily sauced fish dishes.

16.5

RED £7.49

Montes Reserve CHILE
Cabernet Sauvignon 2002

Ripe but upright (thanks to superb tannins). The
berries are very classy, firm, spicy and bold.

16.5

WHITE £6.99

Oyster Bay Chardonnay 2002 NEW ZEALAND

One of the Kiwis' top Chardonnays with its stylish
take on the clichéd melon/lemon recipe.

16.5

RED £9.99

Pirramimma Premium Cabernet AUSTRALIA
Sauvignon 2001

Perfectly mature berries which crowd the palate with
huge flavours of berries and chocolate. Sweet/dry
finish is superb.

16.5
RED £9.99

Pirramimma Premium Shiraz 2001 AUSTRALIA
Burned licorice finish ends a frighteningly delicious
performance where the strings (sweet berries) are
superbly accompanied and indeed counterpointed by
the brass (tannins).

16.5
WHITE £7.99

Sticks Chardonnay 2003 AUSTRALIA
It has what fine white wine must have: balance yet
individuality, richness yet dryness (without
impetuosity of acidity) and a lingering citrus finish.

16.5
WHITE £4.69

Argento Chardonnay 2003 ARGENTINA
More chaotic than previous vintages but still excitingly
biting with its ripe melon/citrus fruit.
Also at Asda, Budgens, Somerfield, Tesco.

16.5
WHITE £4.99

Concha y Toro Casillero del Diablo CHILE
Chardonnay 2003
Flavoursome yet delicate.
Also at Asda, Budgens, Majestic.

16
RED £4.69

Cono Sur Pinot Noir 2003 CHILE
Superb gamy cassis – very firm and compressed. Very
baby bouncy.
Also at Budgens, Morrison's, Somerfield, Tesco,
Waitrose.

16

RED £5.85

Alamos Malbec 2002 ARGENTINA
Very rich, ripe and finely balanced with a big finish of
chocolate and blackberries.

16

RED £4.69

Argento Malbec 2003 ARGENTINA
Superbly well-textured berries with a chocolate
undertone. Marvellously biteable fruit.
Also at Budgens, Somerfield, Tesco.

16

RED £7.49

Bourgueil Les Cent Boisselées, FRANCE
Pierre-Jacques Druet 2002
I like the stealth of the wine – it proceeds with cherry-
rich caution and then, at the finish, releases savoury
tannins.

16

RED £5.99

Beaumes de Venise La Chapelle FRANCE
Notre Dame d'Aubune 2002
Soft plums which gather pace to reveal frisky tannins.

16

RED £5.49

Château Guiraud, St-Chinian, Languedoc 2002 FRANCE
Very firm, almost solid, cassis richness with gripping
tannins. Really combative liquid here.

16

RED £5.99

Château du Luc Corbières, Languedoc 2001 FRANCE
Mature, ripe (tending to show its age here) with fleshy
plums and once-craggy tannins.

16   WHITE   £4.99

Cono Sur Gewürztraminer 2002   CHILE

A gorgeous aperitif tipple with the lychee given a
lemon coating.

---

16   WHITE   £14.99

Chardonnay 2001   AUSTRALIA

High powered richness which turns delicately dry.
Also at Sainsbury's.

---

16   RED   £6.49

Côtes du Rhône-Villages Sablet,   FRANCE
Domaine de Paiugier 2001

Vigorous yet calm, rich yet slow to develop and reveal
all its sides, rustic yet couth.

---

16   ROSÉ   £5.29

Château Guiot Rosé, Costières de Nîmes 2003   FRANCE

Superbly brash cherry fruit – excellent well chilled,
with grilled fish.

---

16   RED   £10.99

Catena Cabernet Sauvignon 2001   ARGENTINA

Delicious – so ripe and ready yet so unashamedly
chic.

---

16   WHITE   £4.99

Chardonnay di Sicilia, Cantine Settesoli 2003   ITALY

Lovely plump melon and citrus. Sheer delight.

16

WHITE £4.99

Cono Sur Viognier 2003   CHILE

Very demure white peach fruit (touch smoky).
Also at Somerfield.

16

WHITE £8.49

Gavi di Gavi Raccolto Tardivo, Villa Lanata 2002   ITALY

Late harvest but emphatically not sweet. It displays
warm peach and peach, thickly knitted admittedly, but
they finish dryly. Thai food candidate.

16

WHITE £6.99

Domaine des Ormousseux, Coteaux du   FRANCE
Giennois 2003

Sheer satin delight. Lovely dry citrus/melon/pear –
over-ripe.

16

WHITE £4.99

Griffin Vineyards Chardonnay 2003   AUSTRALIA

Thunderingly delicious bargain. The fruit melts in the
mouth and clings.

16

WHITE £4.99

Griffin Vineyards Verdelho 2003   AUSTRALIA

Bargain pear/apricot tippling.

16

WHITE £7.99

Gavi di Gavi Raccolto Tardivo, Villa Lanata 2003   ITALY

What a delightful change from Chardonnay. Melon
yes, but the hint of grapefruit is very appealing.

16

WHITE £8.99

Kangarilla Road Viognier 2003 AUSTRALIA

Majestic parcel! Young, still developing in bottle, so
decant 2-3 hours ahead to get the full impact of the
subtle apricot.

16

RED £7.49

Montes 'Limited Selection' Pinot Noir 2002 CHILE

Lovely cassis and cherry crunchiness with deft
tannins, a hint of wood, a touch of spice.

16

RED £6.99

Montes 'Limited Selection' Cabernet/ CHILE
Carmenere 2002

Floods the palate with grilled berries, herbs and
tannins and gently releases cobnuts and chocolate.

16

WHITE £3.99

Montgomery Creek Chardonnay 2003 USA

Lovely plump ripe fruit which lingers lushly yet dryly.

16

WHITE £7.99

New Dog Sauvignon Blanc 2003 NEW ZEALAND

Screwcap. Deliciously complex gooseberry and lime.

16

WHITE £7.99

Oyster Bay Sauvignon Blanc 2003 NEW ZEALAND

Screwcap. Deliciously refreshing yet less immediate
than that suggests. It has real tangy richness.
Also at Co-op.

16

WHITE £9.99
FRANCE

**Pouilly-Fumé Domaine des Rabichattes,
'Les Champs de Cri' 2002**
Very elegant, opulent yet dry Sauvignon with
firm peach fruit, gooseberry and lemon. Classily
complete.

16

WHITE £6.49

Pirramimma Hillview Chardonnay 2002   AUSTRALIA
It's the sheer polished opulence of the liquid which
impresses. Silky peach and fine citrus in harmony.

16

RED £7.99
AUSTRALIA

**Pirramimma Stock's Hill
Cabernet Sauvignon 2001**
Yes it's ripe. Yes it's brash. Yes, it's all over you like a
puppy dog. But it's deliciously gamy and jammy.

16

WHITE £7.49
FRANCE

Quincy Jean-Charles Borgnat 2002
One of the most charming Quincys I've tasted for a
while. The Sauvignon grape has smooth cream and
citrus and is terrific with spiced shellfish.

16

RED £5.49
FRANCE

Réserve Luc St Roche, Montepeyroux 2002
Proceeds slowly (and this unshowily) from plums to
dry blackberries, herbs and tannins on the finish.

16   WHITE   £6.99
    Riff Pinot Grigio, Alois Lageder 2003   ITALY
    Very firm apricot ripeness.

16   WHITE   £7.69
    Ravenswood Vintners Blend Chardonnay 2002   USA
    Tangy and yet complex with fine smoky pear and
    citrus fruit.

16   RED   £7.99
    Riserva Alentejo Vinhos Sogrape 2001   PORTUGAL
    Has excellent, attentive tannins serving brisk plums,
    gently grilled, and the texture is classy (ripe but
    controlled).

May I put in a word for water? I am inspired to do so by Mr Greenwood of Ingleton in Yorkshire (*Guardian* letters, June 28th 2003). He wrote to say that though his tap water tasted awful he could not justify paying the high prices charged for the bottled stuff. Neither can I, Mr Greenwood. I have not bought any mineral water for over three years now, but my guests regularly remark how much they like the Evian, Badoît and San Pellegrino served at my house because it is these bottles I use to contain the stuff I pay those outrageous water rates to have flow from my taps. It is all a question of perception. I advise Mr Greenwood to think and glug again and see if a dose of tap in a trendy mineral water bottle might not do wonders for the taste.

16

WHITE £6.99

Santa Rita Reserva Chardonnay 2002 CHILE
Demure, at first, then high-class lemon and peach
strike.

16

ROSÉ £5.49

Santa Rita Cabernet Sauvignon Rosé 2003 CHILE
Always one of Chile's most pertinent rosés.
Also at Sainsbury's.

16

WHITE £5.99

Sauvignon de Touraine, Joel Delaunay 2003 ITALY
Superbly crisp and classic.

16

WHITE £4.99

Tatachilla Breakneck Creek Chardonnay 2002 AUSTRALIA
Wonderfully dry yet superbly full of flavour and
under-ripe fruit. Classy melon, shrewd lemon, touch
of pineapple.

16

WHITE £8.99

Waimea Estate Sauvignon Blanc 2003 NEW ZEALAND
Screwcap. Chewy style of Sauvignon Blanc with
limpid citrus giving the gooseberry an appealing
fresh edge.

16

WHITE £6.03

Wynns Coonawarra Estate Riesling 2001 AUSTRALIA
18.5 points in 5–8 years.

16

RED £18.99
AUSTRALIA

Yalumba Signature Cabernet/Shiraz, Barossa 1999
Rich, broad, deep, complex, well-muscled – and it'll do the washing up and replace the lavatory seat. Makes the perfect husband.

16

RED £7.49
USA

Ravenswood Vintners Blend Zinfandel 2001
Chunky berries with cool tannins, a hint of spice, a touch of savourily grilled plum.
Also at Asda, Booths, Somerfield, Waitrose.

16

RED £4.99
CHILE

Concha y Toro Casillero del Diablo Carmenere 2003
Chewy plums, tart blackberries, ripe tannins. Superb recipe.
Also at Sainsbury's.

OTHER WINES 15.5 AND UNDER

15.5

WHITE £8.49
SPAIN

Albarino Martin Codax, Rias Baixas 2002

RED £4.99
CHILE

Cono Sur Syrah 2001

RED £2.99
FRANCE

Cuvée de Richard Rouge, Vin de Pays de l'Aude 2003

RED £6.49

Château de l'Abbaye de St Ferme,   FRANCE
Bordeaux Supérieur 2002

WHITE £2.99

Cuvée de Richard Blanc,   FRANCE
Vin de Pays d'Oc 2003

WHITE £5.99

Château de Cray, Bourgogne Aligoté 2003   FRANCE

ROSÉ £3.49

Cuvée des Amandiers Rosé,   FRANCE
Vin de Pays d'Oc 2003

RED £14.99

Château Plaisance,   FRANCE
St-Emilion Grand Cru Classé 2001

WHITE £7.49

De Wetshof Limestone Hill Chardonnay,   SOUTH AFRICA
Danie de Wet 2003

WHITE £4.49

Les Fontanelles Sauvignon Blanc,   FRANCE
Vin de Pays d'Oc 2003

WHITE £3.99

Lyeth Chardonnay 1997   USA

RED £4.99

Michel Laroche Pinot Noir,   FRANCE
Vin de Pays de l'Ile de Beauté 2002

Torres Viña Sol 2003
WHITE £4.99
SPAIN
Screwcap. Also at Asda, Thresher.

Verdicchio Croce del Moro 2002
WHITE £4.49
ITALY

Verdicchio dei Castelli di Jesi,
Coste del Molino 2003
WHITE £5.49
ITALY

15

Coldridge Estate Merlot 2003
RED £3.79
AUSTRALIA

Cuvée des Amandiers Blanc,
Vin de Pays d'Oc 2003
WHITE £3.49
FRANCE

Catena Barrel Fermented Chardonnay 2002
WHITE £10.99
ARGENTINA

Grange du Midi Merlot, Vin de Pays d'Oc 2003
RED £3.99
FRANCE

Kangarilla Road Shiraz 2002
RED £9.99
AUSTRALIA

Kangarilla Road Cabernet Sauvignon 2001
RED £9.99
AUSTRALIA

Michel Laroche Chardonnay,
Vin de Pays d'Oc 2002
WHITE £4.99
FRANCE

	WHITE	£8.49
Menetou-Salon, Domaine Henry Pelle 2003		FRANCE

	WHITE	£3.69
Neblina Sauvignon Blanc 2003		CHILE

	RED	£7.99
Oyster Bay Merlot 2002		NEW ZEALAND
Screwcap.		

	WHITE	£7.99
Pinot Grigio San Angelo Vineyard 2003		ITALY

	RED	£6.99
Pepi Merlot 2002		USA

	FORTIFIED	£14.99
Quinta da Roeda Vintage Port, Croft 1987		PORTUGAL

	WHITE	£9.99
Riesling Grand Cru Eichberg, Zinck 2002		GERMANY
Limited parcel.		

	RED	£5.99
St Hallett Gamekeeper's Reserve 2003		AUSTRALIA

	RED	£4.99
Tatachilla Breakneck Creek		AUSTRALIA
Cabernet Sauvignon 2001		

	WHITE SPARKLING	£8.99
Yellowglen Pinot Noir/Chardonnay NV		AUSTRALIA

14.5

WHITE £8.49
AUSTRALIA
Amberley Estate Sémillon 2002

WHITE £3.49
USA
Christophe Chardonnay 1997

WHITE £8.49
FRANCE
Chablis, Domaine Servin 2002

RED £12.00
SOUTH AFRICA
Kanontop Pinotage 2001

RED £3.29
SPAIN
Tempranillo, Finca Tempranal 2002

WHITE £15.99
FRANCE
Vire Clesse 'La Verchère',
Christopher Cordier 2003

RED £9.99
AUSTRALIA
Wynns Coonawarra Estate
Cabernet Sauvignon 1999

14

RED £4.99
ITALY
Aglianico Rosso di Sicilia,
Cantine Settesoli 2002

WHITE £8.49
AUSTRALIA
Amberley Estate Sémillon 2003

ROSÉ £7.99
FRANCE
Château de Sours Rosé, Esmé Johnstone,
Bordeaux 2002

RED £19.99
FRANCE
Château de Sales, Pomerol 1997

ROSÉ £4.49

Château La Gravette Rosé, Minervois 2003   FRANCE

WHITE £4.99

Chapelle du Bois Colombard/Sauvignon,   FRANCE
Vin de Pays des Côtes de Gascogne 2003

RED £9.99

Delegat's Wine Estate Oyster Bay   NEW ZEALAND
Pinot Noir 2002

WHITE £4.99

Falkensteiner Riesling Mosel 2000   GERMANY
17 points in 2010. One to cellar.

RED £5.99

Les Douze, Fitou 2002   FRANCE

WHITE £4.49

Marc Ducournau,   FRANCE
Vin de Pays des Côtes de Gascogne 2003

RED £3.99

Montgomery Creek Cabernet Sauvignon 2003   USA

RED £7.99

Ochoa Tempranillo Crianza, Bodegas Ochoa 2000   SPAIN

WHITE £6.99

Pepi Chardonnay 2001   USA

RED £8.49

Premier Vin du Château de Pitray,   FRANCE
Côtes de Castillon 1999

RED £9.99

Waimea Estate Pinot Noir 2002   NEW ZEALAND

MARKS & SPENCER

Waterside House,
35 North Wharf Road,
London W2 1NW

Tel: (020) 7268 1234
Fax: (020) 7268 2380

Customer Services: (0845) 302 1234

E-mail: customer.services@marks-and-spencer.com
Website: www.marksandspencer.com

For Marks & Spencer wines 14 points and under visit
www.superplonk.com

17   WHITE £7.99
Banwell Farm Riesling 2003   AUSTRALIA
Superb tangy of chalky minerals, citrus and pineapple
with under-ripe gooseberry. Hugely immediate, highly
classy.

17   RED £6.99
Clos Roques d'Aspes Faugères,   FRANCE
Cave de Lauren, Languedoc 2000
Combines three elements of arousing deliciousness:
catering chocolate, burned berries (raspberry and
blackberry) and superbly lithe tannins. Class by the
bucketful here.

17   WHITE £5.99
Sierra Los Andes Gewürztraminer 2003   CHILE
An extraordinarily lean, individual specimen of brisk
lychee, spice and citrus. Very elegant.

17   RED £13.99
Villalta Amarone della Valpolicella DOCG 1998 ITALY
Stunning bitter almond and black cherry richness
with chocolate tannins.

16.5   RED £7.99
Côte de Brouilly Cuvée Godefroy,   FRANCE
Domaine de la Croix Dessaigne, Beaujolais 2003
So, Claude! You've cracked it! Claude Geoffrey who
makes this wine, once insisted on showing me his
vines at night with a torch. This specimen of his
midnight vines and his pride in them, is one of the

most focused I've tasted for years, offering simple sensuality and delicious tannins. Very classy, very complete.

16.5   RED £4.99
Domaine Le Cazal Minervois,   FRANCE
Château Cazal, Languedoc 2001
Performs on several levels and is a superb sum of many parts: cocoa, tea, tannins, berries and a texture which oozes class as it slowly evolves.

16.5   WHITE £5.99
Darting Estate Riesling   GERMANY
Durkheimer Michelsberg 2003
Superbly crisp and finely balanced. Will rate 18.5 points in 5 years but already its delicate richness is immense (yet subtle, if you see what I mean). Superb lemon and very spicy peach.

16.5   RED £6.50
Gold Label Reserve Cabernet Merlot,   FRANCE
Domaine Virginie, Vin de Pays d'Oc 2001
Superb chocolate richness here with savourily subtle berries, and warm tannins.

16.5   WHITE £5.99
Kaituna Hills Riesling 2003   NEW ZEALAND
18 points in 3 years. Sheer satin delight. Very forward – the petroleum undertone usually acquired with age is here, and it has lovely minerally citrus.

16.5
RED   £9.99

Leon d'Oro Merlot/Cabernet, Viña La Rosa 2002   CHILE
A bonfire of leaves burns subtly in the back but only
as the wine opens up. Then the classy berries assert
themselves and the tannins announce themselves and
we get a raucously delicious finish.

16.5
WHITE   £6.99

Pirque Estate Chardonnay 2003   CHILE
Wonderfully invigorating crisp, under-ripe Charentais
melon, citrus and pear.

16.5
WHITE   £6.99

Pinot Grigio Podere, La Prendina Estate 2003   ITALY
Delicious plump apricot with citrus edging.

Dr Schofield of Lincoln wrote to me enclosing a cutting from the
Guardian dated December 16th 1976 (for which, Doc, huge
thanks). The author is John Arlott who writes of the low-priced fine
wines to be found at the Tate Gallery restaurant. I remember Mr
Arlott's article when it appeared. I was furious. I wished to destroy
every copy of that day's *Guardian.* How dare this man tell the
world about the incredible wines to be found at the Tate? I was
eating there at least once a week at the time. It was my secret (and
had been for a few years before Mr Arlott spilled the beans). I
learned a lot about wine at the Tate (and still do, for the wine list
remains terra extraordinaire). I shared Mr Arlott's astonishment at
magnums of 1964 Lafite and Margaux for a tenner and bottles of
Mouton and Haut-Brion 1962 for a little over a fiver each.

16.5

WHITE SPARKLING £6.99

Prosecco NV ITALY

Superb! Has cheeky cherry richness which goes crisp
and clean – offering extreme elegance. It really is
superior to so many champagnes in its classic
allusions (without underlying or emphasis).

16.5

WHITE £8.99

Rudesheim Estate Riesling 2002 GERMANY

Combines crisp immediacy with lemon/apricot/hint
of pineapple finesse. Will age to 19 points by 2009.

16.5

RED £5.99

Tupungato Cabernet/Malbec 2003 ARGENTINA

Superb buzz from the chocolate berries, the burned
tannins, and the deep, rich-textured finish.

16

WHITE £5.99

Alsace Riesling 2003 FRANCE

Beautifully subtle lemon, orange peel and melon richness.

16

WHITE £3.29

Bianco Beneventano 2003 ITALY

Screwcap. A stunningly crisp and fresh white wine
with a subtle floral undertone.

16

WHITE £4.99

Bordeaux Sauvignon Blanc, Promocom 2003 FRANCE

Chewy, opulent, slightly herby (almost smoky) pear
with subdued citrus. Lovely glugging here.

16

RED £9.99

Canale Estate Reserve Merlot 2002 ARGENTINA
Were the grapes slow-roasted first? Superbly savoury
and gripping.

16

WHITE £4.99

Casa Leona Sauvignon Blanc 2003 CHILE
Lovely layered citrus and melon.

16

WHITE £4.99

Casa Leona Chardonnay, Viña La Rosa 2003 CHILE
Charming citrus and under-ripe Ogen melon.

16

WHITE £9.99

Ernst Loosen Zeltinger Himmelreich GERMANY
Vineyard Riesling 2003
Has sweet honey mitigated by a herby undertone of
subtlety yet presence. Will rate 18.5 in 2010.

16

WHITE £7.99

Father Oak Paso Robles Chardonnay 2002 USA
And oaky it is, but not at all excessively so. It
performs like a creamy lemon balm. More avuncular
than fatherly, then, and a witty uncle at that.

16

WHITE £4.99

Gold Label Sauvignon Blanc, FRANCE
Domaine Virginie 2003
A superbly dry, slightly vegetally leafy Sauvignon of
class and concentration. Sancerre, eat your heart out.

16

WHITE £8.99

Grüner Veltliner Gebling Vineyard 2003　　　AUSTRIA

Sheer dry brilliance. It's difficult to put into words
how a wine, a liquid, can be dry. Only Grüner
Veltliner can achieve this level of finesse. 18 in 2007.

16

WHITE £3.99

Hungarian Pinot Grigio 2003　　　HUNGARY

Lovely class here, has dry apricot and lemon.

16

RED £6.99

Houdamond Pinotage 2000　　　SOUTH AFRICA

Terrific tangy berries, chocolate tannins, spicy
cherries and superb tannins. A brilliantly vivacious
red.

16

RED £9.99

Leon d'Oro Gran Merlot/Cabernet Sauvignon 2002　　CHILE

Lay it down for another 2 years to achieve 17.5 points.

16

WHITE £6.99

Mineralstein Riesling 2003　　　GERMANY

And it has lovely minerals and subtle gooseberry,
lemon and peach! Will rate 18 in 3 years.

16

WHITE £9.99

Martin Estate Riesling 2003　　　AUSTRIA

Severe, prim, very dry! The restraint is cunning,
however, and by 2007 will reveal 17.5-point
richness.

16   RED £5.99

Mandorla Syrah MGM, Mondol del Vino 2003   ITALY
What a delightful exuberance here: big-berried
richness with a sweetness beautifully tempered by the
tannins.

16   RED £6.99

Pirque Estate Cabernet Sauvignon/Merlot 2001   CHILE
Ripe catering chocolate and grilled plums.

16   WHITE £6.99

Pirque Estate Sauvignon Blanc 2003   CHILE
Chewy, nervous lime. Brilliant oriental fish wine.

16   WHITE £3.99

Pinot Grigio, Akos Kamocsay 2003   HUNGARY
Superbly tangy-to-finish. Smoky apricot.
Also at Asda.*

On corks and corkscrews (No. 5)

It would help if all wine was screwcapped. It would eliminate cork
taint and bottle variation; and I guess (I do not know for absolutely
sure) that it would eliminate oxidation. It would also help, until
screwcaps are the norm, for wine waiters to know more about cork
taint and spoilage of wines. In America, wine waiters are
discouraged from smelling corks. But it is essential. A cork is
supposed to be a neutral seal. The end of it which has touched the
wine should smell only of wine. If it smells of anything else it may,
and I emphasise 'may', have contaminated the wine or taken the
edge off it in some way.

16

RED £7.99

Rasteau Côtes du Rhône-Villages, FRANCE
Perrin Frères 2001

Nicely mature, slightly crusty berries with a rustic richness of depth and gently baked richness.

16

RED £4.99

Rustica Primitivo MGM, Mondol del Vino 2003 ITALY

Lovely jammy berries coated in savoury tannins of class and concentration.

16

RED £5.99

Sierra Los Andes Merlot 2002 CHILE

Dry, rich, very nicely compacted red with cocoa-edged tannins to the very warm berries. Has a finish of chewy chocolate.

16

WHITE £5.99

Sierra Los Andes Chardonnay 2003 CHILE

Very classy, crisp and fresh with layers of soft light melon (under-ripe).

16

RED £6.99

Secano Leda Valley Pinot Noir, Leyda Estate 2003 CHILE

I think they held the berries over a barbecue before jumping on them with leathery calloused feet, for surely this is a very warm, human Pinot.

16

WHITE £7.99

Twin Wells Hunter Valley Sémillon, Tyrells 1999 AUSTRALIA
18 in 3–4 years. What a captivating grape Sémillon is.

Offers dry under-ripe pear and pineapple with a hint
of minerals. Classy, textured, very individual.

16

RED £6.99

Torres Scalza Montepulciano d'Abruzzo MGM, ITALY
Mondol del Vino 2003
Juicy plums with undertones of charred berries and
elongated tannins.

16

RED £4.99

Viña Casablanca Pinot Noir 2003 CHILE
Develops deliciously slowly to show gamey cassis.

OTHER WINES 15.5 AND UNDER

15.5

WHITE (3 litre box) £15.99

Alta Mira Sauvignon Blanc NV CHILE

WHITE £6.99

Banwell Farm Barossa Valley Sémillon 2002 AUSTRALIA

ROSÉ £4.99

Casa Leona Rosé 2003 CHILE

RED £4.99

Casa Leona Cabernet Sauvignon 2003 CHILE

RED £7.99

Darting Estate Pinot Noir 2003 AUSTRIA

RED £9.99

Domaine de Fontsèque Corbières 2001 FRANCE

WHITE SPARKLING £18.99
De Saint Gall Blanc de Blancs NV   FRANCE

WHITE £4.99
Dry Muscat 2003   FRANCE

WHITE £4.99
Gold Label Chardonnay, Domaine Virginie,   FRANCE
Vin de Pays d'Oc 2003

RED   (3 litre box) £13.99
Gaston de Veau Merlot, Vin de Pays d'Oc NV   FRANCE

WHITE   (3 litre box) £13.99
Gaston de Veau Chardonnay, Vin de Pays d'Oc NV FRANCE

WHITE £4.99
Grüner Veltliner Niederösterreich 2003   AUSTRIA

WHITE £3.99
Moscatel de Valencia Schenk 2003   SPAIN

WHITE £4.99
Pfalz Riesling 2003   GERMANY

RED £6.99
Pirque Estate Cabernet Sauvignon 2001   CHILE

WHITE   (3 litre box) £17.99
Pheasant Gully Chardonnay/Sémillon,   AUSTRALIA
Bin 109 NV

RED £6.99
San Pablo Estate, Bodegas Salentein 2002   ARGENTINA

WHITE £9.99
St Romain Les Senteurs, Nicholas Potel 2002   FRANCE

WHITE (3 litre box) £13.99
South African Chenin Blanc NV   SOUTH AFRICA

RED £9.99
Twin Wells McLaren Vale Shiraz, Tyrells 2001   AUSTRALIA

WHITE £4.99
Vin de Pays des Portes de la Mediterranée   FRANCE
Chardonnay/ Vermentino 2003

15

RED (3 litre box) £15.99
Alta Mira Cabernet Sauvignon NV   CHILE

ROSÉ £7.99
Bluff Hill Rosé NV   NEW ZEALAND

RED £4.99
Burra Brook Shiraz 2003   AUSTRALIA

RED £6.50
Casa Leona Cabernet Sauvignon Reserva 2003   CHILE

RED £5.50
Mantrana Vivanco Crianza Rioja,   SPAIN
Telma Rodrigues 2002

WHITE £7.50
St Véran Les Monts Bourgogne,   FRANCE
Cave de Prisse 2002

WHITE £10.99
Sancerre Hubert Brochard 2002   FRANCE

WHITE £7.99
Shepherds Ridge Sauvignon Blanc, NEW ZEALAND
Brent Marris 2003

RED £6.99
Secano Estate Pinot Noir 2003 CHILE

WHITE £3.29
Vin de Pays du Gers, Plaimont 2003 FRANCE

WHITE £13.00
Yarra Barn Chardonnay 2002 AUSTRALIA

14.5

WHITE £3.99
Domaine Mandeville Viognier 2003 FRANCE

WHITE £5.99
Friuli Sauvignon 2003 ITALY

14

RED £7.99
Bush View Shiraz, Evans & Tate 2002 AUSTRALIA

WHITE £5.99
Basilicata Dry Muscat 2003 ITALY

RED £6.99
Bourgogne Pinot Noir Les Senteurs 2002 FRANCE

RED £4.99
Casa Leona Cabernet, Viña La Rosa 2003 CHILE

RED £7.99
FRANCE

Château Gallais Bellevue Cru
Bourgeois Médoc 2001

WHITE £5.49
AUSTRALIA

Coonawarra Vineyards Riesling 2003

WHITE £12.99
FRANCE

Domaine La Crozes
Châteauneuf-du-Pape Blanc 2003

RED £9.99
FRANCE

Domaine des Garennes,
Minervois La Livinière 2001

RED £5.99
GREECE

Dipnon Merlot 2003

WHITE £5.99
GREECE

Dipnon Roditis Riesling 2003

FORTIFIED £4.99
SPAIN

Fino Sherry NV

RED £7.99
NEW ZEALAND

Kaituna Hills Reserve Cabernet/Merlot 2002

WHITE SPARKLING £3.99
ITALY

Moscato d'Asti NV

WHITE £7.99
AUSTRALIA

Marabee Point Hunter Valley Chardonnay 2001

WHITE £5.99
FRANCE

Macon Villages 2003

FORTIFIED £4.99
Manzanilla Sherry NV — SPAIN

WHITE £4.99
Quadro Sei Gavi 2003 — ITALY

RED £3.99
Palacio del Marqués Tempranillo/Syrah 2003 — SPAIN

WHITE £4.99
Racina Lanca, Grillo 2003 — ITALY

WHITE (3 litre box) £11.99
Spanish White NV — SPAIN

RED (3 litre box) £11.99
Spanish Red NV — SPAIN

WHITE £5.99
Tupungato Chardonnay 2002 — ARGENTINA

WHITE £5.50
Vouvray Domaine de la Pouvraie 2003 — FRANCE

RED £4.99
Vin de Pays des Portes de la Mediterranée — FRANCE
Niellucciu Merlot, Corsica 2003

RED £4.99
Weandre Stream Shiraz 2002 — AUSTRALIA

MORRISON'S

Hillmore House,
Thornton Road,
Bradford,
West Yorkshire BD8 9AX

Tel: (01274) 494166
Fax: (01274) 494831

Website: www.morereasons.co.uk

For Morrison's wines 14 points and under visit
www.superplonk.com

16.5

WHITE £4.99

Inycon Chardonnay 2002
ITALY
The sheer luxury texture of this oily white wine is
superb.
Also at Tesco.

16.5

RED SPARKLING £7.99

Wyndham Estate Bin 555
AUSTRALIA
Sparkling Shiraz NV
A superb bubbly of vivid richness and dryness. Offers
tannins, light raspberries and blackberries – a touch
of confected sweetness about it. It can be used to
dunk strawberries in or, even better, to partner game
dishes with a fruit sauce.

16.5

RED £4.99

Inycon Merlot 2002
ITALY
Sheer velvet plums and strawberries with firm
tannins.
Also at Tesco.

16

RED £6.99

Bellevue Pinotage 2002
SOUTH AFRICA
A soft, discreetly succulent debutante's Pinotage, it's
very easy to drink.

16

WHITE £5.50

Chardonnay 2003
CHILE
Completely delicious Charentais melon and lemon
with a finely textured rich, yet delicate finish.

16

WHITE £4.99

CHILE

Cono Sur Chardonnay 2003

A sum of many subtleties (dry peach/lemon/apple),
which finishes dryly.
Also at Tesco.

16

RED £4.99

CHILE

Cono Sur Pinot Noir 2003

Jammy, true, but it has a glint in its eye – a true Pinot
warrior.
Also at Budgens, Majestic, Somerfield, Tesco, Waitrose.

16

WHITE £2.99

ARGENTINA

Casa Latina Chardonnay 2003

Has the texture of wines costing five times as much.
The fruit is dry, elusive but very elegantly under-ripe.

16

RED £3.99

CHILE

Condor Chilean Shiraz 2003

I'm not sure there is a single Aussie Shiraz with
tannins this savoury and lingeringly tangy.

16

RED £5.99

SPAIN

Durius Tempranillo 2002

One of the best of Spain's under-six-quid Tempranillos.
Also at Budgens.

16

WHITE £2.99

GERMANY

Franz Reh Auslese 2002

The bargain aperitif of the year. Well chilled, the dry
honey is most charming.

16   WHITE £4.99
Garganega Terre in Fiore 2003   ITALY
Stunning apricot richness with lemon peel.

16   WHITE £4.99
Hill & Dale Chardonnay 2003   SOUTH AFRICA
Delicious fresh berried dryness and real elegant
restraint. Even has tannins.

What happens when a Knutsford wine buff encounters, labels
obscured, a bottle of Château Pétrus 1997 (10 points out of 20,
£575, Selfridges) from Bordeaux alongside Casa Lapostolle Cuvée
Alexandre Merlot 2000 (18.5 points, £12.99, Majestic, Safeway,
Booths, and Sainsbury's Online) from Chile?
That's right. The Merlot from Chile is preferred. Not that the
Pétrus, the world's most expensive Merlot, is utterly routed. It is
tannic and woody, perhaps a touch raw, and it would benefit from
several hours' complete decantation to soften its moodiness by
exposure to air; but unless you are a wine snob utterly obsessed
with status symbols and perceived exemplars of excellence, it
really is a scandalous waste of money. The Chilean, on the other
hand, provides the near ultimate in Merlot magic: coffee, roasted
berries, elongated elegant tannins, richly textured finishing
complexity, and a profoundly delicious memory when the bottle is
empty. When did this confrontation between the wines take place?
On ITV's *Tonight with Trevor MacDonald* on the 20th of October
2003 (a programme principally about credit card debt, in which I
took a small part). The wine buff's name was Mrs Victoria Christie
and apart from her strange affliction (her blind obeisance to the
Pétrus legend), she was a terrific personality.

16

ROSÉ £4.99

Inycon Cabernet Sauvignon Rosé 2003 ITALY

One of the most seriously delicious rosés on sale.

16

WHITE £5.99

Kingston Empiric Selection Viognier 2002 AUSTRALIA

Screwcap. Dry, very dry apricot with a lovely, faraway
hint of lemon.

16

RED £5.99

Kingston Empiric Selection 2001 AUSTRALIA

Magnificent soupy stuff. The fruit is sheer nectar
(with chocolate), but is rescued, brilliantly, from
soppiness by strident, clinging tannins.

16

WHITE £5.99

Montana Sauvignon Blanc 2003 NEW ZEALAND

Satin-textured gooseberry – so simple! So lingeringly
fresh and clean cut.
Also at Tesco.

16

RED £5.99

Marqués de Griñon Rioja 2002 SPAIN

Charming dusky richness and civilised tannins.
Also at Thresher.

16

ROSÉ £2.99

Paso del Sol Rosé 2003 CHILE

Screwcap. Delicious cherry/plum fruit of dryness and
firm richness yet delicacy.

16   RED £2.99

Paso del Sol Carmenere 2003   CHILE
Screwcap. The sassiest red in Morrison's for the
money. Real character and bite here.

16   WHITE £2.99

Paso del Sol Chardonnay 2003   CHILE
Firmly textured, hint of spice, dry under-ripe
melon and lemon with a vague peach edge to the
finish.

16   RED £2.99

Paso del Sol Cabernet Sauvignon 2003   CHILE
Hint of chocolate to the sweet berries. Delicious for
the money.

16   RED £2.99

Paso del Sol Merlot 2003   CHILE
Juicier than its sisters, and more suited to really spicy
food.

16   WHITE £4.99

Peter Lehmann The Barossa Riesling 2003   AUSTRALIA
Screwcap. 18.5 in 2009. Superb tangy lime and
pineapple fruit which will concentrate still further
over time.

16   WHITE £2.99
San Camino Sémillon/Sauvignon 2003   CHILE
One of the bargain whites of the year. Offers superb
pineapple, soft pear and tangy, almost chewy, lemon
fruit. Delicious.

16   RED £2.99
San Camino Carignan/Merlot 2003   CHILE
16 with a fiery curry. 13 with anything else.

16   RED £3.99
Santerra Tempranillo Utiel-Pequeña 2002   SPAIN
Lovely silky fruit with character on the finish thanks
to genteel yet persistent tannins. Very smooth, stylish,
accomplished.

16   WHITE £3.99
Santerra Dry Muscat 2003   SPAIN
Superbly delicate. Offers daintiness on the tongue of
lightly brushed lemon peel and artichoke with very faint
spice. Too coy for food, it makes an excellent aperitif.

On corks and corkscrews (No. 6)

One reason why cork taint is not so widely recognised as it should be
is because most faults are subtle. An edge has been removed, that is
all. Many so-called experts fail to see these faults, so the normal
customer is even less likely to recognise them as errors. Why should
we meekly accept faults in wine, almost exclusively but not entirely
caused by contaminated corks, that we do not for one second tolerate
in other products? Wines should be how their makers intend. No
other product carries the uncertainty a wine does, if it is cork sealed.

16

RED £5.99

Viña Albali Gran Reserva 1997   SPAIN

Surprisingly, it's still in good shape and the tannins
biting.

16

WHITE £4.99

Yellow Tail Verdelho 2003   AUSTRALIA

Tangy, oriental-food-friendly lemon and pear.

16

RED £7.95

Reserve Pinot Noir 2002   CHILE

17 points in 18 months. Superb cherried richness and
tannins.
Also at Small Merchants (Bacchanalia).

16

WHITE £5.99

Sauvignon Blanc, Marlborough 2003   NEW ZEALAND

Very lengthy experience from gentle gooseberry to
chalky tanginess of pineapple on the finish.
Also at Thresher, Oddbins, Tesco, Safeway,
Somerfield, Sainsbury's, Co-op, Booths, Small
Merchants (Unwins, Londis).

16

WHITE £4.99

7th Moon Chardonnay 2001   USA

Brilliant artefact: lemon, gooseberry, lime and oily
melon. Excellent with complex shellfish dishes.
Also at Tesco.

OTHER WINES 15.5 AND UNDER

15.5

WHITE £4.99
Edward Pfeiffer Mosel Riesling Kabinett 2002   GERMANY

WHITE £4.99
Hardy's Bin 769 Chardonnay 2003   AUSTRALIA

WHITE £4.99
Jindalee Chardonnay 2003   AUSTRALIA

WHITE £8.99
Kendall Jackson Vintners Reserve Chardonnay 2001   USA

15

WHITE £2.99
Antonio Barbadillo White 2003   SPAIN

WHITE £4.99
Atlantique Touraine Sauvignon Blanc 2003   FRANCE
Also at Sainsbury's.

WHITE £7.49
Chablis Chardonnay 2002   FRANCE

RED £2.99
Casa Latina Shiraz/Tempranillo 2003   CHILE

WHITE £4.49
Distinto Catarratto/Chardonnay 2003   ITALY

WHITE SPARKLING £9.99
De Brégille Champagne NV   FRANCE

WHITE £6.49
Edward Pfeiffer Mosel Riesling Spätlese 2002   GERMANY

WHITE £6.49
Gewürtztraminer Tradition Preiss   FRANCE
Zimmer d'Alsace 2002

WHITE £4.99
Oxford Landing Sauvignon Blanc 2003   AUSTRALIA
Screwcap. Also at Budgens, Somerfield, Tesco.

RED £4.99
Peter Lehmann The Barossa Grenache 2002   AUSTRALIA
Screwcap.

RED £6.99
Wyndham Estate Bin 555 Shiraz 2001   AUSTRALIA
Also at Tesco.

14.5
RED £4.49
Antu Mapu Merlot 2002   CHILE

WHITE £7.99
Edward Pfeiffer Mosel Riesling Auslese 2002   GERMANY

RED £3.49
Falcon Ridge Merlot 2003   FRANCE

RED £4.69
Romanian Special Reserve Merlot 2000   ROMANIA

RED £10.99
Volnay Le Meurger 2000   FRANCE

RED £6.99
Yellow Tail Reserve Shiraz 2002   AUSTRALIA

14

Casablanca Cabernet Sauvignon 2002

RED £4.99
CHILE

Château Saint Galier Graves 2003

WHITE £5.49
FRANCE

Casablanca Sauvignon Blanc 2003

WHITE £4.99
CHILE

Fetzer Pacific Bay Chardonnay/Pinot Grigio 2002

WHITE £3.99
USA

Fetzer Pacific Bay Merlot 2002

RED £4.99
USA

Jindalee Shiraz 2002

RED £4.99
AUSTRALIA

KWV Barrel Fermented Chenin 2003

WHITE £4.99
SOUTH AFRICA

Lo Tengo Malbec 2003

RED £4.99
CHILE

Pink Fizz Cava Sparkling Rosé

ROSÉ SPARKLING £4.99
SPAIN

Romanian Special Reserve Cabernet 1999

RED £4.29
ROMANIA

Southern Collection Côtes du Roussillon 2002

RED £3.99
FRANCE

Southern Collection Minervois 2002

RED £3.99
FRANCE

Southern Collection Corbières 2002

RED £3.99
FRANCE

ODDBINS

31–33 Weir Road,
Wimbledon,
London SW19 8UG

Tel: (020) 8944 4400
Fax: (020) 8944 4411

E-mail: customer.service@oddbinsmail.com
Website: www.oddbins.com

For Oddbins' wines 14 points and under visit
www.superplonk.com

17.5

RED £6.29

Château de Valcombe, Costières de Nîmes 2003   FRANCE
Limited availability. Superb chocolate mustiness, rich
complex tannins and huge depth of class.

17.5

RED £16.99

Domus Aurea Cabernet Sauvignon 1998   CHILE
Perhaps the most eccentrically delicious Chilean
Cabernet Sauvignon.

17.5

WHITE £8.49

D'Arenberg Last Ditch Viognier 2003   AUSTRALIA
Screwcap. It has dryly smoky apricot, a hint of spice, a
suggestion of fruity opulence as it finishes. Very, very
classy stuff.

17.5

WHITE £14.99

Petaluma Piccadilly Valley Chardonnay 2000   AUSTRALIA
A real treat of a Chardonnay with hugely charming,
oily richness which offers us sunlight glimpsed
through old leaves, of vegetality, melons and a fatty
citrussiness. An outstandingly civilised version of the
international whore of grape varieties.

17.5

WHITE £7.99

Vergelegen Chardonnay 2003   SOUTH AFRICA
The Cape's top Chardonnay for the money. Hugely
stealthy and complex including smoked pear.

17.5

WHITE £8.99

Wither Hills Chardonnay 2001   NEW ZEALAND
Wonderfully warm yet with a delicate creamy

richness. Engages the palate with several layers of
fruit, melon, mango, lime, apricot.

17.5   WHITE £9.19

Wither Hills Sauvignon Blanc 2003   NEW ZEALAND
Screwcap. Unusual complexities here offering lime,
pear, pineapple and a hint of spice. More perfume,
friskier minerals and chewiness of texture.
Also at Booths, The Wine Society.

17   WHITE £7.49

D'Arenberg Hermit Crab Marsanne/   AUSTRALIA
Viognier 2003
Screwcap. 18 points in 3 years (if cellared).
Wonderfully eccentric dryness to the fruit, an oily
textured apricot and lime (with a hint of herb), and
the finish is very elegant. Superbly classy.
Also at Booths.

17   WHITE £9.99

Catena Chardonnay 2002   ARGENTINA
Creamy yet delicate, dainty yet, very emphatic, this
specimen of Chardonnay is a master class.
Also at Waitrose, The Wine Society.

17   WHITE £4.99

Concha y Toro Casillero del Diablo Viognier 2003 CHILE
Superbly subtle (apricot and sesame seeds), brilliantly
slurpable, ineffably thought-provoking.
Also at Safeway.

17

WHITE £9.49

Domaine des Deux Roches, St-Véran 2002   FRANCE

One of my favourite, if not complete favourite, under-a-tenner Burgundies. Lovely plumpness yet finesse here.

17

RED £6.99

Domaine Le Serp, Madiran 2002   FRANCE

Oddbins parcel, limited availability. Sheer naked Rabelaisian richness and dark burned fruitiness.

17

RED £5.79

Labeye Cuvée Guilhem Syrah, Minervois 2002   FRANCE

Screwcap. Wonderfully committed berries, deep yet delicate here. The wine simply brooks no argument. It is a miracle of deliciously berried depth for the money.

17

WHITE £5.59

Labeye Viognier/Chardonnay,   FRANCE
Vin de Pays d'Oc 2001

I simply adore the calm flood of nuttiness, peachiness and gooseberryish subtleties. Hugely apricotty yet utterly restrained.

17

RED £6.99

Moulin de Ciffre, Faugères 2000   FRANCE

Limited availability. Big, chewy, firmly roasted berries with great concentration on the finish.

17

WHITE £10.99

Montana 'R' Renwick Estate   NEW ZEALAND
Chardonnay 2000

The mild butteriness is coated in chewy citrus. Wonderful.

17

WHITE £10.99

Montana 'O' Ormond Estate   NEW ZEALAND
Chardonnay 2000
Superbly classy, elegant (yet emphatically rich to
finish).

17

WHITE £9.49

Nepenthe Pinot Gris 2002   AUSTRALIA
Screwcap. Superb muted spice with under-ripe melon
and citrus with soft pear.

17

RED £18.99

Petaluma Coonawarra   AUSTRALIA
Cabernet Sauvignon/Merlot 1999
This is expensive, I concur, but it is a wily, mature,
wise-headed blend with the typical under-tone of
Coonawarra (a tangy thyme and mintiness). It is
very finely balanced, sveltly tannic, and not too
alcoholic.

17

RED £9.99

Stella Aurea Cabernet Sauvignon 1998   CHILE
Superbly mature, bitingly tannic, magnificently sleek.

17

RED £9.99

Villa Maria Cellar Selection Syrah 2002   AUSTRALIA
Screwcap. A wonderful juicy Syrah/Shiraz with
character and bite. Chocolate, cherries, roasted
almonds and fine tannins. 18.5 in 3 years.

17 RED £8.99

Villa Maria Private Bin Merlot/ NEW ZEALAND
Cabernet Sauvignon 2002
Immediate smoky plums, chunky tannins. Will
develop greater suaveness but its briskness, for me, is
perfect now.

17 WHITE £12.99

Villa Maria Keltern Vineyard NEW ZEALAND
Chardonnay 2002
Screwcap. Delicious fruity white.

17 WHITE £12.99

Villa Maria Waikahu Vineyard NEW ZEALAND
Chardonnay 2002
Screwcap. Deliciously gooseberryish, classy and
elegant.

17 WHITE £5.99

Villa Maria Private Bin Chardonnay 2002 NEW ZEALAND
Screwcap. Has such beautiful footwork as it dances on
the tongue with subtlety, leafy melon and lemon. So
calm, so insouciant, so classy.
Also at Asda, Waitrose.

17 WHITE £7.99

Villa Maria Private Bin Sauvignon Blanc 2003 NEW ZEALAND
Screwcap. Wonderful coating of lime to the ripe
gooseberry. The texture is delicate yet incisive.
Also at Somerfield, Tesco.

17   RED £8.49

D'Arenberg D'Arry's Original   AUSTRALIA
Shiraz/Grenache 2001
Superb freshness and fullness here – roasted berries
with brisk tannins and a tangy, textured finish.
Also at The Wine Society.

---

17   WHITE £7.99

D'Arenberg Money Spider Roussanne 2003   AUSTRALIA
Screwcap. Gorgeous apricot/peach/lemon. Will age
5–8 years and reach 20 points in 2008.
Also at Small Merchants (Bibendum).

16.5   WHITE £7.49

Annie's Lane Riesling 2003   AUSTRALIA
Screwcap. 18.5 in 3 years. Simply one of the snazziest
Rieslings in the world. Complex, textured, complete.
Deliciously delicate lemon-peel-edged fruit with subtle
minerals. Very fine.

'Am I the only reader who doesn't have any idea what Malcolm
Gluck is on about?' asked Bob Cockshott (*Guardian* letters, March
22nd 2003). Mr Cockshott could not understand what I meant
when I referred to a wine as quitting 'the throat like Gielgud
leaving the stage'. I am not surprised he is baffled. Few people
saw Gielgud leave a stage, he loved hogging it so much. But when
he did, his throaty presence still hung, unforgettably, in the air –
as did the wine in question even though it was no longer on
the tongue.

16.5   WHITE £9.99

Albert Mann Muscat, Alsace 2002   FRANCE

Impishly spicy, grapey, delicious, and dry.

16.5   WHITE £9.99

Blind River Sauvignon Blanc 2003   NEW ZEALAND

Limited availability. Screwcap. The texture supports
two contrasting opulences: rich gooseberry and
striking citrus.

16.5   WHITE £5.99

Blue Ring Chardonnay 2002   AUSTRALIA

Screwcap. Intensely dry and elegant but it bites
back on the finish with a lovely undertone smoky
fruit.

16.5   RED £8.49

Clos Petite Bellane Valreas,   FRANCE
Côtes du Rhône-Villages 2001

Delicious dusky fruit, spicy berries, soft unguent
tannins with a brisk overtone, and lovely chewy
texture.

16.5   RED £9.99

Château Charron 'Les Gruppes',   FRANCE
Premières Côtes de Blaye 2001

Superb! Why can't more under-a-tenner clarets
have this precision, this aroma, these spicy, roasted
berries and tannins which, though vivid, are also
elegant.

16.5   RED £7.49
    Concha y Toro Lot 77 Merlot 2002   CHILE
    Develops slowly on the palate to reveal finely toasted
    cherries, warm berries and savoury tannins.
    Wonderful berries and tannins. Real leathery lushness
    and tannic tenacity.

16.5   RED £6.99
    Concha y Toro Lot 130 Syrah 2002   CHILE
    Superb! Oz, watch your backs! Freshness and richness,
    beautifully purposeful fruit, will age 2–3 years.

16.5   RED £5.99
    Concha y Toro Lot 34 Malbec 2002   CHILE
    Delicious layers of chocolate plum.

16.5   RED £7.99
    Concha y Toro Lot 175 Carmenere 2002   CHILE
    Redefines what fruity means. Stunning.

16.5   RED £9.99
    Concha y Toro Lot 230 Cabernet Sauvignon 2002   CHILE
    Wonderfully rich berries, prunes and spice (and
    tannins). Manages to be juicy yet stylishly bold and
    complex.

16.5   RED £11.99
    D'Arenberg The Bonsai Vine 2001   AUSTRALIA
    Incredible jamminess yet serious complex richness.
    Sweet chocolate, licorice and vibrant tannins.

16.5   WHITE £7.49

Dashwood Sauvignon Blanc 2003   NEW ZEALAND
Screwcap. Superb richness and incisive
citric/pineapple edging.

16.5   RED £6.49

Domaine de l'Arjolle, Côtes de Thongue 2002   FRANCE
Oddbins parcel: limited availability and not in store
yet. Vigour and depth, richness and rousingly roasted
berries.

16.5   WHITE £8.99

Flagstone 'Two Roads' Chardonnay 2002   SOUTH AFRICA
It is like a whacky (in a benevolently genteel way)
Puligny Montrachet in a great year from a master
eccentric.

16.5   WHITE £9.99

Green on Sémillon 2002   SOUTH AFRICA
18 points in 5 years. Gorgeous oily richness, dry yet
polished, calm yet characterful.

16.5   RED £7.50

Heartland Limestone Coast Shiraz 2002   AUSTRALIA
Terrific personality. Hearty without being clammy,
rich but not showy, warm but not overheated.

16.5   RED £10.50

Heartland Director's Cut Shiraz 2002   AUSTRALIA
An outstandingly generous-hearted red.

16.5   RED £13.99

Knappstein Enterprise Cabernet Sauvignon 1999 AUSTRALIA
Curiously delicious and more a marriage of California
and northern Italy than pure Australia – but this is to
compliment the wine. It has lithe tannins, sweet black
cherry and roasted plum fruit with that sweetness
containing a hint of licorice. Immensely versatile with
food (from chicken to cheese, tandoori prawns to
pasta).

16.5   WHITE £6.99

Knappstein Hand Picked Riesling 2001   AUSTRALIA
Screwcap. Superb flatly-tissued lime and very dry
under-ripe Charentais melon. Brilliant with shellfish.

16.5   RED £5.69

Labeye Grenache/Syrah, Vin de Pays d'Oc 2003   FRANCE
Oh joy! Edouard Labeye's red under screwcap! So the
lovely hearty fruit stays pure and untainted and richly
berried for hours (in the glass).

16.5   RED £5.79

Labeye Cuvée Gauthier Carignan, Minervois 2003 FRANCE
Screwcap. More bustling and perhaps brasher than its
Syrah brother, it nevertheless has a plummy ripeness
buttressed by deep tannins.

16.5   RED £11.99

McLaren Vale/Padthaway Shiraz 2000   AUSTRALIA
Real softly softly class here. Real elegance and ripeness.

16.5
WHITE £13.99

Margaret River Sauvignon Blanc/Sémillon,   AUSTRALIA
Cullen Wines 2002

Classy blend uniting subtlety with ripeness.

16.5
WHITE £22.99

Margaret River Chardonnay, Cullen Wines 2001   AUSTRALIA

Ripe but the delicacy's like lace: intricate, impactful,
gorgeous.

16.5
WHITE £7.49

Nepenthe Tryst Sauvignon Blanc/Sémillon 2003   AUSTRALIA

Screwcap. Terrific blend of lime, a hint of raspberry,
touch of pineapple. Very classy.

Also at Sainsbury's.

16.5
WHITE £8.99

Pewsey Vale Riesling 2003   AUSTRALIA

Screwcap. 18.5 points in 2–4 years. Lovely citrus
coating to peach and gooseberry.

Also at Sainsbury's, Thresher.

16.5
WHITE £6.59

Tokay Pinot-Gris Turckheim Cuvée Réserve 2001   FRANCE

Very demure apricot fruit but it deceives by flattering
our susceptibilities to subtlety because it then springs
a surprise: a citrus edge, and some minerals, which
develop with decanting (up to 12 hours is not
excessive). The texture gains hugely from exposure
to air.

16.5

Sieur de Camandieu Viognier,
Vin de Pays d'Oc 2002

Fills the mouth with under-ripe peach and lemon.

WHITE £5.49
FRANCE

16.5

Turckheim Gewürtztraminer, Alsace 2002

How massively entertaining in this vigorous yet
elegant vintage. Super lychee and nuts, melon and
spicy pineapple.

WHITE £7.49
FRANCE

16.5

Villa Maria Clifford Bay
Sauvignon Blanc 2003

Screwcap. Finely textured and balanced. Very fine
now but 18 points in 2–3 years.

WHITE £11.99
NEW ZEALAND

16.5

Wynns Coonawarra Estate Shiraz 2001

Perfect sensually textured berries with high stepping
tannins.

RED £7.03
AUSTRALIA

16.5

Zonnenbloem Chardonnay 2002

Creamy, ripe, almost brash but it's just gusto. Superb
with chicken and tarragon.

WHITE £5.99
SOUTH AFRICA

16.5

Vergelegen Cabernet Sauvignon 2000

Intense burned berries. Great length and vivacity.
Also at Safeway.

RED £13.99
SOUTH AFRICA

16   WHITE £6.99
Annie's Lane Sémillon 2003   AUSTRALIA
Screwcap. Intensely elegant, neatly tailored, subtly rich fruit.

16   WHITE £5.99
Peter Lehmann Sémillon 2002   AUSTRALIA
Screwcap. 18 in 2008–2009. Deliciously oily,
gooseberry/grapefruit flavoured. Will improve, thanks
to its screwcap, dramatically over half a decade (and
beyond). Utterly superb thirst-quencher.
Also at Asda, Booths, Tesco.

16   WHITE £7.99
Concha y Toro Winemaker's Lot 20 Riesling 2002   CHILE
Screwcap. 16.5 in 2005–6.

16   RED £4.99
Aradon Rioja 2002   SPAIN
Delicious cocoa-edged concentrated ferocity.

16   WHITE £7.99
Annie's Lane Chardonnay 2002   AUSTRALIA
17.5 points in 3 years. Very classy, complete, confident,
concentrated Chardonnay.

16   WHITE £7.99
Annie's Lane Chardonnay 2003   AUSTRALIA
Screwcap. It is a delicious wine of so many subtle
touches from dry lemon to apricot.

16   RED £5.99
Blue Ring Shiraz/Grenache 2002   AUSTRALIA
Screwcap. Has a soft side (which time, 18 months say,
will soften), but its briskness is charming now.

16

WHITE £8.49
Brokenwood Cricket Pitch AUSTRALIA
Sauvignon/Sémillon 2002
Screwcap. 17.5 in 2006–7. Really very dry but it has
great charm, if a trifle starched at the moment. It will
deepen superbly with a few years of development in
bottle.

16

RED £6.99
Concha y Toro Winemaker's Lot 130 Syrah 2002 CHILE
Real class in a glass. Has a Rhône feel to the
undertone, an Aussie touch to the ripeness and
a uniquely Chilean dimension to the smoky
texture.

16

RED £9.99
Comte Cathare Dioscorea, FRANCE
Minervois La Livinière 2000
Deliciously soft berries, hint of raspberries, touch of
spice, more than a suggestion of tenacious tannin.

16

RED £6.99
Capcanes Mas Picosa, Monsant 2001 SPAIN
Sturdy, meaty, dry, deep fruit of some class and clout.
Roasted berries, chewy tannins.

16

WHITE £6.79
Clos Petite Bellane Blanc, Côtes du Rhône 2003 FRANCE
Lovely rich nuttiness undercut by touches of spicy
melon.

16

RED £8.99
AUSTRALIA

Brokenwood Cricket Pitch Red
(Cabernet Sauvignon/Merlot/Shiraz) 2001
Delicious charred berries and soft tannins.

16

WHITE £8.19
AUSTRALIA

Brokenwood Cricket Pitch White
(Sauvignon Blanc/Sémillon) 2001
Screwcap. Classy lemon and lime.

16

WHITE £9.49
FRANCE

Domaine Vessigaud Macon-Fuissé,
Maconnais 2001
Better than many a Puligny – decisively Burgundian
yet classy and creamy.

16

RED £8.69
AUSTRALIA

D'Arenberg High Trellis
Cabernet Sauvignon 2001
Great concentration and complex classiness.
Also at Booths.

16

WHITE £7.99
AUSTRALIA

D'Arenberg Olive Grove Chardonnay 2003
Screwcap. 17 in 2006. Stylish understatement and
coolness.

16

WHITE £4.99
AUSTRALIA

Deakin Estate Colombard/Chardonnay 2002
The clash of the opulent melon with the fresh lemon
is most striking.

16

WHITE £6.99

Etoile Filante Chardonnay, Vin de Pays d'Oc 2002   FRANCE
What amazing elegance and dry, dry fruit!

16

RED £19.32

Flagstone 'Dragon Tree' Pinotage 2001   SOUTH AFRICA
Cabernet 50%, Pinotage 50%. The most expensive
screwcapped red wine in the UK? Wonderful. And what
a safe, rich, warm, generous, pure-fruited wine it is.

16

WHITE £9.99

Flagstone 'The Berrio' Sauvignon Blanc 2003   SOUTH AFRICA
Screwcap. Unusual complexities here offering lime,
pear, pineapple and a hint of spice.

16

RED £9.99

Flagstone 'Writers Block' Pinotage 2002   SOUTH AFRICA
Screwcap. Very vivacious berries, creamy, slightly
smoky, very rich, energetic, hugely food friendly.

16

RED £8.99

Flagstone 'Strata Series' Cape Blend 2002   SOUTH AFRICA
Screwcap. Very deeply burned berries. Brilliant
casserole red of great bravura fruit.

16

WHITE £8.99

Frostline Riesling 2003   SOUTH AFRICA
Screwcap. 18 points in 2007. Deliciously rich,
oriental food friendly, chewy, lime, pineapple, melon.

16
RED £14.99
FRANCE

Gorilla Comet Cathère, Minervois La Livinière 2002
Limited availability. Delicate yet forceful, it has a rich delicacy which presents a contradiction, civilised and couth yet rustic.

16
WHITE £10.49
FRANCE

Hugel Riesling, Alsace 2001
17 in 2 years. Classy, rich yet tangy, full yet delicate. Superb with fish dishes.

On corks and corkscrews (No. 7)

A Vin de Pays d'Oc red which I was given to sample at a wine tasting organised by a wine retailer last year was tasted by two Masters of Wine employed as buyers and neither of them spotted it was corked until it was pointed out. Likewise, the Californian wine maker (the man who actually made the wine, no less!) who refused to accept the verdict of Oddbins' then wine buyer, Steve Daniel, when Steve said the man's wine was corked. The Californian said absolutely it was not; the wine was perfect the way it tasted. Steve refused to accept this and submitted samples for laboratory analysis. Back came the scientific proof: the wine was minutely polluted with cork taint. You see, unless the fault is so horrendously obvious that the wine is disgusting and undrinkable, many people do not accept it as tainted but merely 'different' or part of the charm (!) of bottle variation. But horrendous pongs and tastes from a wine do not occur very often. Most faults, as I say, merely rob the wine of its bloom, the freshness of its fruit, the pertness of its acidity.

16

RED £14.99

Lost Valley Merlot 2001 AUSTRALIA

Sheer chocolate magic.

16

WHITE £6.99

Knappstein Hand Picked Riesling 2002 AUSTRALIA

Screwcap. More fruit here, the tanginess still to develop.
Wholly decant 5–7 hours beforehand. The wine
developed from the opened bottle in fridge for 3 days.

16

RED £14.99

Mount Ida Heathcote Shiraz 2001 AUSTRALIA

Screwcap. Classic Aussie jamminess here sveltely
tempered by craggy avuncular tannins.

16

WHITE £9.99

Nepenthe Riesling 2001 AUSTRALIA

Fine Wine branches. Screwcap. Nice tangy soapstone
and lime nuances developing. Good wine to read
Dickens with.

16

WHITE £9.49

Nepenthe Sauvignon Blanc 2003 AUSTRALIA

Screwcap. Has an edge of ripe gooseberry to vague
lemon and surprising chalky undertone, magnificent
news for shellfish.
Also at Waitrose.

16

WHITE £8.99

Nepenthe Riesling 2003 AUSTRALIA

Screwcap. Delicious tangy lime and gooseberry.

16

WHITE £7.99

Nepenthe Unwooded Chardonnay 2003 AUSTRALIA
Screwcap. Pure, clean, fresh, under-ripe melon and
lime.

16

WHITE SPARKLING £21.99

Delbeck Brut Heritage Champagne NV FRANCE
Really stylish stuff – full of interesting twists and
turns of lemon, pineapple and pear.

16

WHITE £5.99

Peter Lehmann Sémillon 2001 AUSTRALIA
Screwcap. 18 in 2008. Delicious smoky, almost
charred fruit.

16

RED £5.49

Peter Lehmann Grenache 2002 AUSTRALIA
Screwcap. Chewy, slightly roasted berries of bustle
and bounce.

16

RED £17.99

Peregrine Pinot Noir 2002 NEW ZEALAND
Screwcap. Delicious twists and turns this wine offers
the palate as it provides truffles, chocolate, burned
cherries and a touch of bitter licorice to the tannins.

16

WHITE £9.99

Petaluma Clare Riesling 2002 AUSTRALIA
Screwcap. Delicious under-ripe melon and citrus.
Very young, cellar for 2–4 years.

16

WHITE   £6.99

Raats Original Chenin 2003   SOUTH AFRICA

Delightfully insouciant, chalky peach and lemon.

16

WHITE   £9.99

Scotchman's Hill Chardonnay 2001   AUSTRALIA

A cross between Burgundy and southern Italy – a.k.a.
uniquely Aussie richness.

16

WHITE   £9.99

Scotchman's Hill Chardonnay 2003   AUSTRALIA

Screwcap. Dry, elegant, very gentlemanly fruit.

16

WHITE   £5.99

St Hallett Poachers Blend 2003   AUSTRALIA

Screwcap. 18 in 2006. Hints at many things:
succulence, tanginess, richness, depth. But it
sidesteps 'head-on' concentration and settles for a
citrussiness which will deepen over the years.

16

WHITE   £6.99

Snake Creek Marsanne 2002   AUSTRALIA

Screwcap. 17.5 in 2007–8. Delicious lime/peach fruit
of insistent tanginess. The hint of lemon peel is classy.

16

WHITE   £3.99

Snake Creek Chardonnay/Sémillon 2003   AUSTRALIA

Brilliant ripe melon, touch of mango, with a lively
textured richness.

16

WHITE £7.99

Siyabonga Severney 2002   SOUTH AFRICA

One-off parcel, limited availability. Unusual four-grape
blend for oriental food.

16

WHITE £9.59

St Véran, Les Deux Roches 2002   FRANCE

One of the most complete of white Burgundies under
a tenner. Has elegance and subtle richness.

16

RED £24.99

The Vergelegen 2000   SOUTH AFRICA

Naked unashamed luxury.

16

WHITE £5.79

Torres Viña Esmeralda 2003   SPAIN

Screwcap. Brilliant touches of peach, nut, citrus and
pineapple. Excellent with Thai food.
Also at Thresher, Waitrose.

16

WHITE £8.99

Villa Maria Cellar Selection   NEW ZEALAND
Chardonnay 2002

Screwcap. The concentration of melon and lemon
needs total decantation to achieve.

16

WHITE £9.19

Villa Maria Cellar Selection Riesling 2002   NEW ZEALAND

Screwcap. Gentle muskiness to the lemon. Will age
gloriously and will reach 18.5 in 3-7 years and then
beyond.

16
WHITE £9.99
NEW ZEALAND

**Villa Maria Cellar Selection
Sauvignon Blanc 2003**
Screwcap. Intense, almost clotted richness.

16
RED £9.99
SOUTH AFRICA

Writers Block Pinotage 2002
Screwcap. Very vivacious berries, creamy, slightly
smoky, very rich, energetic, hugely food friendly.

16
RED £3.99
USA

Walkers Pass Cabernet Sauvignon 2002
Very rich charred berries with tannins with a hint of
very subtle nut chocolate.

16
WHITE £3.99
USA

Walkers Pass Chardonnay 2001
Amazing value here, for such silky class. Has touches
of apricot and apple, grilled nut and lemon.

16
RED £15.99
NEW ZEALAND

Wither Hills Pinot Noir 2002
Screwcap. Red forceful elegance and Pinot personality.
Also at Booths, Small Merchants (Jeroboams, Thos
Peatling, Ballantynes of Cowbridge), Waitrose, The
Wine Society.

16
WHITE £5.99
SOUTH AFRICA

Zonnenbloem Sauvignon Blanc 2003
Elegant, citric, charming.

16

Sauvignon Blanc, Marlborough 2003   NEW ZEALAND
Very lengthy experience from gentle gooseberry to
chalky tanginess of pineapple on the finish.
Also at Thresher, Booths, Tesco, Safeway, Somerfield,
Sainsbury's, Co-op, Morrison's, Small Merchants
(Unwins, Londis).

OTHER WINES 15.5 AND UNDER

15.5

RED £8.99
Annie's Lane Cabernet/Merlot 1999   AUSTRALIA

WHITE £8.99
Brookland Verse 1 Sémillon/Sauvignon 2003   AUSTRALIA

RED £24.99
Clonakilla Shiraz/Viognier 2002   AUSTRALIA

RED £4.69
Cruz de Piedra Garnacha 2002   SPAIN

RED £6.99
Ferngrove Shiraz 2001   AUSTRALIA

RED £5.99
Flagstone 'Longitude' Red 2003   SOUTH AFRICA
Screwcap.

Haras Character Chardonnay 2001

WHITE £8.49
CHILE

Heartland Limestone Coast Petit Verdot 2002

RED £7.99
AUSTRALIA

Musella Valpolicella 1998

RED £9.49
ITALY

Orangutan, Comte Cathare Limoux 2002

WHITE £8.49
FRANCE

Snake Creek 'Almudj' Merlot 2001

RED £7.99
AUSTRALIA

Salomon Groovay Grüner Veltliner 2003

WHITE £5.99
AUSTRIA

Tukulu Groenekloof 2002

RED £7.99
SOUTH AFRICA

Viña Herminia Excelsus Rioja 2001

RED £8.99
SPAIN

Wolf Blass Gold Label Shiraz/Viognier 2002
Screwcap.

RED £14.99
AUSTRALIA

Waipara West Chardonnay 2000

WHITE £9.99
NEW ZEALAND

Xeroloithia Peza 2002

WHITE £5.49
GREECE

Deakin Estate Merlot 2002
Also at Waitrose.

RED £6.49
AUSTRALIA

15

WHITE £7.99
AUSTRALIA

Bleasdale Verdelho 2003
Screwcap. 17 in 2008.

WHITE £7.99
SPAIN

Burgans Albariño, Rias Baixas 2003

WHITE £4.69
FRANCE

Colombelle Vin de Pays des
Côtes du Gascogne 2003
Screwcap.

RED £7.99
SPAIN

Cosme Palacio Tinto, Bodegas Palacio 2001

RED £9.99
ARGENTINA

Catena Malbec 2001

WHITE £5.49
AUSTRALIA

Deakin Estate Sauvignon Blanc 2004
Screwcap.

RED £6.69
FRANCE

Domaine de Grangeneuve Vieilles Vignes,
Coteaux de Tricastin 2000

RED £12.99
SPAIN

El Vinculo La Mancha 2001

WHITE SPARKLING £20.99
FRANCE

F. Bonnet Champagne NV

WHITE £6.49
GREECE

Gaia Estate Notios, Peleponnese 2003

WHITE £5.59

Gooseberry Patch Sauvignon Blanc, Touraine 2002 FRANCE

RED £7.95

Heartland Limestone Coast   AUSTRALIA
Cabernet Sauvignon 2002

WHITE £9.99

Katnook Estate Sauvignon Blanc 2002   AUSTRALIA

WHITE £6.99

Knappstein Hand Picked Riesling 2003   AUSTRALIA
Screwcap. 17 in 2008.

RED £7.99

Knappstein Cabernet/Merlot 2000   AUSTRALIA

WHITE £8.49

Mulderbosch Chenin 2003   SOUTH AFRICA

WHITE £11.99

Macon-Bussières 'Le Clos' Verget 2002   FRANCE

RED £7.49

Nepenthe Tryst Red 2003   AUSTRALIA
Screwcap. Also at Asda, Waitrose.

RED £24.99

Observatory Syrah 2001   SOUTH AFRICA

RED £4.99

Oracle Pinotage 2003   SOUTH AFRICA

RED £3.99

Obikwa Shiraz 2002   SOUTH AFRICA

WHITE £5.69

Penfolds Rawsons Retreat Riesling 2002   AUSTRALIA
Screwcap. 16.5 in 2006.

RED £11.99

Pesquera Crianza, Ribera del Duero 2001   SPAIN

WHITE £7.99

Reuilly, Claude Lafonde 2003   FRANCE

RED £9.99

Terrunyo Carmenere 2001   CHILE

RED £11.49

Voyager Estate Shiraz 2002   AUSTRALIA
Screwcap.

WHITE £6.69

Verdicchio, Marotti Campi 2002   ITALY

WHITE £7.49

Wakefield Promised Land Unwooded   AUSTRALIA
Chardonnay 2003
Screwcap.

14.5

RED £8.99

Annie's Lane Shiraz 2002   AUSTRALIA
Screwcap.

RED £8.49

Bleasdale Shiraz/Cabernet 2001   AUSTRALIA

RED £7.89

Château Cru Cantemerle, Bordeaux   FRANCE
Supérieur 2000

RED £15.99

Château Pontet-Chappaz, Margaux 2001   FRANCE

WHITE £5.99

Domaine de Montine, Coteaux de Tricastin 2003   FRANCE

RED £11.99

D'Arenberg The Sticks and Stones 2002   AUSTRALIA

WHITE £3.99

El Furioso Albillo, Castilla y Leon 2002   SPAIN

WHITE £4.99

Flagstone 'Noon Gun' 2004   SOUTH AFRICA
Screwcap.

RED £38.95

'Graveyard Vineyard' Hunter Valley Shiraz 2001   AUSTRALIA

WHITE £10.99

Lost Valley Reserve Verdelho 2001   AUSTRALIA

WHITE £9.99

Mulderbosch Sauvignon Blanc 2003   SOUTH AFRICA
Fine Wine branches only.

WHITE SPARKLING £18.99

Pierre Grimonnet & Fils Brut, 1er Cuvée   FRANCE
Gastronome Champagne NV

RED £5.99

Piana del Sole Primitivo Salento 2001   ITALY

RED £29.99

Peter Lehmann Stonewall Shiraz 1997   AUSTRALIA

Scaranto Rosso, Colli Euganei 1999

RED £7.49
ITALY

Wakefield Riesling 2003
Screwcap.

WHITE £8.99
AUSTRALIA

14

Amarande, Bordeaux 1998

RED £8.99
FRANCE

Annie's Lane Shiraz 2001

RED £8.99
AUSTRALIA

Annie's Lane 'Coppertail' Riesling 2003
Screwcap. 16 in 2008.

WHITE £16.99
AUSTRALIA

Brokenwood Shiraz 2000

RED £12.49
AUSTRALIA

Berganorio Orvieto Classico Secco,
Tenuta le Velette 2003

WHITE £6.29
SPAIN

Château Charron Acacia, Premières Côtes
de Blaye 2001

WHITE £8.99
FRANCE

Château Plain-Point, Fronsac 2000

RED £13.99
FRANCE

Colombelle, Vin de Pays des Côtes de
Gascogne 2002

WHITE £4.99
FRANCE

	RED £19.99
De Toren V 2001	SOUTH AFRICA

	RED £19.99
D'Arenberg The Coppermine Road Cabernet Sauvignon 2001	AUSTRALIA

	WHITE £4.99
Deakin Estate Colombard/ Chardonnay 2004 Screwcap.	AUSTRALIA

	RED £9.99
Flagstone 'Dragon Tree' 2002 Screwcap.	SOUTH AFRICA

	RED £12.99
Flagstone 'Music Room' Cabernet Sauvignon 2002 Screwcap.	SOUTH AFRICA

	RED £7.49
Gaia Notios, Peleponnese 2003	GREECE

	RED £9.49
Glen Carlou Pinot Noir 2002	SOUTH AFRICA

	RED £7.99
Heartland Limestone Coast Shiraz 2001	AUSTRALIA

	RED £9.99
J. & K. 'The Outsider' Shiraz 2002	SOUTH AFRICA

	WHITE £5.99
Lingenfelder 'Bird Label' Riesling, Pfalz 2002	GERMANY

WHITE £15.99

Leitz Rudesheimer Berg Schlossberg Spätlese, GERMANY
Mosel 2002
Fine Wine branches only.

WHITE £12.99

Lost Valley Cortese 2002 AUSTRALIA

RED £14.99

Lost Valley Shiraz 2001 AUSTRALIA

RED £8.99

Montana Reserve Merlot 2002 NEW ZEALAND

RED £6.99

Nepenthe Tryst AUSTRALIA
Cabernet/Tempranillo/Zinfandel 2002

WHITE SPARKLING £15.99

Henri Harlin Champagne Brut NV FRANCE

WHITE SPARKLING £17.49

F. Bonnet Champagne Brut Heritage NV FRANCE

WHITE SPARKLING (37.5cl) £5.29

Nivole Moscato d'Asti 2002 ITALY

WHITE £9.99

Nepenthe Pinot Gris 2003 AUSTRALIA
Screwcap. 16 points in 2007.

WHITE £7.49

Nepenthe Tryst Sauvignon Blanc 2003 AUSTRALIA
Screwcap.

WHITE £3.89

Obikwa Chenin Blanc 2003   SOUTH AFRICA

WHITE £9.99

Petaluma Riesling 2003   AUSTRALIA
Screwcap.

WHITE £9.99

Reichsgraf von Kesselstatt Graacher Domprobst   GERMANY
Riesling Kabinett, Mosel 2002
16.5 points in 3–4 years and beyond.

RED £24.95

'Rayner Vineyard' McLaren Vale Shiraz 2000   AUSTRALIA

WHITE £5.99

Snake Creek Mount Benson Pinot Gris 2003   AUSTRALIA
Screwcap. 16 in 2006.

RED £7.99

Swan Bay Pinot Noir 2003   AUSTRALIA
Screwcap. 15.5 in 2008.

RED £7.99

Tokolosh Cabernet Franc/Shiraz 2002   SOUTH AFRICA

WHITE £13.99

Voyager Estate Chardonnay 2002   AUSTRALIA
Screwcap.

WHITE £8.99

Wakefield Gewürztraminer 2003   AUSTRALIA
Screwcap.

ROSÉ £7.99

Wirra Wirra 'Mrs Wigley' Rosé 2003   AUSTRALIA
Screwcap. Also at Sainsbury's.

SAFEWAY

This retailer is now owned by William Morrison,
another entrant in this book. However, I have retained
Safeway as a separate entry until all stores have
converted to the Morrison format (which may take
until well into 2005).

Safeway House,
6 Millington Road,
Hayes,
Middlesex UB3 4AY

Tel: (020) 8848 8744
Fax: (020) 8573 1865

E-mail: safewaypressoffice@btclick.com
Website: www.safeway.co.uk

For Safeway wines 14 points and under visit
www.superplonk.com

17.5
RED £12.99

Casa Lapostolle Cuvée Alexandre Merlot 2000   CHILE
Superb, world-class, complex, astonishing, beautiful.
Also at Booths, Majestic.

17
RED £12.99

Crescent Shiraz/Mourvèdre/Grenache 2001   AUSTRALIA
A blend of Shiraz, Mourvèdre, Grenache. Very
sensually perfumed, fruited, textured and finished.

17
RED £9.99

Errazuriz Max Reserva Syrah 2000   CHILE
Stridency with elegance. Superb polish, purpose with
berries of huge class and concentration.
Also at Tesco.*

17
WHITE £4.99

Concha y Toro Casillero del Diablo Viognier 2003   CHILE
Superb smoky apricot.
Also at Oddbins.

16.5
RED £12.99

Vergelegen Cabernet Sauvignon 2000   SOUTH AFRICA
It has that casual brilliance of first-class New World
Cabernets. (New World! The Cape planted its fine vines
in 1633!) It's soft yet craggy, rich yet delicate, aromatic,
yet hugely back-edged with beautifully tasty berries.
Also at Oddbins.

16.5
WHITE £4.99

Araldica La Luciana, Gavi 2002   ITALY
What a great change from Chardonnay and Sauvignon
Blanc the Contese grape here makes: dry, elegant,

textured, aromatic, plump yet spry – this is great
tippling indeed.

16.5

WHITE £3.49

Cserszegi Fuszeres, Akos Kamocsay 2003   HUNGARY

So delicate yet so emphatic. Gooseberry, melon and
pear. If Hungary could produce an abundance of
wines of such quality as this one it could rock the
white-wine world.

16.5

WHITE £11.99

Concha y Toro Ameila Chardonnay 2001   CHILE

Big, thick, rich – the perfect companion for a fish stew.

16.5

RED £5.99

Chateau Bouisset, Coteaux du Languedoc 2001   FRANCE

Well structured chocolate with cherry berries and
some lengthy incisiveness from the tannins. A hint of
smokiness on the finish completes a well-rounded,
delicious performance.

16.5

WHITE £3.49

Irsai Oliver, Akos Kamocsay 2003   HUNGARY

Beautiful pure fruit, slightly spicy, fresh, grapey, hint
of under-ripe gooseberry. Wonderful with scallops and
minted pea purée.

16.5

RED £4.99

La Paz Tempranillo,   SPAIN
Co-op Nuestra Señora de la Paz 2001

Fine cherry, berry fruit, touch of prune, terrific toasted
tannins.

16.5

Simon Gilbert Hunter Verdelho 2002 AUSTRALIA

A lovely sum of highly charming yet demure points:
lychee, peach, lemon and pineapple with a floral echo
of spice. Too delicate for spicy food but superb to lift a
blue mood.

Piat d'Or has long been a presumptuous brand, from its sleek,
seductive TV commercials of the 70s and 80s through to the
revelation that hypermarkets in the French ferry ports shoved the
stuff on the Wines-From-Countries-Other-Than-France shelves
because staff had never heard of it (whatever the TV commercials
were trying to kid the gullible into believing). In 2003, Piat d'Or
came up with its latest line in entertaining wheezes with an idea
which compared, in so-called independent taste tests all over the
UK, its products with two others, both French, one selling at £5.99
and the other at £11.99.

'Participants were,' the Piat d'Or's PR company said, 'asked to
select their preference for red or white, they tasted the three
options blind, and finally, one simple question was put to them:
which wine tastes good to you?'

As a result of this travesty of a trial, naturally enough the
£3.99 Piat d'Or specimen came out top. Well, why wouldn't it? Any
bloody fool can choose a hundred French wines, at any price, to
which even a bottle of Piat d'Or would be preferable. Note that only
French contenders were chosen. I'd like to see this test replicated,
with half-a-dozen New World wines and see what people's real
taste preferences were. I'd like to see Piat d'Or stacked up against
supermarket own-label cheapies. It would get slaughtered.

16.5   WHITE £4.99

35 South Sauvignon Blanc 2003   CHILE
Superbly textured and subtle (yet has tang and
tenacity).
Also at Somerfield.

16.5   RED £13.49

Villa Maria Cellar Selection   NEW ZEALAND
Merlot/Cabernet Sauvignon 2002
Very brisk tannins, finely balanced cherries, plums
and blackberries.

16   RED £4.99

Big Rivers Durif de Bortoli 2003   AUSTRALIA
Big, rich chocolate-mousse rich fruit with a hint of
candied cherry. A simply superb wine to unleash on to
curried dishes.

16   WHITE £7.99

Cono Sur Vision Riesling 2002   CHILE
Screwcap. 18 points in 5–6 years.
Also at Sainsbury's, Thresher.

16   RED £4.99

Concha y Toro Casillero del Diablo Pinot Noir 2002   CHILE
Fresh cherries with gamey spice.

16   RED £15.95

Caballo Loco No. 6 NV   CHILE
One of the best blends yet with its ruffled velvet texture.

SAFEWAY

16
RED £5.99
DFJ Touriga Nacional/Touriga Franca 2001   PORTUGAL
16.5 points if £4.49. Delightfully rich yet elegant
with very gracious, subtly gritty tannins and soft
cherry/plum richness with a hint of spice.
Also at Tesco.

16
WHITE £6.29
Fetzer Chardonnay/Viognier 2002   USA
Exotic multi-toned gooseberry and apricot with fine
citrus and pineapple. Superb Thai food wine.
Also at Thresher.

16
RED £6.00
Kanonkopp Kadette 2001   SOUTH AFRICA
Pinotage 60%, 40% Cabernet, Cabernet Franc and
Merlot. Lovely, simple, unpretentious plum fruit with
graceful tannins.
Also at Small Merchants (SWIG).

16
WHITE £4.99
La Palma Chileña Chardonnay/   CHILE
Sauvignon Blanc 2002
Lip smackin'. Melon and lemon.

16
RED £7.49
Montgras Syrah Limited Edition 2002   CHILE
Broad-shouldered richness.

16

RED £6.29

Neethlingshof Lord   SOUTH AFRICA
Neethling Pinotage 2001
Superb energy from the tannins which have complex
layers offering chocolate on the finish.
Also at Waitrose.

16

RED £4.99

35 South Cabernet Sauvignon 2002   CHILE
Very calm almost haughty fruit of direct berried
softness and slightly grilled richness. It has an
effortless, unhurried style.
Also at Asda, Morrison's, Somerfields, Sainsbury's.

16

RED £4.99

Viña Morande Merlot 2003   CHILE
Wonderfully fleshy food wine.

16

RED £14.99

Valdivieso Caballo Loco No. 6 NV   CHILE
The best blend yet.

16

WHITE £5.99

Sauvignon Blanc, Marlborough 2003 NEW ZEALAND
Very lengthy experience from gentle gooseberry to
chalky tanginess of pineapple on the finish.
Also at Thresher, Oddbins, Tesco, Booths, Somerfield,
Sainsbury's, Co-op, Morrison's, Small Merchants
(Unwins, Londis).

SAFEWAY

OTHER WINES 15.5 AND UNDER

15.5   WHITE £5.99
Chilensis Reserva Sauvignon Blanc 2003   CHILE

WHITE £5.99
Chilensis Casablanca Valley Sauvignon   CHILE
Blanc 2002

RED £7.89
Stellenzicht Golden Triangle Pinotage 2001 SOUTH AFRICA
Also at Waitrose.

WHITE £3.99
Riverview Gewürztraminer, Akos   HUNGARY
Kamocsay 2003
Also at Asda, Sainsbury's, Waitrose.

15   RED £4.99
La Chasse du Pape Grande Réserve,   FRANCE
Côtes du Rhône Rouge, Gabriel Meffre 2001

RED £8.99
Nederburg Private Bin Pinotage 2001 SOUTH AFRICA
Also at Waitrose.

WHITE £5.99
Sauvignon Blanc Virgin Vintage,   HUNGARY
Akos Kamocsay 2003

14.5   RED £5.99
Fetzer Zinfandel/Shiraz 2002   USA
Also at Budgens.

RED £4.99

Portada Castelao Tinta Doriz 2001 PORTUGAL

WHITE £13.99

The Lane 'Beginning' Chardonnay 2000 AUSTRALIA

14

WHITE £6.99

Booarra Chardonnay/Viognier 2002 AUSTRALIA

WHITE £3.99

Eden Collection La Mancha, SPAIN
Co-op Jesús del Perdon 2002

WHITE £4.99

Fat Bastard Chardonnay, FRANCE
Fat Bastard Wine Company, Languedoc 2003
Also at Asda.

SAINSBURY'S

Head Office:
33 High Holborn,
London EC1N 2HT

Tel: (020) 7695 6000
Fax: (020) 7695 7610

Customer Careline: (0800) 636262

Website: www.sainsburys.co.uk.

For Sainsbury's wines 14 points and under visit
www.superplonk.com

17.5

WHITE £8.99

Springfield Estate Wild Yeast
Chardonnay 2002

SOUTH AFRICA

On line only: www.sainsburys.co.uk(sainsburyswine).
Utterly bewitchingly delicious. Offers so many layers
of depth and delicacy. Sheer satin class and
complexity.

Also at Small Merchants (Bibendum, SWIG, Charles
Stevenson, Magnum).

17

WHITE £9.99

Errazuriz Wild Ferment Chardonnay 2001

CHILE

Has layers of beguiling, slightly chalky flavours with
spice, melon, pear and citrus.

17

WHITE £14.99

Springfield Estate Méthode
Ancienne Chardonnay 2002

SOUTH AFRICA

On line only: www.sainsburys.co.uk(sainsburyswine).
Like the above in character but has more pineapple
richness on the finish.

17

WHITE £9.99

Villa Maria Reserve Sauvignon Blanc 2003   NEW ZEALAND
On line only: www.sainsburys.co.uk(sainsburyswine).
Screwcap. Wonderful coating of lime to the ripe
gooseberry. The texture is delicate yet incisive.
Also at Thresher.

16.5   WHITE   £5.99
Bert Simon Serrig Wurtzberg Kabinett,   GERMANY
Mosel-Saar-Ruwer 2001
Lovely delicacy of lime, pineapple and peach. Will rate
18 in 5 years.

16.5   RED   £7.99
Doña Dominga Carmenere Reserve 2002   CHILE
Very velvety berries, couth yet hinting at cragginess,
with superb cocoa-edged tannins.

16.5   RED   £8.99
Don Reca Limited Release Merlot 2002   CHILE
Distinguished, high-class, hearth-felt richness (old
slippers, leather chair, pipe, ashes).

16.5   WHITE   £6.99
Leasingham Magnus Riesling 2003   AUSTRALIA
18.5 in 3 years. Screwcap. So elegant and self-
possessed. Superb crisp, minerally citrus.

On corks and corkscrews (No. 8)
It would also help if all wine waiters, restaurateurs and chefs
running restaurants immediately changed wines without demur.
One reason why so many people feel so reluctant to complain, or
simply wonder if the wine is as good as it ought to be, is that the
reaction from some restaurant staff is so hostile (at worst) or
indifferent (at best). 'Send back a bad wine, just as you would if
you were served a bad egg,' wrote Alexis Lichine in his classic 1952
The Wines of France (quoted from memory so I apologise if I have
remembered it inexactly).

16.5   RED £7.99
Marqués de Casa Concha Merlot 2002   CHILE
Delicious cherry/plum fruit with savoury tannins. Gripping berries of substance and sensuality. Hint of cocoa to the sweet plums, and the tannins add a dry-textured richness to the deep finish.

16.5   WHITE £8.99
Pewsey Vale Riesling 2003   AUSTRALIA
18.5 in 2–4 years. Dry yet has a restrained peach undertone.
Also at Oddbins, Thresher.

16.5   WHITE £4.49
Réserve St Marc Sauvignon Blanc, Vin de Pays d'Oc 2003   FRANCE
Delicious, dainty, dry, perfectly formed. Fantastic shellfish plonk.

16.5   WHITE £4.99
Sainsbury's Australian Riesling 2003   AUSTRALIA
18.5 in 3–5 years.

16.5   WHITE £10.99
Sonoma Coast Chardonnay, La Crema 2002   USA
Brilliantly textured chewy melon, gooseberry and citrus.

16.5   WHITE £6.99
Nepenthe Tryst Sauvignon Blanc/Sémillon 2003   AUSTRALIA
Screwcap. Delicious tangy apricot and pear with citrus stitching.
Also at Oddbins.

16   RED   £8.99

Barco Reale di Carmignano,   ITALY
Tenuta di Capezzana 2002
Lovely aroma of roasted berries and flowers. Rich fruit
is not a let-down – slight savoury ripeness.

16   WHITE   £4.99

Castel Chardonnay/Viognier,   FRANCE
Cuvée Réservée, Vin de Pays d'Oc 2003
Lovely dry apricot teases out the citrus. Superbly fresh
and keen.

16   WHITE   £5.29

Canepa Winemaker's Selection   CHILE
Gewürztraminer 2003
Very crisp, slow-to-evolve-to-fruit – a Gewürz of
elegance and bite.

16   RED   £4.99

Concha y Toro Casillero del Diablo   CHILE
Carmenere 2002
Lovely cassis and tannins.

16   RED   £4.99

Concha y Toro Casillero del Diablo   CHILE
Carmenere 2003
Chewy plums, tart blackberries, ripe tannins. Superb
recipe.
Also at Majestic.

16   WHITE   £6.99
Chardonnay 2001   AUSTRALIA
Classy ripeness, hint of mango to the lemon/melon.
Also at Majestic.

16   WHITE   £5.99
Dr L. Riesling, Mosel-Saar-Ruwer 2003   GERMANY
Screwcap. The touch of peach-stone to the apricot-
fleshed fruit is superb.

16   WHITE   £9.99
Jekel Chardonnay 2001   USA
Bargain! Creamy lemon zest and pineapple. Hint of
mango.

16   RED   £7.99
Matua Valley Wines 'Innovator' Syrah 2002   NEW ZEALAND
Lovely rich rolling fruit, beautifully polished yet would
be craggy.

16   RED   £4.99
Pinno 2003   SOUTH AFRICA
Pinotage as Beaujolais Nouveau! Great chilled with its
fresh plummy chutzpah.

16   WHITE   £8.49
Querbach Hallgartener Halbtrocken Riesling,   GERMANY
Rheingau 2002
18 points in 3–4 years. Sheer class. Satin-textured
minerals.

16

WHITE £6.99

Rueda Verdejo, Bodegas Veracruz 2003 SPAIN
Delicious harmony between plump peach and pert
citrus.

16

WHITE SPARKLING £29.99

Ruinart Blanc de Blancs Champagne NV FRANCE
It cannot be denied – it is lovely: dry, classically lean
yet consummately moreish.

16

WHITE £4.99

Sainsbury's Classic Selection Muscadet, FRANCE
Sèvre et Maine 2003
A most unusual specimen of the breed: it has real
fruit, yet keeps its classic dryness and crispness.

16

WHITE £3.99

Sainsbury's California Chardonnay 2002 USA
Better, classier than many a white Burgundy at five
times the price.

16

WHITE £3.19

Sainsbury's Chilean Sauvignon Blanc NV CHILE
Delicious under-ripe peach and lemon.

16

RED £5.79

Sainsbury's Reserve Selection Chilean CHILE
Cabernet Sauvignon 2001
Lovely ripe yet delicately layered berries.

16   WHITE £9.99

Shaw & Smith Unoaked Chardonnay 2003   AUSTRALIA
Very pure and classy.

16   RED £6.99

Shiraz 2001   AUSTRALIA
Immensely soft and yielding berries.

16   RED £10.99

Sonoma Coast Pinot Noir, La Crema 2001   USA
Delicious gamey cherry and plum.

16   WHITE £6.99

Stepping Stone Padthaway Chardonnay 2003   AUSTRALIA
Has a most unusual chewy lime/peach/pineapple
richness which never creeps OTT.

16   RED £7.99

St Hallett Shiraz 2002   AUSTRALIA
Real tangy fruit (raspberries, plums and a touch of
roast nut) with generous yet vegetal tannins.
Also at Tesco.

16   WHITE £10.99

Torres Fransola Sauvignon Blanc 2002   SPAIN
On line only: www.sainsburys.co.uk (sainsburyswine).
Very complete and classy.

16   RED £6.99

Tabali Syrah Reserva 2002   CHILE
Sheer satin jam with firm, gently roasted tannins.

16 RED £13.99

SOUTH AFRICA

The Foundry Double Barrel 2001

On line only: www.sainsburys.co.uk (sainsburyswine).
Thrillingly sensuously rich, and rolling in dainty yet
emphatic fruit. Tinto Barocca and Cabernet
Sauvignon.

16 WHITE £5.99

CHILE

**Villa Montes Sauvignon Blanc
Reserve 2003**
Superbly crisp.

16 RED £6.99

CHILE

Valdivieso Reserve Cabernet Sauvignon 2002
Delightful hint of spice to the cassis.

16 WHITE £4.99

SOUTH AFRICA

**Graham Beck Wines
Waterside White 2003**
A lovely texture to peach and pineapple. Stunning for
the money.

16 RED £9.99

AUSTRALIA

**Wirra Wirra Church Block
Cabernet Sauvignon/Shiraz/Merlot 2002**
Screwcap. Like picking fresh damsons and black
cherries, roasting them, and adding coal dust.

16

WHITE £4.99

Wolf Blass Eaglehawk Riesling 2003 AUSTRALIA

Screwcap. Terrific potential here (18 in 3–5 years) but already a tangy specimen of cool class.

16

WHITE £6.99

Bernard Germain Anjou Chenin Blanc, FRANCE
Signature Collection 2001

Most individual white wine of suppressed, dry honey/peach fruit. Has a textured, acquired-taste dryness and a hint of sherry on the finish. A delicious surprise.

16

WHITE £4.99

Wolf Blass Eaglehawk Chardonnay 2003 AUSTRALIA

Delightfully creamy, melony and yet fresh to finish. Also at Asda.

16

WHITE £5.99

Sauvignon Blanc, Marlborough 2003 NEW ZEALAND

Very lengthy experience from gentle gooseberry to chalky tanginess of pineapple on the finish. Also at Thresher, Oddbins, Tesco, Safeway, Somerfield, Booths, Co-op, Morrison's, Small Merchants (Unwins, Londis).

When the director of the London office of the Australian Wine Bureau went to see the head of wine buying at a leading UK supermarket chain in 1980, she was told that 'Australian wine will never catch on.'

16   RED £4.99
  La Baume Merlot, Vin de Pays d'Oc 2003   FRANCE
  Screwcap. Delicious chewy plums, gently leathery and
  very faintly wrinkled.
  Also at Budgens.

16   WHITE £4.99
  La Baume Sauvignon Blanc,   FRANCE
  Vin de Pays d'Oc 2003
  Screwcap. Utterly cracking Sauvignon and crackle it
  does with live-wire gooseberry and citrus.
  Also at Budgens.

16   WHITE £7.99
  Cono Sur Vision Riesling 2002   CHILE
  Screwcap. 18 points in 5–6 years.
  Also at Safeway, Thresher.

OTHER WINES 15.5 AND UNDER

15.5   WHITE £8.99
  Alois Lageder Gewürztraminer 2002   ITALY
  On line only: www.sainsburys.co.uk(sainsburyswine).

                                                          RED £9.00
  Beyerskloof Pinotage Reserve 2002   SOUTH AFRICA

                                                          WHITE £4.99
  Custodio del Mar Chardonnay/Sauvignon   CHILE
  Blanc 2003

RED £9.99

Errazuriz Wild Ferment Pinot Noir 2002 CHILE

17.5 points in 2 years.

WHITE £7.99

Jordan Estate Chardonnay 2003 SOUTH AFRICA

On line only: www.sainsburys.co.uk(sainsburyswine).
Also at Booths.

RED £6.99

Stonehaven Stepping Stone AUSTRALIA
Cabernet Sauvignon 2001

WHITE £4.99

Kumala Organic Colombard/Chardonnay 2003 SOUTH AFRICA
Also at Asda, Booths.

RED £2.99

Sainsbury's Chilean Cabernet Sauvignon NV CHILE

RED £6.99

Sainsbury's Classic Selection AUSTRALIA
Barossa Shiraz 2003

RED £4.99

Sainsbury's Reserve Selection Minervois 2002 FRANCE

ROSÉ £5.99

Santa Rita 120 Cabernet Sauvignon Rosé 2003 CHILE

RED £7.99

St Hallett Faith Cabernet Sauvignon 2001 AUSTRALIA

WHITE £6.99

Skuttlebutt Sauvignon Blanc/Sémillon/ AUSTRALIA
Chardonnay 2003
16.5 in 3–5 years.

WHITE £9.99
Starvedog Lane Sauvignon Blanc 2002   AUSTRALIA

RED £4.99
Viña Albali Reserva, Bodegas Feliz Solis 1999   SPAIN

WHITE £4.99
Villa Malea Oaked Viura 2002   SPAIN

WHITE £6.99
Zonte's Footstep Verdelho 2003   AUSTRALIA

RED £6.99
Wirra Wirra Sexton's Acre Shiraz 2002   AUSTRALIA
Screwcap.

WHITE £3.99
Riverview Gewürztraminer, Akos Kamocsay 2003   HUNGARY
Also at Asda, Safeway, Waitrose.

15

RED £4.99
Sainsbury's Reserve Selection Corbières 2002   FRANCE

WHITE £6.99
Sanctuary Sauvignon Blanc 2004   NEW ZEALAND
Screwcap. 16.5 in 18 months.

WHITE £5.99
Domaine Belle-Croix Bourgogne Aligoté 2003   FRANCE

WHITE £5.79
Sainsbury's Reserve Selection   CHILE
Chilean Chardonnay 2002

RED £5.79
Sainsbury's Reserve Selection Chilean Merlot 2002   CHILE

WHITE £10.99
Enate Gewürztraminer, Somontano 2003   SPAIN
On line only: www.sainsburys.co.uk (sainsburyswine).

WHITE £9.99
Gran Araucano Chardonnay 2002   CHILE

RED £8.99
Las Brisas Pinot Noir Reserve 2002   CHILE

RED £4.49
Réserve St Marc Grenache/Malbec,   FRANCE
Vin de Pays d'Oc 2003

WHITE £13.99
Stonehaven Limited Vineyard Release   AUSTRALIA
Chardonnay 2000

RED £5.99
Santa Rita 120 Carmenere 2003   CHILE

WHITE £5.99
Sainsbury's Classic Selection   ITALY
Pinot Grigio delle Venezie 2003

RED £3.99
Sainsbury's California Merlot 2003   USA

RED £2.99
Sainsbury's Chilean Merlot NV   CHILE

WHITE £4.99

Atlantique Touraine Sauvignon Blanc 2003 FRANCE
Also at Morrison's.

14.5 ROSÉ £3.99

Big Frank's Deep Pink, Vin de Pays d'Oc 2003 FRANCE

RED £5.99

Campaneo Old Vines Garnacha 2002 SPAIN

RED £5.99

Campaneo Old Vines Garnacha 2003 SPAIN

WHITE £7.99

Cono Sur Vision Gewürztraminer 2003 CHILE
Screwcap.

RED £4.99

Castel Cabernet Sauvignon, FRANCE
Cuvée Réservée, Vin de Pays d'Oc 2003

RED £5.99

Domaine des Coccinelles, Côtes du Rhône 2002 FRANCE

ROSÉ £5.49

Domaine de Sours Rosé 2003 FRANCE

WHITE £8.99

Gran Araucano Sauvignon Blanc 2002 CHILE

RED £5.99

Grande Réserve Les Vignerons des FRANCE
Trois Terroirs, St-Chinian 2003

RED £4.99

Jacob's Creek Cabernet/Merlot 2002   AUSTRALIA

RED £5.99

Kumala Organic Pinotage/Shiraz 2003   SOUTH AFRICA
Also at Asda.

WHITE £3.99

Le Petit Sommelier Fruity White 2003   FRANCE

WHITE £4.49

Lurton Sauvignon Blanc,   FRANCE
Vin de Pays du Jardin de la France 2003

WHITE £2.85

Sainsbury's California White Wine NV   USA

RED £7.99

St-Emilion, Réserve des Remparts Calvet 2002   FRANCE

RED £6.99

Stepping Stone Coonawarra   AUSTRALIA
Cabernet Sauvignon 2001

WHITE £6.99

Michel Torino Limited Edition Torrontes 2003   ARGENTINA

RED £14.99

Wolf Blass Gold Label Cabernet Sauvignon/   AUSTRALIA
Cabernet Franc 2001

ROSÉ £4.99

Santa Julia Syrah Rosé 2004   ARGENTINA
Screwcap.

RED £7.99

Zonte's Footstep Shiraz/Viognier 2003   AUSTRALIA

WHITE £6.99

Stonehaven Stepping Stone Chardonnay 2003   AUSTRALIA

RED £2.99

Sainsbury's Bulgarian Cabernet Sauvignon NV   BULGARIA

RED £2.99

Sainsbury's Vin de Pays d'Oc Rouge NV   FRANCE

14

ROSÉ £3.99

Agramont Garnacha Rosado 2003   SPAIN

ROSÉ £7.99

Wirra Wirra 'Mrs Wigley' Rosé 2003   AUSTRALIA
Screwcap. Also at Oddbins.

RED £10.99

Brolio Chianti Classico, Barone Ricasoli 2002   ITALY

RED £6.49

Carneby Liggle Red 2002   AUSTRALIA

ROSÉ £4.99

Côtes du Rhône Rosé, Enclave des Papes 2003   FRANCE

ROSÉ £4.99

Domaine de Pellehaut Rosé,   FRANCE
Côtes de Gascogne 2003

FORTIFIED £7.49

Domecq La Ina Very Pale Fino Sherry   SPAIN

RED £7.99

Leasingham Magnus   AUSTRALIA
Shiraz/Cabernet Sauvignon 2000

RED £3.99

Marquises Réserve Merlot/Grenache,   FRANCE
Vin de Pays d'Oc 2003

RED £7.49

Montgras Single Vineyard Zinfandel 2001   CHILE

WHITE £5.99

Michel Laroche Chardonnay,   FRANCE
Vin de Pays d'Oc 2003

RED £4.99

Réserve des Tuileries, Côtes du Roussillon 2003   FRANCE

RED £12.99

Starvedog Lane Shiraz 1999   AUSTRALIA

WHITE £8.49

Steenberg Sémillon 2003   SOUTH AFRICA

WHITE £7.99

Santa Rita Medalla Real Sauvignon Blanc 2003   CHILE

WHITE £6.99

Sainsbury's Classic Selection   AUSTRALIA
Western Australia Sauvignon Blanc/ Sémillon 2003
Screwcap.

RED £4.79

Sainsbury's Douro 2001   PORTUGAL

WHITE £10.99

Two Hands The Wolf Riesling 2003 AUSTRALIA

On line only: www.sainsburys.co.uk(sainsburyswine).
Screwcap.

RED £2.99

Vin de Pays des Côtes Catalanes, FRANCE
Vignerons Catalans NV

RED £2.99

Sainsbury's Bulgarian Merlot NV BULGARIA

RED £2.89

Sainsbury's Merlot, Vin de Pays d'Oc 2003 FRANCE

RED £2.89

Sainsbury's Cabernet Sauvignon, FRANCE
Vin de Pays d'Oc NV

RED £5.49

Chinon Domaine du Colombier 2002 FRANCE

WHITE £5.99

Sainsbury's Classic Selection Riesling 2003 GERMANY

WHITE £3.99

Chenin Blanc, FRANCE
Vin de Pays du Jardin de la France 2003

WHITE £2.99

Sainsbury's Vin de Pays d'Oc Blanc NV FRANCE

SMALL MERCHANTS

ADNAMS WINE MERCHANTS
Sole Bay Brewery,
East Green, Southwold,
Suffolk IP18 6JW

Tel: (01502) 727222
Fax: (01502) 727223

E-mail: wines@adnams.co.uk
Website: www.adnamswines.co.uk

JOHN ARMIT WINES
5 Royalty Studios, 105 Lancaster Road,
London W11 1QF

Tel: (020) 7908 0600
Fax: 020 7908 0601

E-mail: info@armit.co.uk
Website: www.armit.co.uk

BACCHANALIA
90 Mill Road,
Cambridge CB1 2BD

Tel/Fax: (01223) 576 292

E-mail: paul.bowes@ntlworld.com

BALLANTYNES OF COWBRIDGE
3 Westgate,
Cowbridge,
South Glamorgan CF71 7AQ

Tel: (01446) 774 840
Fax: (01446) 775 253

E-mail: richard@ballantynes.co.uk
Website: www.ballantynes.co.uk

BENNETS FINE WINES
High Street,
Chipping Campden,
Glos GL55 6AG

Tel: (01386) 840 392

BERRY BROS & RUDD
3 St James Street,
London SW1A 1EG

Tel: (020) 7396 9600 or (0870) 900 4300
Fax: (0870) 900 4301

E-mail: orders@bbr.com
Website: www.bbr.com

BIN TWO
South Quay,
Padstow,
Cornwall PL28 8BL

Tel: (01841) 532022
Fax: (01208) 862267

E-mail: wine@bintwo.com
Website: www.bintwo.com

D. BYRNE & CO.
Victoria Buildings,
12 King Street,
Clitheroe,
Yorkshire BB7 2EP

Tel: (01200) 423152
Fax:(01200) 429 386

HANDFORD HOLLAND PARK

12 Portland Road,
Holland Park,
London W11 4LE

Tel: (020) 7221 9614
Fax: (020) 7221 9613

Website: www.handford.net

HEDLEY WRIGHT WINE MERCHANTS

11 Twyford Centre,
London Road,
Bishop's Stortford,
Herts CM23 3YT

Tel: (01279) 465 818

E-mail: justin@hedleywright.co.uk
Website: www.hedleywright.co.uk

JEROBOAMS

Head Office:
43 Portland Road,
London W11 4LJ

Tel: (020) 7259 6716 (shop information)

E-mail: sales@jeroboams.co.uk
Website: www.jeroboams.co.uk

LAY & WHEELER

Gosbecks Park, 117 Gosbecks Road,
Colchester,
Essex CO2 9JT

Tel: (0845) 330 1855
Fax: (01206) 560002

E-mail: sales@laywheeler.com
Website: www.laywheeler.com

LIBERTY WINES UK LTD
Unit A53, The Food Market,
New Covent Garden,
London SW8 5EE

Tel: (020) 7720 5350
Fax: (020) 7720 6158

E-mail: info@libertywine.co.uk
Website: www.usda.org.uk

LONDIS (HOLDINGS) LTD
Eurogroup House, 67–71 High Street,
Hampton Hill,
Middlesex TW12 1LZ

Tel: (020) 8941 0344
Fax: (020) 8941 6499

E-mail: marketing@londis.co.uk
Website: www.londis.co.uk

MAGNUM FINE WINES
43 Pall Mall,
London SW1Y 5JG

Tel: (020) 7839 5732
Fax: (020) 7321 0848

E-mail: wine@magnum.co.uk
Website: www.magnum.co.uk

NISA-TODAY'S
Ambient Warehouse,
Nisa Today's Ltd,
Park Farm Road,
Foxhills Industrial Estate,
Scunthorpe,
North Lincolnshire DN15 8QP

Tel: (0845) 6044999
Fax: (01724) 278727

E-mail: info@nisa-todays.com
Website: www.nisa-todays.com

REX NORRIS

50 Queen's Road,
Haywards Heath,
West Sussex RH16 1EE

Tel/Fax: (01444) 454756

PALMERS WINE

West Bay Road,
Bridport DT6 4JA

Tel: (01308) 422396
Fax: (01308) 421149

Website: www.palmersbrewery.com

PARTRIDGES

24–25 Drury Lane,
London WC2B 5RJ

Tel: (020) 7240 1336
Fax: (020) 7497 5601

Website: www.partridges.co.uk

THOS PEATLING FINE WINES

Westgate House,
Bury St Edmunds,
Suffolk IP33 1QS

Tel: (01284) 755948
Fax: (01284) 714483

E-mail: sales@thospeatling.co.uk
Website: www.thospeatling.co.uk

PORTLAND WINE COMPANY
16 North Parade,
Sale Moor N33 3JS

Tel: (01619) 962 8752

E-mail: info@lcb.com.uk

CHARLES STEVENSON
11 Plymouth Road Industrial Estate,
Havestock,
Devon PL19 9QN

Tel: (01822) 616272
Fax: (01822) 617094

E-mail: sales@stevensonwines.co.uk

STRATFORD'S WINE AGENCIES
High Street,
Cookham,
Berkshire SL6 9SQ

Tel: (01628) 810 606

E-mail: sales@stratfordwine.co.uk
Website: www.stratfordwine.co.uk

SWIG
188 Sutton Court Road,
London W4 3HR

Tel: (020) 8995 7060
Fax: (020) 8995 7069

E-mail: imbibe@swig.co.uk
Website: www.swig.co.uk

TANNERS WINE MERCHANTS
26 Wyle Cop,
Shrewsbury SY1 1XD

Tel: (01743) 234455
Fax: (01743) 234456

E-mail: sales@tanners-wines.co.uk
Website: www.tanners-wines.co.uk

UNWINS
Birchwood House, Victoria Road,
Dartford,
Kent DA1 5AJ

Tel: (01322) 272 711
Fax: (01322) 294469

E-mail: admin@unwinswines.co.uk
Website: www.unwins.co.uk

VINCEREMOS WINES & SPIRITS
74 Kirkgate,
Leeds LS2 7DJ

Tel: (0113) 2440002
Fax: (0113) 2884566

E-mail: info@vinceremos.co.uk
Website: www.vinceremos.co.uk.

WIMBLEDON WINE CELLARS
1 Gladstone Road,
Wimbledon,
London SW19 1QU

Tel: (020) 8540 9979
Fax:(020) 8540 9399

E-mail: enquiries@wimbledonwinecellar.com
Website: www.wimbledonwinecellar.com

WINE IMPORTERS OF EDINBURGH LTD

7 Beaverhall House,
27 Beaverhall Road,
Edinburgh EH7 4JE

Tel: (0131) 556 3601
Fax: (0131) 557 8493

E-mail: wineimporters@dial.pipex.com

THE WINE LIBRARY

43 Trinity Square
London EC3

Tel: (020) 74810415

NOEL YOUNG WINES

56 High Street,
Trumpington,
Cambridge CB2 2LS

Tel: (01223) 844744

E-mail: admin@nywines.co.uk

For all Small Merchants' wines 15.5 points and under
visit www.superplonk.com

18.5

RED   £16.49

Torres Manso de Velasco 2000   CHILE

Thos Peatling, Portland Wine Company

This is one of those masterpieces every bit as
satisfying as a Mozart piano sonata: effortless, tuneful,
silky, surprisingly elongated and very, very restful.
The wine is composed of smooth berries and tannins
as svelte as taffeta with a very soft (sotto voce?)
suggestion of creamy coffee. Yet in spite of these
delicate nuances I enjoyed it, and the wine showed all
its sides with a simple slab of real mature Cheddar.
Cellar it? If you enjoy greater vegetality, yes. But how
can this wine improve? It is magnificent now.
Also at London Stores (Harrods).

18

RED   £11.99

The Derelict Vineyard Grenache 2002   AUSTRALIA

Bibendum

Wonderfully invigorating, life-enhancing richness.

17.5

RED   £5.29

Casa Rivas Merlot 2002   CHILE

Adnams

Stunning level of chocolate, tannins, tobacco and
spicy roasted plums. Its length is extraordinary.

17.5

RED   £5.29

Casa Rivas Cabernet Sauvignon 2002   CHILE

Adnams

Layers of spice, cherry, cocoa and real tannic genius.

17.5   RED £7.99
    Casa Rivas Merlot Reserva 2002   CHILE
    Adnams
    Excellent chocolate and grilled berries.

17.5   RED £11.95
    The Laughing Magpie Shiraz/Viognier 2002   AUSTRALIA
    Bibendum, Charles Stevenson, Magnum, Palmers
    Chocolate richness without sweetness. Superb length
    to the tannins.

All manner of virtues are claimed for Burgundy and for
Burgundies, not least by Burgundians themselves, but it seems to
me that the King of France got it right in Lear when he referred to
it as 'waterish'. True, le roi was referring to the fact that Burgundy
has a lot of streams, rills and rivers, but the derision is not inapt
particularly if Burgundy, at anywhere near the same price, is
compared with Chilean Pinot Noir (the latter being the same grape
as red Burgundy's). The best Chilean Pinots are cheap (a fiver to
eight quid), compact and well structured with classic gamey
cherries appearing on the finish as the tannins dry out in the
throat. A touch exotic here? Perhaps. The jejune liquid from
Burgundy does not perform half so daringly on the delicate high-
wire which stretches between overt vegetality and sweet berried
richness which is the challenge Pinot poses.

17.5   RED £10.00
The William Wine 2000   SOUTH AFRICA
Bibendum
Huge 30% Pinotage, 40% Cabernet Sauvignon, 30%
Cabernet presence on the palate.

17.5   WHITE £9.50
Springfield Estate Wild Yeast   SOUTH AFRICA
Chardonnay 2002
Bibendum, SWIG, Charles Stevenson, Magnum
No wood, no nonsense, no kidding. This is a
magnificently textured, complex, smooth yet
characterful white wine.
Also at Sainsbury's.

17.5   WHITE £15.00
Reserve Chardonnay Marlborough 2001   NEW ZEALAND
Philglas & Swiggot, Wimbledon Wine Cellars
Finesse, flavour, fabulous technique. The
genteel touches of charred hay and melon are
wonderful.
Also at London Stores (Selfridges).

17   WHITE £7.95
Alto Palena Reserve Viognier 2002   CHILE
Bibendum
Superb apricot fruit, sheer silk.

17

WHITE £11.67
NEW ZEALAND

Chardonnay Marlborough
Seresin Estates 2002
Wimbledon Wine Cellars
So elegant it hurts as it consoles. Utterly superb,
subtle touches of smoke, melon, lemon etc.

17

RED £14.99
SOUTH AFRICA

Cornerstone Cabernet 2000
Bibendum
A blend of 55% Cabernet Sauvignon, 30% Pinotage,
15% Cabernet, which contrives bite, bounce and
superb characterful richness.

17

RED £5.29
CHILE

Casa Rivas Carmenere 2002
Adnams
Simply superb spicy cocoa.

17

RED £7.99
CHILE

Casa Rivas Cabernet Sauvignon Reserva 2002
Adnams
Chewy baked cocoa and spice.

17

WHITE £14.99
FRANCE

Domaine de la Bongran, Macon-Villages,
J.Thevenet 2000
Adnams
A white Burgundy to better Pulignys and Meursault.
Justifies its price with real fruit, creamy consistency
and a finely wrought texture.

17

WHITE DESSERT (37.5cl) £13.50

De Trafford Straw Wine 2002 SOUTH AFRICA
Bibendum, SWIG
Sheer silken honied peach and pastry-edged richness.

17

WHITE (50cl) £8.49

'La Beryl Blanc' Chenin Blanc, Fairview 2002 SOUTH AFRICA
Liberty Wines
Stunning ripeness of spicy pineapple, honey and
peach. Will cellar for 10–12 years and reach 20 points.

17

WHITE £15.95

Méthode Ancienne SOUTH AFRICA
Chardonnay Springfield Estate 2002
Bibendum, SWIG
Creamy, subtly rich, ripe, elegant, smoky, complete.
Superb with mildly spicy fish dishes.

17

RED £14.99

Old Road Pinotage 2000 SOUTH AFRICA
Bibendum
I've never tasted before a 4-year-old Pinotage with
such lively presence and tannic fulsomeness.

17

WHITE £15.50

Pinot Gris Marlborough, NEW ZEALAND
Seresin Estates 2003
Wimbledon Wine Cellars
Stunning dry apricot and citrus. High-class act from
nose to throat.

17   WHITE £8.95
The Money Spider Roussanne 2003   AUSTRALIA
Bibendum
Screwcap. Gorgeous apricot/peach/lemon. Will age
5–8 years and reach 20 points in 2008.
Also at Oddbins.

17   WHITE £7.50
The Hermit Crab Marsanne/Viognier 2002   AUSTRALIA
Magnum
Screwcap. Superb dry apricot, pineapple and pear.
Wonderfully well textured.
Also at Booths.

17   WHITE £5.99
Villa Maria Private Bin Chardonnay 2003   NEW ZEALAND
Unwins
Has such beautiful footwork as it dances on the
tongue with subtly leafy melon and lemon.
Also at Oddbins, Asda, Sainsbury's, Waitrose.

17   RED £17.95
Vacqueyras 'Lao Muse',   FRANCE
Domaine Le Clos de Caveau 2000
Adnams
Superbly polished yet brisk and characterful. Utterly
delicious tannins, hint of chocolate.

17   WHITE £9.95
Viognier Fairview 2003   SOUTH AFRICA
Noel Young Wines, Bennets Fine Wines, Hedley Wright
Wine Merchants, Liberty Wines
'We put a lot of effort into this one,' said Charles

Back, the estate's proprietor, to me. And it shows.
Beautiful apricot/peach/lychee complexities and
superb texture.

16.5

WHITE £8.75

Armit Wines New Zealand   NEW ZEALAND
Sauvignon Blanc 2003
John Armit Wines
Superb, classic, towers above Sancerres with its biting
citricity and minerality.

16.5

RED £39.00

Châteauneuf-du-Pape, Domaine du Vieux   FRANCE
Télégraphe, H. Brunier et Fils 2000
Tanners Wine Merchants
Highly perfumed, ripe yet the tannins are still
frisky.

16.5

WHITE £16.80

Chardonnay by Farr, Geelong Victoria 2001   AUSTRALIA
Tanners Wine Merchants
A supremely elegant, genteel Chardonnay of superb
balance of minerally citrus and buttery melon. Lovely
wine, delicate yet hugely emphatic.

16.5

WHITE £6.99

Domaines Paul Mas,   FRANCE
Vignes de Nicole Chardonnay/Viognier, Languedoc 2003
Stratford's Wine Agencies, Bacchanalia
Has the added sexiness of grilled seeds and hay.

16.5
WHITE £6.45
FRANCE

Domaine Coudoulet Muscat,
Vin de Pays d'Oc 2003
Lay & Wheeler
Very plump as it opens and finishes (with the further
requirement of a touch of grilled peach-stone). In
between it offers a grapey ripeness and deliciously
unpretentious dryness.

16.5
WHITE £4.99
FRANCE

'Les Bastions' Blanc, Côtes de Saint-Mont,
Producteurs Plaimont 2002
Adnams
A wine to give you a headache before you drink it as
you try to decipher the small print of the deliciously
chaotic label. The wine matches this deliciousness but
not the chaos, for here is a lovely marriage of
crispness with richness of great pith and moment. A
truly individual bargain.

On corks and corkscrews (No. 9)
I believe our ancestors – recently, not just in the 1950s or before the
war – regularly drank wine that was corked. The great wines then,
indeed all wines, were exclusively the purchasing province of the
toff or the successful professional and they were invariably
consumed old. It is only with the contemporary advent of New
World wines, especially Australian, Californian, New Zealand, South
African, Chilean and so forth, that the problem has been seen to be
so pernicious, so widespread, so damaging. The freshness and
vibrancy of these wines' fruit is one of their most attractive features
and the merest degree of cork taint mars the wines measurably.

16.5

RED £8.49

Montgras Quatro 2002   CHILE

Unwins

Intense cocoa, licorice, berries and ripe tannins.

16.5

RED £5.95

Marselan, Vin de Pays de l'Hérault,   FRANCE
Domaine Coudoulet 2003

Lay & Wheeler

So new! So modern! So well-mannered. Perhaps that's
the surprise in this genteel partner to roasts and
cheese dishes. Plainly delicious berries.

16.5

WHITE £6.95

Picpoul de Pinet, Coteaux du Languedoc,   FRANCE
Domaine Felines Jourdan 2003

Lay & Wheeler

Why these wines aren't more widely appreciated is a
mystery to me – especially now when they've become
so fruity and vivacious (without being OTT). This
specimen has apricot and pineapple and even a hint
of paw-paw.

16.5

RED £7.99

Pinotage Fairview 2002   SOUTH AFRICA

Liberty Wines

15% Shiraz gives it more breadth, greater
chutzpah. Lively roasted berries with soft tannins.
A most unusually delicious Pinotage. Far from
typical.

16.5   RED £7.95
    Reserve Shiraz 2002   CHILE
    Bibendum
    Charming fruit with firm tannins – will it cause any
    sleepless nights in Oz?

16.5   RED £5.95
    The Stump Jump Grenache/   AUSTRALIA
    Shiraz/Mourvèdre 2002
    Bibendum, Magnum
    Screwcap. What a brilliant exercise in classy jam making.

16.5   RED £13.95
    The Work of Time Springfield Estate 2001   SOUTH AFRICA
    Bibendum
    Intense leather, spice, long tannins with an overall
    terrific texture.

16.5   WHITE £6.49
    Casa Lapostolle Sauvignon Blanc 2003   CHILE
    Partridges
    Super dry, under-ripe fruit yet this subtlety is
    amazingly emphatic and suggestive of richness rather
    than achieving it full on. A classic Sauvignon Blanc.
    Also at Booths, London Stores (Selfridges), E-tailers
    (Everywine, Barrels and Bottles).

16.5   RED £6.29
    Torres Santa Digna Cabernet Sauvignon 2002   CHILE
    Noel Young Wines, Tanners Wine Merchants, Wimbledon
    Wine Cellars
    Intense berries which hold a very calm, assured centre

of mild cassis. But as the wine opens up in the glass
a tanginess develops – of some kind of fresher berry.
This is the young acidic side of the wine asserting
itself and it betokens great compatibility with rich
food. After 20 hours of breathing the wine shows dark
milk chocolate with nuts – very chewy.
Also at Booths.

16.5

WHITE £9.99
AUSTRALIA

**Knappstein Lenswood Vineyards
Sauvignon Blanc 2003**
Handford Holland Park
Screwcap. Simply light years fresher and tangier than
any Sancerre.
Also at London Stores (Harrods).

16.5

WHITE £7.95
SOUTH AFRICA

**Springfield Estate Life from Stone
Sauvignon Blanc 2003**
*SWIG, Palmers, Rex Norris, Bin Two, Charles Stevenson,
Magnum*
Stunningly classy and chewy. Tight minerals and fine
extended gooseberry. In this vintage it has an
appealing vegetality.
Also at Booths.

16.5

RED £9.30
SOUTH AFRICA

**Springfield Estate Whole Berry
Cabernet Sauvignon 2001**
SWIG, Rex Norris
Startlingly ripe and ready yet complex and serious.
Its appeal lies in its paradox of texture, tannins, and

tenacity with such vivid immediacy. Total
commitment to plummy pleasure. Fine tannins, hint
of jam, touch of chocolate.
Also at Booths.

16   WHITE £9.99
Knappstein Lenswood Vineyards   AUSTRALIA
Sémillon 2000
The Wine Library, Wine Importers of Edinburgh
Hints of many things and the sum of those delicate
subtleties is sheer pleasure-giving liquid.
Also at London Stores (Harrods).

16   RED £7.95
Reserve Pinot Noir 2002   CHILE
Bacchanalia
17 points in 18 months. Superb cherried richness and
tannins.
Also at Morrison's.

16   RED £15.95
Beacon Shiraz, Fairview 2002   SOUTH AFRICA
Liberty Wines, Bennets Fine Wines
Gripping yet soft, genteel yet highly characterful. Very
feisty and savoury.

16   RED £9.49
Billi Billi Creek Mount Langi Ghiran 2000   AUSTRALIA
Unwins
Spreads itself oozingly deliciously over the tastebuds
with jam and grilled seeds.

16

RED £5.75

FRANCE

Cabernet Sauvignon, Vin de Pays des Côtes de Thongues, Domaine de Mont d'Hortes 2003
Lay & Wheeler
Delicious gently roasted plums with a touch of raspberry. Very gentle tannins which, as they dry out, show some real tangy class. Has a plastic cork, so don't cellar it.

16

RED £7.45

FRANCE

Cuvée Tradition, Costières de Nîmes, Domaine des Canterelles 2001
Lay & Wheeler
Stands up well to chilling, the cherry/blackberry fruit. It also takes agreeably to a pea and ham risotto.

16

WHITE £11.00

FRANCE

Complazens Viognier, Château Complazens, Vin de Pays d'Oc 2002
Philglas & Swiggot, D. Byrne
Delightful apricot and lime.

16

ROSÉ £5.50

CHILE

Cabernet Sauvignon Rosé 2003
Bibendum
Delicious cherry/strawberry fruit with tannins.

16

WHITE £5.29

CHILE

Casa Rivas Sauvignon Blanc 2003
Adnams
Simply superb tangy gooseberry.

16

WHITE £5.29
CHILE

Casa Rivas Chardonnay 2003
Adnams
Lovely lemon and ripe pineapple with a refreshing
food-friendly edge.

16

ROSÉ £5.29
CHILE

Casa Rivas Cabernet Sauvignon Rosé 2003
Adnams
Delicious sticky, cherry fruit. Brilliant with barbecue
food.

16

RED £5.76
FRANCE

Clot de Gleize,
Vin de Pays des Bouches du Rhône 2002
Berry Bros & Rudd
Organic. Brisk tannins, juicy berries. Excellent sturdy
quaffing.

16

WHITE £10.45
FRANCE

Domaine Jean-Louis Denois,
Grande Cuvée, Vin de Pays d'Oc 2001
Berry Bros & Rudd
What a lovely ripe yet delicate piece of wine making.
A fine Rhône/Burgundy mixed style plus wit.

16

WHITE £4.99
FRANCE

Eden Collection Organic Chardonnay,
Jacques Frélin 2002
Nisa-Today's, Vinceremos
Very calm, classy, gently tangy melon/lemon.

16   RED £8.45

Faugères, Château Moulin de Ciffre 2001   FRANCE
Lay & Wheeler
A very civilized, rustically engaging red of herby
berries, sweet plums and smooth tannins.

16   RED £12.99

Fairview Primo Pinotage 2002   SOUTH AFRICA
D.Byrne
Deliciously calm, plum/cassis fruit with elegant
tannins.

I am grateful to the range of Bordeaux wines called Mouton Cadet.
They made me laugh my head off. Since they are widely on sale I
am, in defiance of this book's fiat that only high-rating wines
feature here, going to comment on these wines made by the Baron
Philippe de Rothschild's corporation. Normally Mouton Cadet
products do not pass my purview, no retailer ever bothers to put
them in a tasting for wine writers, and no wine writer ever asks for
samples, but last year I received. Mouton Cadet Blanc 2001 (10
points out of 20, £5.99, Asda, Thresher, Sainsbury, Unwins, Tesco,
Oddbins) is faintly reminiscent of lemon washing-up liquid.
Mouton Cadet Rouge 2000 (9 points, £7.99, Asda, Thresher,
Safeway, Unwins, Somerfield, Sainsbury, Tesco) is heartless and
barren. Mouton Cadet Rosé 2001 (10 points out of 20, £5.99, small
local merchants) offers a medicinal aroma and thin cherry fruit.
Mouton Cadet Reserve Blanc 1997 (8 points, £7.49, who cares who
sells it? - no-one you've ever heard of) is oxidised, bare, ugly.
Mouton Cadet Médoc 1999 (10 points, £9.49) is...oh, this is
intolerable. No more of this insipid range!

16

RED £21.99
Ridge Vineyards Geyserville USA
Zinfandel/Carignan/Petite Sirah 2001
Adnams
Drink it now, don't cellar it. It has urgency, class and
bite.

16

WHITE £11.95
Julius Riesling, Henschke 2002 AUSTRALIA
Lay & Wheeler
Screwcapped immediacy and bite. Lovely lemon peel
with a hint of melon lushness. Will cellar for 10–15
years.

16

RED £8.95
Kuyen Syrah/Cabernet Sauvignon 2001 CHILE
Adnams
Nicely textured, warmly layered.

16

WHITE £6.99
La Forge Estate Chardonnay, FRANCE
Domaines Paul Mas, Languedoc 2003
Stratford's Wine Agencies
Pleasingly plump and has the Chardonnay recipe,
melon and lemon, off pat.

16

RED £5.99
Luis Felipe Edwards Estate Carmenere 2002 CHILE
Unwins
Delicious toasty undertone to chewy berries. Has a
Lebanese pastry echo on the finish.

16

RED £7.95

Lay & Wheeler Rioja 2001   SPAIN

Lay & Wheeler

Well, nothing overblown or OTT here. Good plummy
fruit, all at one with itself, and treading a nice balance
between sweetness and crustiness. A handsome Rioja
of firm gluggability.

16

ROSÉ £6.95

Minervois Rosé, Château Villerambert-Julien 2003   FRANCE

Lay & Wheeler

One of the more pleasant of the rosés which plague
the shelves of UK retailers. Offers textured cherries,
dry and classy.

16

RED £4.99

Morande Pinot Noir 2003   CHILE

Unwins

Bargain gamey cherries.

16

WHITE £12.00

Riesling, Marlborough   NEW ZEALAND
Seresin Estates 2002

Wimbledon Wine Cellars

Lovely texture and citrus bite. Has great high-class texture.

16

WHITE £8.45

Sanz Rueda Sauvignon 2002   SPAIN

Lay & Wheeler

Lovely oily fruit with touches of peach, melon and
lemon peel (almost an echo of marmalade indeed).
Utterly delicious with the right book.

16

WHITE £6.99

Fairview Sauvignon Blanc 2003   SOUTH AFRICA

Liberty Wines, Bennets Fine Wines, Hedley Wright Wine Merchants

Delicious hint of peachy spice to the citrus.

16

RED £15.95

Fairview Solitude Shiraz 2002   SOUTH AFRICA

Liberty Wines, Bennets Fine Wines

Very full, deep, gently peppery hint of stature and richness.

16

WHITE £7.99

Sauvignon Blanc 'Vineyard Selection'   NEW ZEALAND
Forrest Estate, Marlborough 2002

Adnams

Very firm, rich (yet stylishly chic) Sauvignon of wit and fruit.

16

WHITE £5.95

The Stump Jump Riesling/Marsanne/   AUSTRALIA
Sauvignon 2002

Bibendum, Magnum

Screwcap. Brilliant Thai-food fruit.

16

RED £11.95

The Galvo Garage 2001   AUSTRALIA

Bibendum, Magnum

A blend of 66% Cabernet Sauvignon, 20% Merlot, 14% Cabernet which achieves feistiness with daintiness.

16

RED £6.75
SOUTH AFRICA

Springfield Estate Firefinch
What the Birds Left Ripe Red 2002
Bin Two, Rex Norris
A blend of 50% Merlot, 30% Ruby Cabernet, 20%
Cabernet Sauvignon, which manages to be jammily
ripe yet dry to finish with a touch of spice.
Also at Booths.

16

WHITE £5.35
SOUTH AFRICA

Springfield Estate Firefinch
Colombard/Chardonnay 2003
Magnum
'A nice summer wine,' says its maker – which damns
it with faint praise, for it has lovely refreshing peach/
lemon fruit.
Also at Booths.

16

WHITE £5.99
NEW ZEALAND

Sauvignon Blanc, Marlborough 2003
Unwins, Londis
Very lengthy experience from gentle gooseberry to
chalky tanginess of pineapple on the finish.
Also at Thresher, Oddbins, Tesco, Safeway,
Somerfield, Sainsbury's, Co-op, Morrison's, Booths.

16

RED £13.99
NEW ZEALAND

Wither Hills Pinot Noir 2002
Jeroboams, Thos Peatling, Ballantynes of Cowbridge
Screwcap. One of the most convincing Kiwi Pinots.

Has a gaminess, feral berried richness and aromatic
intensity, and finishes well.
Also at Booths, Oddbins, Waitrose, The Wine Society.

16

RED £45.99

Pinot Noir Bouchard Finlayson, SOUTH AFRICA
Tête du Cuvée Galpin Peak 2001
Hedley Wright Wine Merchants, SWIG
Outstanding, perhaps the most complete Pinot I've
tasted from the Cape. Beautiful tannins and high-class
fruit.
Also at Waitrose.

16

RED £6.00

Kanonkopp Kadette 2001 SOUTH AFRICA
SWIG
Pinotage 60%, 40% Cabernet, Cabernet Franc and
Merlot. Lovely, simple, unpretentious plum fruit with
graceful tannins.
Also at Safeway.

SOMERFIELD

Somerfield House,
Whitchurch Lane,
Bristol BS14 OTJ

Tel: (0117) 935 9359
Fax: (0117) 978 0629

E-mail: customer.service@somerfield.co.uk
Website: www.somerfield.co.uk

For Somerfield wines 14 points and under visit
www.superplonk.com

17

RED £6.49

Chianti DOCG, Cantina Leonardo 2003   ITALY

Superb grip of tannic black cherry and grilled plums.

17

RED £4.99

Concha y Toro Casillero del Diablo Shiraz 2002   CHILE

Superbly chewy, ripe, balanced full and rich, complex
and very highly polished yet somehow craggy. This
brand is available at almost all supermarkets.

17

WHITE £7.99

Villa Maria Private Bin   NEW ZEALAND
Sauvignon Blanc 2003

Wonderful coating of lime to the ripe gooseberry.
The texture is delicate yet incisive.
Also at Oddbins, Tesco.

16.5

RED £13.95

Château Pontet Fumet, St-Emilion 1999   FRANCE

A 60% Merlot, 40% Cabernet Franc blend of class
and concentration. The harmony of leathery soft
Merlot and peppery Cabernet Franc is superb.

16.5

WHITE £5.99

Danie de Wet Barrel Fermented   SOUTH AFRICA
Chardonnay 2002

Screwcap. A lovely layer of leafy citrus is added to the
calm, gently smoky Ogen melon.

16.5

WHITE £8.99
FRANCE

Fouassier Sancerre Les Grand Groux 2003
Catch it whilst it's young and feisty. Superbly classy,
perfect weight of alcohol (12.5%), dry, slightly vegetal
edge. Very, very classy and dry.

16.5

WHITE £4.99
ITALY

Inycon Chardonnay 2003
Superbly oily fruit, beautifully balanced. Has a
slightly smoky richness with citrus and a hint of
orange peel.

16.5

WHITE £5.99
NEW ZEALAND

**Montana East Coast Unoaked
Chardonnay 2002**
Deliciously textured and lingering melon/lemon fruit.
Shows how pure unwooded fruit can appear.
Also at Asda.

16.5

WHITE £5.99
NEW ZEALAND

Montana Marlborough Riesling 2002
A superb example of utterly unpretentious, classic
New World Riesling: tangy, ripe, complex, rich (yet not
without discretion) and complete. Very fine, textured,
deep citric richness and opulence.

16.5

RED £6.99
SOUTH AFRICA

Porcupine Ridge Syrah 2002
Threads a marvellous thick line between chocolate
plums and herby, gently charred berries and tannins.

16.5
RED £4.03

Somerfield Chilean Merlot, Viña Morande 2003 CHILE
Simply stunningly simple yet overwhelmingly
charming. Direct cherries/berries, firm, lithe tannins
and a texture of thickly knitted acids and tannins. A
very classy mouthful.

16.5
RED £4.99

Trivento Reserve Syrah 2001 ARGENTINA
Literally pulsates with classy berries offering chocolate
and tobacco-edged berries.

16.5
RED £5.99

The Wolf Trap 2002 SOUTH AFRICA
Wonderful chocolate-edged berries and cherries with
complex acids and tannins. Superbly complete, deep,
well-roasted fruit.
Also at Asda.

16.5
WHITE £4.99

Argento Chardonnay 2003 CHILE
Oozes class from every sun-drenched pore of its being
(which is grapefruit, citrus and very slightly smoky
pear).
Also at Asda, Budgens, Majestic, Tesco.

16.5
RED £6.99

Goats do Roam in Villages 2002 SOUTH AFRICA
Vivacity with finesse. That rare, that deliciously rare,
combination.
Also at Majestic, Tesco.

16.5 WHITE £4.89
35 South Sauvignon Blanc 2002 CHILE
Superbly textured and subtle (yet has tang and tenacity).
Also at Safeway.

16.5 WHITE £5.99
Errazuriz Chardonnay 2002 CHILE
Lovely oily texture, superb spicy pineapple and melon
fruit with a touch of oregano.

16 RED £5.99
Errazuriz Cabernet Sauvignon 2002 CHILE
Outstandingly entertaining, serious yet playful, soft
yet leathery, fruity yet possessing finesse.
Also at Asda.

16 RED £4.99
Argento Malbec 2003 ARGENTINA
Soft spicy berries of great charm.
Also at Budgens, Majestic, Tesco.

16 WHITE £4.99
Brown Brothers Dry Muscat 2003 AUSTRALIA
Superbly restrained yet emphatic. Provides delicious
hints of spicy melon, lemon and apricot, and the
overall theme is very elegantly expressed.
Also at Tesco.

16 RED £5.79
Beaumes de Venise, Côtes du Rhône 2001 FRANCE
Bitter black olives and cherries with earthy tannins.
Very full yet deeply dry.

16   RED   £8.49

Château Fongaban Puisseguin-St-Emilion 2001   FRANCE
Dry, almost hard baked berries with cocoa and
tobacco. Brilliant with game and rare meats.

We hear a lot about marine influences on wines and how
beneficial it is for vineyards to enjoy a littoral climate. However,
one producer in South Africa, Springfield Estate of Robertson, run
by brother and sister Abrie and Jeanette Bruwer, took marine
influence to a new, unique level (six fathoms to be precise), by
dumping some of their finest Cabernet Sauvignon, from the richly
tannic 1997 vintage, in the Atlantic off the Cape. It was bottled, I
hasten to add, and the corks were covered in wax. The wine was
donated to Davy Jones' locker in March 2000. It was fished up on
New Year's Eve 2003. Miss Bruwer came to London and gave me a
bottle of what she and Abrie now call their 'sea-wine'. The bottle
was encrusted with all sorts of evil-smelling dead marine life and
looked utterly horrendous. Hardly a promising bottle to have
standing on a Valentine's Day dinner table, especially when two of
the guests owned property in Bordeaux and are committed to that
region's Cabernets. The bottle was opened and its contents poured
into a jug and when, an hour or so later, the jug stood empty
along with everyone's glasses, and I was forced to confess my
wine racks could yield nothing comparable to follow, one guest
wistfully remarked 'Not unless you've got the 1982 Lafite.' The
wine in question is Springfield Estate's so-called Méthode
Ancienne Cabernet 1997.

16

WHITE £5.99

Cono Sur Viognier 2003 CHILE
Incredibly satiny apricot.
Also at Majestic.

16

RED £5.03

Cono Sur Pinot Noir 2003 CHILE
An immediate sensation of charred gamey black
cherries hits the nose. The palate is aroused by cassis
and grilled leafiness. Very delicious and composed.
Also at Budgens, Majestic, Morrison's, Tesco, Waitrose.

16

WHITE £4.99

Domaine de Bois Viognier 2002 FRANCE
Superbly subtle apricot.

16

WHITE £6.99

Danie de Wet Limestone Hill SOUTH AFRICA
Chardonnay 2002
And limey it is – a tangy chalkiness is interleaved with
ripe melon and pineapple.

16

WHITE £4.49

Danie de Wet Chardonnay Sur Lie 2004 SOUTH AFRICA
Superb unwooded fruit of great class, bite tanginess
and sheer silky style.

16

WHITE £5.03

Goats do Roam White 2003 SOUTH AFRICA
A really class white Rhône style, elegantly crisp, dry
wine – superb with smoked fish.

16   WHITE £3.99

Hardy's Stamp Riesling/Gewürztraminer 2002   AUSTRALIA
Terrific pace and quick spice. Superb with mussels
(Thai lemongrass).

16   WHITE £5.29

James Herrick Chardonnay,   FRANCE
Vin de Pays d'Oc 2002
Very classy Burgundy style, full of dry finesse and
layered hard/soft fruit flavours.

16   WHITE £4.99

Kiwi Cuvée Chardonnay/Viognier 2002   FRANCE
Classy blend of gooseberry citrus and soft apricot.

16   RED £4.99

La Cetto Petite Sirah 2001   MEXICO
Starts bustlingly, finishes with chewy chocolate.
Superb glug.

16   RED £4.99

Leaping Horse Merlot 2001   USA
Real personality and fire in its belly. Has spice, leather,
prunes and roasted berries – with firm tannins of
weight and class.

16   RED £4.99

Merlot No. 2, Vin de Pays d'Oc 2002   FRANCE
Soft, but seriously kittenish. The tannins don't
scratch.

16

WHITE £3.99

Malambo VR Chardonnay/Chenin 2003   ARGENTINA

Shows a good turn of speed with spicy fish dishes.

16

WHITE £4.99

Misiónes de Rengo Chardonnay 2002   CHILE

Good smoky layers to dry melon.

16

WHITE £4.99

Misiónes de Rengo Chardonnay 2003   CHILE

Dry, incisive, very pert citrus with under-ripe
gooseberry and a vague hint of peach. Superb with
grilled fish. Very classily styled.
Also at Asda.

16

RED £4.99

Misiónes de Rengo Carmenere 2002   CHILE

Why bite nails when you can bite on this?

16

WHITE £6.99

Omrah Unoaked Chardonnay 2002   AUSTRALIA

This is an assertive bundle of fruit which one can
confidently take to the Thai BYOB restaurant.

16

RED £7.99

Omrah Plantagenet Shiraz 2001   AUSTRALIA

Lip-smackin' berries of huge interest to curry dishes.

16

WHITE £4.79

Orvieto Classico Cardetto 2003   ITALY

Deliciously crisp, restrained apricot. Classily textured.

16   WHITE £5.49
Porcupine Ridge Sauvignon Blanc 2003   SOUTH AFRICA
Screwcap. Delicious gooseberry and citrus. Ripe but
delicate.
Also at Asda, Waitrose.

16   WHITE £6.99
Ravenswood Chardonnay 2002   USA
Selected stores only. Dry, delicious well-developed
layers of smoky vegetality, leafy melon and warm
citrus. Very stylish and highly quaffable (or can be
drunk by the bookworm, such is the wine's
wordiness).

16   WHITE £6.99
Somerfield Gewürztraminer d'Alsace 2003   FRANCE
Deeply perfumed, almost fragrantly brash, and with
Chinese food the fruit's Muscat-edged richness and
spicy, congealed floral freshness is stupendous.

16   WHITE £5.99
Somerfield South African Limited Release   SOUTH AFRICA
Chardonnay 2002
Very creamy, offering spiced pear, citrus and
pineapple. Superb with oriental fish dishes.

16   RED £4.29
Somerfield Chilean Cabernet/Merlot 2002   CHILE
Superbly forward yet subtle. Has finely modulated
burned berries, genteel tannins and huge quaffability.

16

WHITE £5.49

Somerfield Domaine St Agathe Chardonnay,   FRANCE
Vin de Pays d'Oc 2002
Superb vegetal overlay to the oily melon fruit.

16

RED £4.99

Santa Julia Oak Aged Tempranillo 2003   ARGENTINA
Superb touches of grilled fig and old stogie (dead
cheroot). Real character and class here. Simply so
much more exciting and sensual than a thousand
Riojas.

16

WHITE £5.03

Viña Casablanca Sauvignon Blanc 2003   CHILE
Selected stores only. Beautifully crisp and fresh.

16

WHITE £6.99

Western Australia Unoaked Chardonnay 2003   AUSTRALIA
Screwcap. Very rich firm fruit, which will grace Thai
food perfectly.

16

WHITE £6.99

Western Australia Sauvignon Blanc 2003   AUSTRALIA
Screwcap. Lively, hint of spice, gooseberry ripeness,
yet has soothing citric acids.

16

RED £7.99

Western Australia Shiraz 2001   AUSTRALIA
This has a determined, though far from soppy,
sweetness which is suited to spicy food, especially
Bangladeshi chicken dishes.

16

WHITE £6.99

Wolf Blass Riesling 2003 AUSTRALIA

Screwcap. 18.5 in 2009. Lovely tangy perfume, firm dry fruit, a crisp clean finish. A classic New World Riesling.

16

RED £6.99

Ravenswood Vintners Blend Zinfandel 2001 USA

Chunky berries with cool tannins, a hint of spice, a touch of savourily grilled plum.

Also at Asda, Booths, Majestic, Waitrose.

16

WHITE £5.99

Sauvignon Blanc, Marlborough 2003 NEW ZEALAND

Very lengthy experience from gentle gooseberry to chalky tanginess of pineapple on the finish.

Also at Thresher, Oddbins, Tesco, Safeway, Booths, Sainsbury's, Co-op, Morrison's, Small Merchants (Unwins, Londis).

On corks and corkscrews (No. 10)

Some wine merchants confronted with a customer with a duff bottle get very hoity-toity. I don't get as many letters on the subject as I used to (perhaps because wine shops are not so bad as they used to be), but it was once a primary theme of my correspondence bag. People who work in wine merchants often know little about cork taint and they are not schooled in the pleasantries of how to treat people properly. In a supermarket, you can bring a bottle back and get a replacement or a refund if you don't like the way the label is stuck on.

OTHER WINES 15.5 AND UNDER

15.5

	WHITE £4.49
Chileño Chardonnay/Sauvignon Blanc 2003	CHILE

Also at Thresher.

	WHITE £3.99
Firefly Verdelho 2002	AUSTRALIA

	RED £6.99
Fetzer Eagle Peak Merlot 2001	USA

	WHITE £6.49
Fetzer Sundial Chardonnay 2003	USA

Selected stores only.

	WHITE £3.99
Hardy's Stamp Chardonnay/Sémillon 2002	AUSTRALIA

	WHITE £4.49
Kiwi Cuvée Sauvignon Blanc 2003	FRANCE

Screwcap.

	RED £4.99
James Herrick Syrah 2002	FRANCE

	WHITE £4.99
Leaping Horse Chardonnay 2002	USA

	FORTIFIED £6.99
Navigators LBV Port 1996	PORTUGAL

	RED £5.99
Primi Rioja 2003	SPAIN

WHITE **£3.99**
Somerfield Pergola Viura 2002 SPAIN

WHITE **£3.99**
Somerfield Argentine Chardonnay 2003 ARGENTINA

WHITE SPARKLING **£13.99**
Somerfield Prince William FRANCE
Premier Cru Champagne

RED **£6.99**
Veramonte Cabernet Sauvignon 2001 CHILE

WHITE **£5.79**
Hardy's Stamp Sémillon/Chardonnay 2003 AUSTRALIA
Also at Asda.

15

RED **£4.49**
Chileño Shiraz/Cabernet Sauvignon 2002 CHILE
Also at Thresher, Tesco.

WHITE SPARKLING **£16.99**
Champagne Victor Brut NV FRANCE

RED **£4.99**
Delicato Shiraz 2002 SOUTH AFRICA

WHITE **£4.99**
Hardy's VR Chardonnay 2003 AUSTRALIA

RED £3.99

Hardy's Stamp Shiraz/Cabernet 2002 AUSTRALIA
Also at Asda.

WHITE £3.99

Malambo Chenin Blanc/Chardonnay 2003 ARGENTINA

RED £5.99

Nottage Hill Cabernet Sauvignon/Shiraz 2002 AUSTRALIA

WHITE £4.99

Oxford Landing Sauvignon Blanc 2003 AUSTRALIA
Screwcap. Selected stores only. Also at Budgens,
Morrison's, Tesco.

WHITE £6.99

Omrah Sauvignon Blanc 2003 AUSTRALIA
Selected stores only.

RED £6.99

Penfolds Koonunga Hill Shiraz/Cabernet 2001 AUSTRALIA
Also at Asda, Tesco.

RED £3.99

Somerfield Pergola Tempranillo 2002 SPAIN

RED £3.99

Somerfield First Flight Shiraz/Cabernet 2002 AUSTRALIA
Screwcap.

WHITE £3.49

Somerfield First Flight AUSTRALIA
Colombard/Chardonnay 2002

WHITE £3.99
AUSTRALIA

Somerfield First Flight
Unoaked Chardonnay 2003
Screwcap.

WHITE £3.99
SOUTH AFRICA

Somerfield South African
Sauvignon Blanc 2003

RED £3.99
ITALY

Somerfield Montepulciano d'Abruzzo 2003

WHITE £4.99
ITALY

Trulli Chardonnay del Salento 2003

WHITE £4.99
ARGENTINA

Terra Organica Chenin 2003

RED £4.99
ARGENTINA

Terra Organica Bonarda/Sangiovese 2003

WHITE £6.99
AUSTRALIA

Wolf Blass Chardonnay 2003

RED £4.49
ITALY

Zagara Nero d'Avola Sangiovese 2003
Selected stores only.

RED £4.99
AUSTRALIA

Hardy's VR Shiraz 2003
Also at Asda.

SOMERFIELD

14.5

		RED £4.99
Bajaz Vino Tinto 2001		SPAIN

		WHITE £3.99
Blueridge Chardonnay 2002		BULGARIA

		RED £4.49
Château St Benoît, Minervois Rouge 2000		FRANCE

		ROSÉ £5.99
Fetzer Valley Oaks Syrah Rosé 2003		USA
Screwcap.		

		RED £6.99
Montana East Coast Cabernet/Merlot 2002		NEW ZEALAND

		FORTIFIED £5.99
Navigators Vintage Character Port NV		PORTUGAL

		RED £4.49
Pedras do Monte 2002		PORTUGAL

		WHITE £6.99
Somerfield Chablis 2003		FRANCE

		WHITE £2.99
Somerfield First Flight Dry White NV		AUSTRALIA

		WHITE £3.29
Somerfield Soave 2003		ITALY

		WHITE £4.99
Somerfield First Flight Reserve Chardonnay 2003		AUSTRALIA

		WHITE £4.99
Trulli Chardonnay 2002		ITALY

14

WHITE £4.99
Altozano Blanco Verdejo 2002   SPAIN

RED £4.99
Altozano Tempranillo/Merlot 2000   SPAIN

WHITE £4.79
Banrock Station Colombard/Chardonnay 2003   AUSTRALIA

WHITE £3.99
Blueridge Chardonnay 2003   BULGARIA

WHITE £4.49
Chardonnay No. 4, Vin de Pays d'Oc 2002   FRANCE

WHITE £4.29
Devil's Rock Riesling 2002   GERMANY

WHITE £6.99
Fetzer Sundial Chardonnay 2002   USA

RED £3.99
Il Padrino Syrah 2002   ITALY

RED £3.99
Jindalee Merlot 2002   AUSTRALIA

WHITE £4.99
Kiwi Cuvée Chardonnay/Viognier 2003   FRANCE

ROSÉ £4.49
Kumala Rosé 2004   AUSTRALIA
Selected stores only.

ROSÉ £4.99
La Palma Rosé 2004   CHILE

RED £5.99
Leonardo Chianti 2003 ITALY

WHITE £3.79
Mainzer Domherr Spätlese 2002 GERMANY

WHITE SPARKLING £7.49
Nottage Hill Sparkling Chardonnay 2001 AUSTRALIA

RED £9.99
Ravenswood Amador County Zinfandel 2000 USA
Selected and fine wine stores only.

WHITE £2.79
Somerfield Vin de Pays de Comte Tolosan 2003 FRANCE

WHITE £4.49
Somerfield Chardonnay delle Venezie 2002 ITALY

RED £2.99
Somerfield First Flight Red 2003 AUSTRALIA

RED £3.99
Somerfield First Flight Cabernet Sauvignon 2002 AUSTRALIA

WHITE SPARKLING £11.99
Somerfield Prince William Blanc de Noirs NV FRANCE

WHITE £4.49
Somerfield Viña Caña Rioja Blanco 2002 SPAIN

WHITE £4.99
Vacqueyras 2002 FRANCE

WHITE £3.79
Winter Hill White, Vin de Pays d'Oc 2003 FRANCE

RED £3.79
Winter Hill Red, Vin de Pays d'Oc 2003 FRANCE

TESCO

Head Office:
Tesco House,
PO Box 18,
Delamare Road,
Cheshunt,
Hertfordshire EN8 9SL

Tel: (01992) 632222

Customer Services helpline: (0800) 505555

Email: customer.service@tesco.co.uk
Website: www.tesco.com

For Tesco wines 14 points and under visit
www.superplonk.com

17

RED £5.07

Concha y Toro Casillero del Diablo
Cabernet Sauvignon 2003   CHILE
Hints of chocolate and cocoa on the finish of a
wonderfully complex red of richness and savour.
Also at Asda, Budgens.

17

RED £9.99

Errazuriz Max Reserva Syrah 2000   CHILE
Stridency with elegance. Superb polish and purpose
with berries of huge class and concentration.
Also at Safeway.

17

RED £9.99

'Q' Tempranillo, La Agricola 2001   ARGENTINA
A fabulous silky allure to the tannins and berries.

17

WHITE £8.00

Villa Maria Private Bin   NEW ZEALAND
Sauvignon Blanc 2003
Screwcap. Wonderful coating of lime to the ripe
gooseberry. The texture is delicate yet incisive.
Also at Oddbins, Somerfield.

17

RED £5.50

Merlot 2003   CHILE
Stunning softness yet characterful tannicity.

16.5

WHITE £5.50

Argento Chardonnay 2003   ARGENTINA
High-class melon/citrus/pear. Real quality tippling of
a very high order.
Also at Asda, Budgens, Majestic, Somerfield.

16.5   RED £5.50
Cabernet Sauvignon 2002   CHILE
It's the sheer taffeta effrontery of the berries into
which are stitched complex tannins which makes it so
fine.

16.5   RED £8.99
Errazuriz Cabernet Sauvignon Max   CHILE
Reserva 2002
Hint of sweet cocoa powder to the richly roasted
berries and ever-so-slightly burned tannins.

16.5   RED £7.99
Faith Shiraz 2002   AUSTRALIA
One of the best-value Aussie Shirazs around under a
tenner with its ripe berries and unguent tannins.

16.5   RED £6.99
Goats do Roam in Villages 2002   SOUTH AFRICA
An outrageous range of extensions from Charles Back
which has 60% Shiraz, 40% Pinotage in superb, rich,
palate-rousing combination. What will the French say
to this latest pun?
Also at Majestic, Somerfield.

16.5   RED £4.99
Inycon Merlot 2002   ITALY
Sheer chocolate (light) and deeply berried delight.
The tannins are classy and incisive.
Also at Morrison's.

16.5
WHITE £4.94
ITALY

Inycon Chardonnay 2002
Superbly oily, elegant fruit reminiscent of a citrussy
Puligny-Montrachet of the 1959 vintage.
Also at Morrison's.

16.5
RED £5.99
CHILE

Isla Negra Cabernet Sauvignon 2003
Screwcap. Wonderfully mouth-filling and ripe with tannic
richness and hint-of-chocolate complexity to the berries.

16.5
WHITE £15.95
AUSTRALIA

**'M3 Vineyard' Adelaide Hills Chardonnay,
Shaw & Smith 2002**
Deliciously classy and textured, finely wrought lemon,
melon and hint of pineapple.

I went to hear the so-called poet laureate of America, Billy Collins, recite some of his stuff and he was entertaining even though he does mash up his vegetables for soft palates. I am very old-fashioned where poetry is concerned, and feel much modern stuff is no more than a cheap alternative to pyschotherapy, but you haven't paid to hear me pontificate about that. The reason I have trespassed is that Mr Collins wrote a poem called 'Osso Buco' in which he says 'The secret marrow, the invaded privacy of the animal prized out with a knife and swallowed down with cold, exhilarating wine.' There are some nice touches in this poem, especially 'the meat soft as the leg of an angel who has lived a purely airborne existence' but I do wonder about that exhilarating wine. What could he have had in mind? A Soave maybe?

16.5   RED £6.99
Pinotage 2002   SOUTH AFRICA
Catch it whilst its raspberry/plum fruit has tannins of
such stridency.

16.5   RED £7.99
St Hallett Faith Shiraz 2001   AUSTRALIA
What scrumptious gently spicy berries here, which
seem ready for anything in spite of the lightness of
the tannins. The sweetness of genteel plums, roasted,
is perfect with spicy food.

16.5   RED £2.97
Tesco Chilean Cabernet Sauvignon NV   CHILE
Screwcap. Utterly superb! The screwcap has kept all
the tannins lively and spicy and the berries are deep
and rewarding, slightly charred.

16.5   RED £2.96
Tesco Chilean Merlot NV   CHILE
Screwcap. Interesting vegetal edge to the firm berries
which have a cheeky immediacy yet serious depth of
richness. Classy finish.

16.5   WHITE £6.03
Lindemans Bin 65 Chardonnay 2003   AUSTRALIA
Always one of Oz's finest Chardonnays, in this
vintage it has some added finesse.
Also at Asda.

16

SPARKLING RED £7.92
Banrock Station Sparkling Shiraz NV   AUSTRALIA
Lovely chocolate edge to the vivacious bubbles.

16

WHITE £4.98
Brown Brothers Dry Muscat 2003   AUSTRALIA
The perfect grapey, spicy aperitif. Utterly enchanting
as a pre-prandial whistle whetter.
Also at Somerfield.

16

RED £4.03
Concha y Toro Copper Merlot 2003   CHILE
Ripe yet never becomes too coarse or too obvious.
Fresh yet elegant, firm yet supple.

16

RED £4.99
Concha y Toro Casillero del Diablo   CHILE
Cabernet Sauvignon 2002
Brand spanking fresh tannins. Widely available brand
at many leading supermarkets.

16

WHITE £4.99
Concha y Toro Casillero del Diablo   CHILE
Sauvignon Blanc 2003
Spirited, tangy, lemonic – and brilliant with shellfish.
Also at Asda.

16

WHITE £7.03
Chapel Hill Unwooded Chardonnay 2002   AUSTRALIA
Very rich yet amazingly tangy. Superb level of fruit
and it'll stay the course with oriental food.

16   RED £5.03
Cono Sur Pinot Noir 2003   CHILE
Burgundy, eat your heart out! Yes, it's a touch brash
this example, but it's so handsome, sleek, lithe,
gamey, and discrete on the finish, it's hugely
quaffable.
Also at Budgens, Majestic, Morrison's, Somerfield,
Waitrose.

16   WHITE £4.53
Douglas Green Chardonnay/   SOUTH AFRICA
Colombard 2003
Deliciously classy and understated gooseberry/melon
with a surge on the finish.

16   WHITE £5.99
Errazuriz Chardonnay 2003   CHILE
It's the hint of under-ripe melon to the gooseberry
and pear which makes it so delicious.
Also at Budgens.

16   RED £5.99
Errazuriz Merlot 2002   CHILE
Bright as a button, fresh as a daisy, hard as nails, rich
as Croesus – all the clichés which, together, make for
an original.

16   WHITE £4.99
French Connection Classic Côtes du Rhône   FRANCE
Blanc, Vignobles du Peloux 2003
A Grenache Blanc, Clairette, Marsanne and

Roussanne blend of great wit and style. Offers lime, melon, pear and pineapple.

16

RED £7.03

Graham Beck Coastal Pinotage 2002   SOUTH AFRICA
Very spicy with roasted berries and classy tannins.

16

WHITE £5.53

Hardy's Stamp Riesling/Gewürztraminer 2003   AUSTRALIA
Wonderful vibrant melon/lychee/mango and citrus.
A real thrill with oriental food.

16

WHITE £5.99

Montana Marlborough Riesling 2003   NEW ZEALAND
Deliciously tangy and fresh yet also wise and
experienced with minerally citrus.

16

WHITE SPARKLING £31.99

Moët et Chandon Imperial Vintage 1996   FRANCE
Truly delicious vintage this, with smoky melon and
citrus with a very vague floral undertone.
Impressively complete.

16

WHITE £5.03

7th Moon Chardonnay 2001   USA
Brilliant artefact: lemon, gooseberry, lime and oily
melon. Excellent with complex shellfish dishes.
Also at Morrison's.

16

WHITE SPARKLING £17.99

Mercier Champagne NV   FRANCE
Very dry, almost chewy fruit but, boy, does it have
class and real presence on the palate!

16

WHITE £6.03

McWilliams Hanwood Estate Chardonnay 2002 AUSTRALIA
The essence of mod-style Aussie Chardonnay where
subdued spicy melon, nicely textured, goes hand-in-
hand with citrus and pear.

16

RED £9.03

Marqués de Griñon Reserva Rioja 1999 SPAIN
Grand, mouth-filling chocolate and blackberry
richness – thick coagulated tannins.
Also at Budgens.

16

WHITE £4.98

Nottage Hill Chardonnay 2002 AUSTRALIA
Superbly well textured and richly classy! Combines
tangy citrus with melon.

On corks and corkscrews (No. 11)

When you smell the end of the cork, will you detect mustiness or a
mushroomy smell? A hint of cardboard or of mouldy wood? But,
hang on, isn't a cork supposed to smell of these things? If the wine
is red, and of some years' age, and if it has been barrel fermented
and/or aged, won't there be the smell of wood? Isn't it natural that
a wine like this should have woody odours on its cork? The answer
is yes, but only to the extent that it does not mar the fruit of the
wine. If the cork is a pure, neutral stopper as it is intended to be,
then what you should smell is the wine - nothing else. The wine
itself may be woody and so naturally this is part of the effect its
maker intends. It may be overwoody, but this may be oenological
cackhandedness, not the sign of a faulty cork. You see how tricky
and how fraught with subtle thorns this field of enquiry is?

16 ROSÉ £3.99

Riverview Cabernet Sauvignon Rosé, HUNGARY
Akos Kamocsay 2003
One of the most delicious rosés around.

16 RED £3.99

Riverview Kekfrankos/Merlot, HUNGARY
Akos Kamocsay 2003
Catch it while it's so frisky and fresh and tannicly
teasingly berried up to its neck.

16 WHITE £3.99

Riverview Chardonnay/Pinot Grigio, HUNGARY
Akos Kamocsay 2003
Million bottles a year sold. 'Just midway between a
light spicy wine and a heaver bodied rich late-harvest
wine,' says the wife of its maker. And she's right.

16 WHITE £3.99

Riverview Sauvignon Blanc, HUNGARY
Akos Kamocsay 2003
Delicious soft gooseberry with under-ripe pear.

16 RED £6.95

Rosemount Shiraz/Cabernet Sauvignon 2003 AUSTRALIA
Hugely sticky and oily, big spice overwhelmed by thick
roasted tannins.

16 RED (3 litre box) £13.84

Stowells of Chelsea Mataro/Shiraz NV AUSTRALIA
Delicious charred plums with blackberries, a hint of
prune, some very deft tannins.

16

WHITE £5.99

St Hallett Chardonnay 2002   AUSTRALIA

Very stylish Charentais melon and mango with a
gritty lemon finish. Superb with fish, poultry, chicken
(no spice).

16

WHITE £5.33

Santa Julia Viognier 2003   ARGENTINA

Delicious apricotty nuttiness.

16

RED £6.03

Sartori Vignetti di Montegradella   ITALY
Valpolicella Classico 2002

Deliciously fresh yet experienced. Has finely toned
berries with tannins of great bite and precision.

16

RED £5.32

Torres Sangre de Toro 2002   SPAIN

Bright, fresh plums with slightly charred tannins.

16

RED £5.48

Torres Coronas Tempranillo 2001   SPAIN

Deliciously elegant, rich, well-berried tannins, dry yet
delicate.

16

RED £3.99

Tesco Australian Merlot NV   AUSTRALIA

Real treat of a liquid: brave, rich, deep, berried up to
its neck in tannins, and genteel spice.

16

RED £3.99

Tesco Picajuan Peak Bonarda 2003 ARGENTINA
Lip-smackingly warm and rich, very firm and roasted.
Superb with casserole-style food.

16

RED £3.99

Tesco Picajuan Peak Malbec 2003 ARGENTINA
Screwcap. Huge amount of sustained class here.
Loads of ripe, roasted plums and with firm tannins to
finish.

16

WHITE £4.99

Tesco Finest Chilean CHILE
Sauvignon Blanc Reserve 2003
Very rich and food friendly.

16

WHITE £4.99

Tesco Finest Chilean Chardonnay Reserve 2002 CHILE
Plump middle of ripe melon to pineapple and pear.

16

RED £4.99

Tesco Finest Italian Merlot 2001 ITALY
Superb dry toffee-edged roasted cherries and plums
with fine tannins.

16

RED £12.99

Tesco Finest Châteauneuf-du-Pape 2000 FRANCE
Deliciously rich and well berried, with complex plums
and cherries. Fine tannins, multi-layered herb, hint of
spice, touch of chocolate.

16

RED £7.53

Valdivieso Cabernet Sauvignon Reserve 2001   CHILE
Lip-smackingly berried and firm with slow-to-evolve,
grilled tannins.

16

WHITE £5.97

Peter Lehmann Sémillon 2002   AUSTRALIA
Screwcap. 18 in 2008–2009. Deliciously oily,
gooseberry/grapefruit flavoured. Will improve, thanks
to its screwcap, dramatically over half a decade (and
beyond). Utterly superb thirst-quencher.
Also at Asda, Booths, Oddbins.

16

RED £4.99

Lindemans Cawarra Shiraz/Cabernet 2003   AUSTRALIA
Lovely spicy richness with burned berries and warm
tannins.
Also at Asda.

16

WHITE £5.03

Penfolds Rawson's Retreat Sémillon/   AUSTRALIA
Chardonnay 2002
A terrific blend of dryness yet witty flavoursomeness.
Also at Asda.

16

WHITE £4.49

Firefinch Sauvignon Blanc 2003   SOUTH AFRICA
Delicious concentrated pure gooseberry with a lime
undertone.
Also at Thresher.

16

WHITE £5.99

Sauvignon Blanc, Marlborough 2003   NEW ZEALAND
Very lengthy experience from gentle gooseberry to
chalky tanginess of pineapple on the finish.
Also at Thresher, Oddbins, Booths, Safeway,
Somerfield, Sainsbury's, Co-op, Morrison's, Small
Merchants (Unwins, Londis).

16

RED £5.05

Argento Malbec 2003   ARGENTINA
Superbly well-textured berries with a chocolate
undertone. Marvellously biteable fruit.
Also at Budgens, Majestic, Somerfield.

16

WHITE £5.03

Cono Sur Chardonnay 2003   CHILE
A sum of many subtleties (dry peach/lemon/apple),
which finishes dryly.
Also at Morrison's.

16

WHITE £5.86

Montana Sauvignon Blanc 2003   NEW ZEALAND
Satin-textured gooseberry – so simple! So lingeringly
fresh and clean cut.
Also at Morrison's.

16

RED £6.03

DFJ Touriga Nacional/Touriga Franca 2001   PORTUGAL
16.5 points if £4.49. Delightfully rich yet elegant with
very gracious, subtly gritty tannins and soft
cherry/plum richness with a hint of spice.
Also at Safeway.

16

RED £6.03
AUSTRALIA

St Hallett Shiraz 2002
Real tangy fruit (raspberries, plums and a touch of
roast nut) with generous yet vegetal tannins.
Also at Sainsbury's.

OTHER WINES 15.5 AND UNDER

15.5

RED £8.03
AUSTRALIA

Brown Brothers Shiraz 2001

WHITE £4.49
AUSTRALIA

Barramundi Sémillon/Chardonnay NV

RED £7.25
FRANCE

Beaumes de Venise, Côtes du Rhône-Villages 2003

RED £5.03
CHILE

Cono Sur Cabernet Sauvignon 2003

RED £4.99
ITALY

Di Notte Valpolicella Valpantena 2002

RED £4.99
SOUTH AFRICA

Douglas Green Merlot 2003

RED £5.99
CHILE

Errazuriz Shiraz 2002

WHITE £6.03
FRANCE

Gaston d'Orléans Vouvray Demi Sec 2002
16.5 points in 4-5 years.

WHITE SPARKLING £18.99

Jacquart NV   FRANCE

WHITE £4.48

Jacob's Creek   AUSTRALIA
Sémillon/Sauvignon/Chardonnay 2003
Screwcap.

WHITE £6.00

Jacob's Creek Dry Riesling 2002   AUSTRALIA
18 in 4–5 years. Screwcap. Also at Asda.

RED £8.03

Montana Reserve Merlot 2001   NEW ZEALAND

WHITE £5.99

Matua Valley North Island Chardonnay 2003   NEW ZEALAND
Screwcap.

RED £6.03

Marqués de Griñon Rioja 2001   SPAIN

RED £6.03

Penfolds Rawson's Retreat   AUSTRALIA
Shiraz/Cabernet 2003

WHITE £7.03

Penfolds Koonunga Hill Chardonnay 2002   AUSTRALIA

WHITE £4.99

Oxford Landing Chardonnay 2002   AUSTRALIA

RED £7.03

Rosemount Grenache/Shiraz 2002   AUSTRALIA
Screwcap.

WHITE £4.02

Riverview Chardonnay/Pinot Grigio,   HUNGARY
Akos Kamocsay 2002

RED £8.03

St Hallett Faith Shiraz 2002   AUSTRALIA

RED £5.03

Santa Julia Oaked Tempranillo 2002   ARGENTINA

RED £8.99

Tim Adams Shiraz 2002   AUSTRALIA

RED £4.99

Tesco Finest Chilean Cabernet Sauvignon   CHILE
Reserve 2002

RED £3.99

Tesco Picajuan Peak Sangiovese 2003   ARGENTINA

WHITE £3.99

Tesco Australian Chardonnay NV   AUSTRALIA

WHITE £5.03

Tempus Two Chardonnay 2003   AUSTRALIA

WHITE £3.23

Tesco Picajuan Peak Chardonnay 2003   ARGENTINA
Screwcap.

WHITE £2.98

Tesco Chilean Sauvignon Blanc NV   CHILE
Screwcap.

RED £5.99

Tesco Chilean Carmenere NV   CHILE
Screwcap.

WHITE £2.81

Tesco Chilean White NV   CHILE
Screwcap.

RED £7.50

Tesco Finest Crozes Hermitage   FRANCE
Red Oak Aged 2001

RED £9.03

Tesco Finest Gigondas, Château de   FRANCE
Ramières 2001

RED   (3 litre box) £14.99

Tesco Chilean Cabernet Sauvignon   NV   CHILE

RED £5.07

Valdivieso Cabernet Sauvignon 2002   CHILE

RED £5.07

Valdivieso Merlot 2003   CHILE

WHITE £6.99

Thandi Chardonnay 2003   SOUTH AFRICA
Also at Co-op.

15

RED £4.53

Douglas Green Cinsault/Pinotage 2003   SOUTH AFRICA

WHITE £5.99

Glen Ellen Chardonnay 2002   USA

WHITE £9.07

Grans Fassian Trittenheimer GERMANY
Riesling Spätlese 2001
17.5 in 2010.

WHITE £3.99

Goiya Kgeisje Sauvignon/Chardonnay 2003 SOUTH AFRICA

WHITE £7.99

Hardy's Crest Chardonnay 2003 AUSTRALIA

WHITE £5.03

High Altitude Chardonnay/ ARGENTINA
Viognier 2002

WHITE £5.03

Jacob's Creek Sémillon Blanc 2003 AUSTRALIA
Screwcap.

WHITE £5.02

Lindemans Cawarra Chardonnay 2003 AUSTRALIA

RED £6.51

Montana Cabernet Sauvignon/Merlot 2002 NEW ZEALAND

RED £5.99

Matua Valley North Island Red 2002 NEW ZEALAND
Screwcap.

RED £5.99

Nottage Hill Shiraz 2001 AUSTRALIA

RED £5.53
Oxford Landing Merlot 2002 AUSTRALIA

RED £6.07
Penfolds Koonunga Hill Shiraz/Cabernet 2001 AUSTRALIA
Also at Asda, Somerfield.

WHITE £5.99
Rosemount Sémillon/Chardonnay NV AUSTRALIA
Screwcap.

RED £7.48
Rosemount Shiraz 2002 AUSTRALIA

WHITE £3.58
Ramada White 2001 PORTUGAL

WHITE £7.03
The Crossings Sauvignon Blanc 2002 NEW ZEALAND

RED £7.03
Calvet Claret Réserve 2001 FRANCE
Screwcap.

RED £5.49
Tesco Finest Fitou Réserve, Baron de la Tour 2002 FRANCE

RED £4.99
Tesco Finest Californian Merlot Reserve 2002 USA
Screwcap.

WHITE SPARKLING £3.82
Tesco Cava Brut   NV SPAIN

RED   £4.02

Tesco Claret Réserve 2002   FRANCE
Screwcap.

WHITE   £4.99

Tesco Finest Reserve Australian   AUSTRALIA
Sauvignon Blanc 2003

WHITE   £3.99

Tesco Australian Sémillon/Chardonnay NV   AUSTRALIA

RED   £4.99

Tesco Finest Reserve Cabernet Sauvignon 2002   AUSTRALIA
Screwcap.

RED   £5.03

Terra Organica Malbec 2003   ARGENTINA

WHITE   £2.81

Tesco Reka Valley Chardonnay NV   HUNGARY

RED   (3 litre box) £14.15

Tesco Australian Shiraz NV   AUSTRALIA

RED   £5.03

Trulli Zinfandel 2002   ITALY

RED   £4.03

Tesco South African   SOUTH AFRICA
Cabernet Sauvignon 2003

WHITE SPARKLING   £3.33

Villa Jolanda Moscato d'Asti DOCG NV   ITALY

RED   £3.99

Veo Cabernet/Merlot 2003   CHILE

WHITE £6.03

Wyndham Estate Bin 777 Sémillon 2002   AUSTRALIA

17.5 points in 2-3 years.

RED £5.53

Jacob's Creek Merlot 2002   AUSTRALIA

Also at Asda.

WHITE £5.03

Oxford Landing Sauvignon Blanc 2003   AUSTRALIA

Screwcap. Also at Budgens, Morrisons, Somerfield.

RED £7.03

Wyndham Estate Bin 555 Shiraz 2001   AUSTRALIA

Also at Morrison's.

WHITE £4.44

Hardy's VR Chardonnay 2003   AUSTRALIA

Screwcap.

14.5

WHITE £4.99

Banrock Station Chardonnay 2003   AUSTRALIA

Screwcap.

WHITE £8.99

Blason de Bourgogne,   FRANCE
Montagny Vieilles Vignes 2000

RED £6.99

Cono Sur Pinot Noir Reserve 2001   CHILE

RED £10.03

Chapel Hill McLaren   AUSTRALIA
Vale and Coonawarra Cabernet Sauvignon 2001

RED £6.99

French Connection Classic Côtes du Rhône Rouge, FRANCE
Vignobles du Peloux 2003

RED £3.99

Goiya Glaan 2003 SOUTH AFRICA

RED £5.33

High Altitude Malbec/Shiraz 2002 ARGENTINA

RED £7.99

Hardy's Crest Cabernet/Shiraz/Merlot 2002 AUSTRALIA

WHITE SPARKLING £17.99
Heidsieck Dry Monopole NV FRANCE

RED £5.53

Jacob's Creek Cabernet Sauvignon 2001 AUSTRALIA

RED £5.03

Le Chic No. 2 Merlot Vin de Pays NV FRANCE

WHITE £9.99

Pouilly Fumé Fouassier, Cuvée Jules 2002 FRANCE

RED £4.99

Tesco Finest Chilean Merlot Reserve 2002 CHILE

RED £3.99

Tesco Australian Cabernet/Merlot NV AUSTRALIA
Screwcap.

Tempus Two Shiraz 2002

RED £5.03
AUSTRALIA

Tesco Finest Chianti Classico Riserva 1999

RED £7.02
ITALY

Tesco Unwind Pinot Grigio NV
Screwcap.

WHITE £5.03
ITALY

Tesco Rosé d'Anjou NV

ROSÉ £2.81
FRANCE

Tesco Premières Côtes de Bordeaux NV

WHITE £4.25
FRANCE

Tesco French Prestige Grenache/
Chardonnay, Vin de Pays d'Oc 2003
Screwcap.

WHITE £4.03
FRANCE

Tesco Vouvray NV

WHITE £4.83
FRANCE

Tesco South African Chardonnay/
Sauvignon Blanc 2003
Screwcap.

WHITE £4.03
SOUTH AFRICA

Tesco South African Merlot/Shiraz 2003
Screwcap.

RED £4.03
SOUTH AFRICA

WHITE £5.03
Tesco Finest South African SOUTH AFRICA
Chenin Blanc Reserve 2003

RED £7.99
Tesco Finest Viña Mara Rioja Reserva 1999 SPAIN

RED £3.99
Tesco Californian Merlot NV USA
Screwcap.

14

ROSÉ £4.98
Beyerskloof Pinotage Rosé 2003 SOUTH AFRICA
Tesco Internet Wine Club.

WHITE £4.99
Beau Mayne Sauvignon, Bordeaux 2003 FRANCE

WHITE SPARKLING £28.99
Bollinger Special Cuvée Brut NV FRANCE

RED £4.99
Banrock Station Shiraz 2002 AUSTRALIA
Screwcap.

ROSÉ £4.99
Banrock Station White Shiraz 2003 AUSTRALIA

RED £4.57
Bela Fonte Baga 2001 NEW ZEALAND

RED £8.03
Château La Raze Beauvallet, Médoc 2002 FRANCE
Screwcap.

RED £4.57

Chileño Shiraz/Cabernet Sauvignon 2003 CHILE
Also at Somerfield, Thresher.

WHITE £5.83

Cottesbrook Sauvignon Blanc 2003 NEW ZEALAND
Screwcap.

WHITE £7.82

Chablis Michel Laroche 2003 FRANCE

WHITE £5.03

French Connection Côtes du Rhône White 2003 FRANCE
Screwcap.

RED £5.99

Glen Ellen Merlot 2002 USA

RED £4.79

Hardy's VR Merlot 2002 AUSTRALIA
Screwcap.

RED £5.53

Jacob's Creek Shiraz 2001 AUSTRALIA

WHITE £4.99

Jacob's Creek Chardonnay 2003 AUSTRALIA

RED £4.48

Jacob's Creek Grenache/Shiraz 2003 AUSTRALIA

RED £5.50

Lindemans Bin 40 Merlot 2001 AUSTRALIA

RED £6.53

McWilliams Hanwood Estate Shiraz 2002 AUSTRALIA

WHITE SPARKLING **£18.97**
Nicolas Feuillatte Champagne Brut NV FRANCE
Also at Thresher.

WHITE SPARKLING **£18.98**
Piper Heidsieck Champagne Brut NV FRANCE

RED **£7.99**
Thandi Pinot Noir 2002 SOUTH AFRICA

RED **£3.53**
Ramada Red 2002 PORTUGAL

RED **£4.99**
Tesco Finest Australian Reserve Shiraz AUSTRALIA
2003
Screwcap.

WHITE **£5.03**
Tesco Organic Australian Chardonnay AUSTRALIA
2002
Screwcap.

WHITE **£2.72**
Tesco Australian Dry White NV AUSTRALIA
Screwcap.

RED **£2.70**
Tesco Australian Red NV AUSTRALIA
Screwcap.

RED £3.99
Tesco Australian Shiraz/Cabernet   AUSTRALIA
Sauvignon NV
Screwcap.

WHITE SPARKLING £14.99
Tesco Demi-Sec Champagne NV   FRANCE

WHITE £3.03
Tesco Simply Riesling 2002   GERMANY

WHITE £3.79
Tesco Kabinett, Rheinhessen NV   GERMANY

RED £13.03
Tesco Finest Barolo 1999   ITALY

RED £5.03
Tesco Finest Valpolicella Classico 2002   ITALY

RED £3.49
Tesco Rosso del Salento NV   ITALY

WHITE £3.68
Tesco Finest Soave Classico 2002-3   ITALY

WHITE £3.99
Tesco Orvieto Classico Abboccato 2002-3   ITALY

WHITE £4.99
Tesco Finest Vina Clara Frascati   ITALY
Classico Superiore 2002-3

RED £3.03
Tesco Reka Valley Merlot 2002   BULGARIA

	WHITE £4.49
Tesco New Zealand Dry White NV	NEW ZEALAND
	RED £8.53
Tesco Finest St-Emilion 2002	FRANCE
	RED £8.03
Tesco Finest Fleurie 2002	FRANCE
	RED £5.03
Tesco Finest Corbières,	FRANCE
Réserve La Sansoure 2002	
	WHITE £9.99
Tesco Finest Sancerre 2002	FRANCE
	RED £3.99
Tesco French Prestige	FRANCE
Merlot/Cabernet, Vin de Pays d'Oc NV	
Screwcap.	
	RED £4.49
Tesco French Grenache Prestige NV	FRANCE
Screwcap.	
	WHITE £3.99
Veo Chardonnay 2003	CHILE
	RED £7.53
Wolf Blass Yellow Label	AUSTRALIA
Cabernet Sauvignon 2002	
Also at Asda.	
	RED £7.03
Wyndham Estate Bin 444	AUSTRALIA
Cabernet Sauvignon 2001	

THRESHER

Enjoyment Hall,
Bessemer Road,
Welwyn Garden City,
Hertfordshire AL7 1BL

Tel: (01707) 387200
Fax: (01707) 387416

For Thresher wines 14 points and under visit
www.superplonk.com

17.5

RED £10.99
FRANCE

**Cazal Viel L'Antienne St-Chinian,
Vin de Pays d'Oc 2000**

A superbly complete red, classier than many a much-vaunted Bordeaux at twice the price. Berried up to its neck in delicious, rich fruit.

17.5

WHITE £9.99
AUSTRALIA

The Willows Sémillon 1996

Very mature, flaxen-hued white of oiliness and beautifully vegetal richness with very dry pineapple and pear. It has a medicinal undertone.

17

RED £29.99
ITALY

Barolo Bussia Dardi La Rose, Poderi Colla 1996

Classic licorice and grilled berries. Terrific burned tannins.

17

WHITE £7.99
FRANCE

**Cazal Viel Viognier Grande Réserve,
Vin de Pays d'Oc 2002**

Makes many Rhône whites very poor value in comparison. Superb dry apricot and soft vegetality.

17

RED £19.99
CHILE

Errazuriz Don Maximiano 1999

Sheer velvet chocolate with burned tannins and complex berries.

17

RED £8.99

**Errazuriz Maximiano Reserve Cabernet
Sauvignon 2001**

CHILE

Unites an incredible level of burned strawberry jam
with tannins and herbs.

17

RED £9.99

Penfolds Bin 128 Coonawarra Shiraz 2000   AUSTRALIA

Delicious oily richness with a tangy mineral edge to
the superb berries. What a superb example of mint
and tannin – married more firmly and sensually than
M. Douglas and C. Zeta Jones. Yet the contrived
passion this suggests is mitigated by superb, un-
Aussie, cool-climate, textured richness.

17

RED £29.99

Penfolds St Henri Shiraz 1998   AUSTRALIA

More gripping than Grange, more complete than
Hermitage, more sensual than Château Lafite. What
are you waiting for? Yes, it's a lot of money. But this
is a lot of wine.

17

WHITE £9.99

Penfolds Thomas Hyland Reserve   AUSTRALIA
Chardonnay 2003

Classy follow-on from the 2002, which it resembles in
fruit but not in acid structure. Really is a delightfully
creamy, classy, complete white wine. It may, though,
cellar better over 18 months.
Also at Asda.

17   RED £8.99
                                            USA

**Ravenswood Amador County
Old Vine Zinfandel 2001**
So this is what Zin can do when it's a perfect age.
Crackles with feisty grilled berries and cherries and
tannins.

17   WHITE £7.99

Special Cuvée Sauvignon Blanc 2003   SOUTH AFRICA
Sancerre growers – eat your hearts out. Tropical but
hugely elegant.

What is so wonderful about the French is their genius for metaphors.
The Aussies can't compete (they think a metaphor is something to do
with mixed doubles). A lot of coverage has been given to the stunning
sales success of New World wines, especially Australian, as they
compete against, and thrash, the French in the UK market, but when
it comes to the telling metaphor the latter are in a class of their own.
What Australian would have the sheer mediaeval brio to utter, as
recently did Monsieur Bernard Laydis, Président du College du Vin du
Saint-Emilion, that 'Quand on goûte un vin, c'est peu comme si on
embrassait une femme: les effleuves de son parfum, les soyeux de ses
lèvres, le fruite de sa peau....'
Now on grounds of good taste I cannot translate this into English. It
can only be printed in French (where it is solely at home and its
hilarious humour understood). For a man to compare tasting a wine
to kissing a woman and feeling her lips and her skin is as entertaining,
and inspirational, as a woman remarking that drinking Jacob's Creek is
like fellatio. But of course no woman would say this (she would keep
the secret to herself for a start) and no Aussie would dare.

17
WHITE £9.99

Villa Maria Reserve Sauvignon Blanc 2003 NEW ZEALAND
Screwcap. 18 in 3–5 years. Chewy, ripe, rich, superbly
Thai food friendly. Very fresh, classic dry
citrus/gooseberry/peach.
Also at Sainsbury's.

16.5
WHITE £9.99

Bonterra Viognier 2002 USA
A superb example of smoky pear, apricot and citrus.
Complex, finely textured, classy.

16.5
RED £4.99

Caliterra Carmenere 2002 CHILE
Juice of a very high order.

16.5
WHITE £8.99

Origin Reserve Sauvignon Blanc 2003 NEW ZEALAND
Superb tang of grapefruit and citrus.

16.5
RED (3 litre box) £14.99

Origin Malbec/Merlot 2003 ARGENTINA
The best red wine 3-litre box on sale in the UK?
Could be. Superb dry, oily fruit with chewy tannins
carrying roasted plums and chocolate.

16.5
RED £4.99

Origin Merlot 2003 SOUTH AFRICA
Stunning level of textured chutzpah. Full on berries,
vibrant tannins, a rich finish of charred fruit.

16.5   WHITE £9.49

Pewsey Vale Riesling 2003   AUSTRALIA
Screwcap. 18.5 points in 2–4 years. Delicious
minerally citrus, slow-to-emerge peach and
gooseberry.
Also at Oddbins, Sainsbury's.

16.5   RED £9.99

Penfolds Thomas Hyland Cabernet 2001   AUSTRALIA
Chewy yet elegant, textured yet subtle, richly
flavoursome yet possessing finesse.

16.5   RED £11.99

Penfolds Bin 407 Cabernet Sauvignon 1998   AUSTRALIA
Chocolate seemed to have been grated on to the
blackberries, licorice and prunes. Mildly amusing,
striving for effect.

16.5   RED £5.99

Pic St Loup Vin de Pays de   FRANCE
Coteaux de Languedoc 2001
Delightfully rich and firm. Lovely plum fruit with a
hint of grilled almond.

16.5   RED £9.99

St Hallett Barossa Shiraz 2000   AUSTRALIA
Sheer chutzpah here. Superbly vibrant, grilled berries
and fine tannins.

16.5

WHITE   £6.99

Tokay-Pinot Gris, Cave de Turckheim,   FRANCE
Alsace 2000
Deliciously understated peach, gooseberry and tart
pineapple. Superb quaffing here.

16.5

WHITE   £12.99

Tokay-Pinot Gris, Grand Cru Brand, Alsace 2000   FRANCE
Lovely opulent, slightly oily apricot – pure and
stunning. Gentle grilled nutty feel on the finish. Very
full – it needs oriental hot food.

16.5

RED   £9.99

Villa Maria Pinot Noir 2002   NEW ZEALAND
18 in 2-3 years. Screwcap. Simply one of the best
under-a-tenner Pinots on earth. Smooth, cherry
richness, cellar it. And it has been raised on good
earth.

16.5

WHITE   £7.03

Wynns Coonawarra Chardonnay 2002   AUSTRALIA
Soft lime and melon with touches of grilled hay and
citrus. Very classy, individual, delicious.

16.5

WHITE   £11.99

Wolf Blass Gold Label Chardonnay 2003   AUSTRALIA
Screwcap. Lovely wood and fruit interpretation here.
Quite delicious. Best Wolf Blass Chardonnay I've ever
tasted.

16   WHITE £8.99
Winemakers Series Sauvignon Blanc 2003   NEW ZEALAND
Classy, rich, balanced gooseberries.

16   WHITE £6.99
Booarra Chenin/Verdelho 2002   AUSTRALIA
Screwcap. I admire the way it presents sleekly
different aspects of its fruit, both texturally and
flavoursomely: peach, pear, grapefruit.

16   WHITE £4.99
Barramundi Chardonnay/Sémillon 2003   AUSTRALIA
Screwcap. What a superb blend of grapes! A
delicious working partnership.

16   WHITE £4.49
Comte Tolosan Colombard/Sauvignon,   FRANCE
Vin de Pays de Comte Tolosan 2002
Excellent blend stretching the under-ripe gooseberry
to better show-up the lime and citrus. Terrific
shellfish wine.

16   RED £5.99
Corallo Primitivo 2001   ITALY
A brilliant spicy food red. Has burned black cherry
fruit, a hint of nut, and a superb layered finish.

16   RED £4.49
Corallo Nero d'Avola 2002   ITALY
Delicious earthy cherry aroused by frisky tannins.

16

RED   £4.99
CHILE

**Concha y Toro Casillero del Diablo
Cabernet Sauvignon 2002**
Fresh and full of frolics.

16

RED   £10.99
FRANCE

Cordier Cuvée Prestige, Bordeaux 2001
What an elegant claret. Offers chocolate and pruney
berries.

16

WHITE   £8.99
CHILE

Cono Sur Vision Gewürztraminer 2002
Screwcap. Spicy, fresh and beautifully controlled
spice.

16

WHITE   £8.99
SOUTH AFRICA

**De Wetshof Limestone Hill
Chardonnay 2002**
Fruity, crisp Chardonnay of great aplomb!

16

RED   £5.99
CHILE

Errazuriz Syrah 2001
Sumptuous berries.
Also at Budgens, Waitrose.

16

RED   £9.99
USA

Estancia Cabernet Sauvignon 1999
What sensual fruit, vivacious yet elegant, bold yet
graceful with finesse and flavour.

16

WHITE £4.49

Eden Collection Torrontes 2003   ARGENTINA

Delicious dry grapey aperitif. Real class and restrained tangy finesse.

16

WHITE £5.35

Firefinch Sauvignon Blanc 2003   SOUTH AFRICA

Delicious concentrated pure gooseberry with a lime undertone.

Also at Tesco.

16

WHITE £4.99

French Connection Chardonnay/Viognier 2001   FRANCE

Very classy, calm, classy, ripe yet dry.

16

RED £6.99

Graham Beck Wines Pinotage 2002   SOUTH AFRICA

Chewy, savoury, brilliant charred berries, herbs and rubbery tannins.

16

RED £4.99

Inycon Sangiovese 2002   ITALY

Beautifully brisk berries with firm tannins.

16

WHITE £6.99

La Chasse du Pape Grande Réserve,   FRANCE
Côtes du Rhône Blanc, Gabriel Meffre 2003

Richness yet acidic balance here. Elegance, richness, style.

16

RED £5.29

Le Catalan Grenache Rouge 2002   FRANCE
Lovely textured prunes, apricots and warm tannins.
What a fabulous food tipple.

16

ROSÉ SPARKLING £8.49

Lindauer Sparkling Rosé   NEW ZEALAND
Crisp and fresh with a delicious touch of dry raspberry
to the finish.

16

WHITE £6.99

Marqués de Casa Concha Chardonnay 2002   CHILE
Superb smoky fruit.

16

RED £6.99

Marqués de Griñon Rioja 2002   SPAIN
Always one of the classiest of Riojas. Let it linger on
the palate. It takes time.
Also at Morrison's.

16

RED £4.79

Montepulciano d'Abruzzo 2001   ITALY
Very herby blackberries with a fine coating of fresh
tannins.

16

RED £5.99

Matua Valley Malbec/Merlot 2002   NEW ZEALAND
Screwcap. Very fresh plums with a hint of raspberry.
Delicious with a fish stew.

16   RED £14.99
Penfolds Bin 389 Cabernet/Shiraz 2000   AUSTRALIA
Dark berries to begin, sweet plums to finish. The
middle-man is tannic and tenacious. Impressively
roasted and savoury, tannicly complex and concentrated.

16   RED £14.99
Penfolds Old Vines Shiraz/Grenache/   AUSTRALIA
Mourvèdre 1997
Very mature, showing its middle-aged spread (of
softening tannins and fruit getting softer). But still a
treat of a liquid.

16   WHITE £7.99
Radcliffes Mosel Riesling 2002   GERMANY
Now much better than previously tasted (and rated).
The minerally almost chewy citrus is superb.

On corks and corkscrews (No. 12)

I believe that anyone who finds a wine not as fruity, as fresh, or as
vivid as it should be, or as he or she has been led to expect,
should complain - because that wine, however mildly, is corked.
Send it packing! It is a fact that the only reason corked wines
continue to exist is because we DO NOT complain enough. If,
every time a restaurant wine or retailer-bought bottle failed to
please because it didn't taste right was returned whence it came,
either for replacement or refund, then corked, faulty wines would
have disappeared years ago. There is so little pressure placed on
restaurants and retailers by their customers that these purveyors
of wine place no pressure on their wholesalers and other
suppliers.

16

WHITE £5.99

Radcliffes Bordeaux Sauvignon 2003   FRANCE

Very elegant, classy, restrained yet deeply satisfying.

16

RED £7.49

St Hallett Cabernet/Shiraz 2001   AUSTRALIA

What's so sexy is the way it slowly peels off layer after
layer of slow-burning berries.

16

WHITE £5.99

Torres Viña Esmeralda 2003   SPAIN

Screwcap. The perfect Thai curry white: rich, fluent
fruit of apricots and a touch of pear.
Also at Oddbins, Waitrose.

16

WHITE £7.99

Terrunyo Sauvignon Blanc 2003   CHILE

Terrific Cox's Orange Pippin freshness.

16

WHITE £6.99

Villa Maria Riesling 2002   NEW ZEALAND

Screwcap. 18.5 points in 4–6 years. Utterly captivating.

16

WHITE £7.99

Vin Five Collection Sémillon/Sauvignon 2002   AUSTRALIA

Screwcap. What layered beauty! Finesse yet flavour,
class with concentration.

16

WHITE £4.79

Verdicchio Moncaro 2002   ITALY

Lovely! Subtle dry apricot daintiness.

16
RED £9.99
NEW ZEALAND

Vidal Estate Syrah 2002
Terrific savoury buzz about this wine. Hums with
energy and flavour

16
WHITE £6.49
NEW ZEALAND

Vidal Estate Sauvignon Blanc 2003
Screwcap. Very fleshy, well developed and fresh.
Lovely crisp, gooseberry fruit. Superb shellfish wine.

16
RED £9.99
CHILE

Veramonte Primus 1999
Very fresh baked tannins. Marvellous.

16
WHITE £5.99
NEW ZEALAND

Sauvignon Blanc, Marlborough 2003
Very lengthy experience from gentle gooseberry to
chalky tanginess of pineapple on the finish.
Also at Booths, Oddbins, Tesco, Safeway, Somerfield,
Sainsbury's, Co-op, Morrison's, Small Merchants
(Unwins, Londis).

16
WHITE £8.99
CHILE

Cono Sur Vision Riesling 2002
Wonderful now, 18.5 points in 5–6 years. Superb
lemonic lushness.
Also at Safeway, Sainsbury's.

16
WHITE £5.99
USA

Fetzer Chardonnay/Viognier 2002
Exotic multi-toned gooseberry and apricot with fine
citrus and pineapple. Superb Thai food wine.
Also at Safeway.

OTHER WINES 15.5 AND UNDER

15.5

Beyerskloof Pinotage 2003	RED	£5.99
		SOUTH AFRICA

Bonterra Chardonnay 2002	WHITE	£9.99
		USA

Chileño Chardonnay/Sauvignon 2003	WHITE	£4.50
Also at Somerfield.		CHILE

Eden Torrontes Organic 2003	WHITE	£4.49
		ARGENTINA

Grenache Noir,	RED	£5.29
Vin de Pays des Côtes Catalans 2002		SPAIN

Kendermann Organic Rosé 2002	ROSÉ	£4.99
		GERMANY

La Chasse du Pape Grande Réserve White 2002	WHITE	£5.99
		FRANCE

Origin Garnacha 2002	RED	£4.99
		SPAIN

Origin Chardonnay 2003	WHITE	£4.99
		CHILE

Torres Viña Sol 2003	WHITE	£4.99
Also at Asda.		SPAIN

WHITE **£5.99**

Terredavino Gavi, Rondanini 2003   ITALY

WHITE **£3.99**

Talaris Chardonnay 2002   BULGARIA

WHITE **£4.99**

Muscat/Viognier, Vin de Pays d'Oc 2002   FRANCE

RED **£4.49**

Vin Five Next Generation   AUSTRALIA
Cabernet/Merlot 2003

RED **£7.99**

Vin Five The Collection   AUSTRALIA
Cabernet Sauvignon 2001

15   RED **£4.50**

Chileño Shiraz/Cabernet Sauvignon 2002   CHILE
Also at Somerfield, Tesco.

RED **£9.99**

Baron de Ley Reserva Rioja 1999   SPAIN

Colombard/Sauvignon,   WHITE **£4.49**
Côtes du Tolosan 2002   FRANCE

RED **£4.49**

Lalaguna Tinto NV   SPAIN

WHITE **£9.99**

Montagny, 'Les Bassets', Château de Cary Potet 2001   FRANCE

RED £4.99

Masterpeace Cabernet/Shiraz/Grenache 2003   AUSTRALIA

RED £3.99

Riverview Merlot/Cabernet Sauvignon,   HUNGARY
Akos Kamocsay 2003

WHITE (half bottle) £7.99

Radcliffes Eiswein 2002   GERMANY
18 points in 3-10 years.

WHITE £6.49

Radcliffes Haut Poitou Sauvignon 2003   FRANCE

RED £3.99

Talaris Pinot Noir 2001   BULGARIA

WHITE £4.99

Van Loveren Sauvignon Blanc 2003   SOUTH AFRICA

14.5   RED £8.99

Fleurie Georges Duboeuf 2002   FRANCE
Screwcap.

WHITE SPARKLING £7.99

Origin Reserve Argentinian Sparkling Wine NV ARGENTINA

WHITE £4.99

Fiordaliso Pinot Grigio 2003   ITALY

RED **£5.99**

La Chasse du Pape, Côtes du Rhône 2002   FRANCE

WHITE **£4.49**

Vin Five Next Generation   AUSTRALIA
Chardonnay/Sémillon 2003

14

RED **£4.99**

Barramundi Shiraz 2002   AUSTRALIA
Screwcap.

WHITE SPARKLING **£19.49**

Nicolas Feuillatte Champagne Brut NV   FRANCE
Also at Tesco.

RED **£9.99**

Estancia Pinot Noir 2001   USA

ROSÉ **£5.99**

Fetzer Valley Oaks Syrah Rosé 2002   USA

WHITE **£8.99**

Fetzer Viognier 2001   USA

RED **£4.99**

Grenache Noir Le Catalan 2002   FRANCE

WHITE **£6.99**

Houghton HWB Dry White 2002   AUSTRALIA

RED **£3.99**

Inti Soft Fruity Red 2003   ARGENTINA

WHITE **£3.99**

Inti Fresh White 2003   ARGENTINA

WHITE £4.99
Kendermann Dry Riesling 2002 GERMANY

WHITE £4.99
Le Catalan Grenache Blanc 2002 FRANCE

WHITE £8.99
Lincoln Winemakers Reserve NEW ZEALAND
Sauvignon Blanc 2003

WHITE (3 litre box) £14.99
Origin Chenin/Chardonnay 2003 ARGENTINA

ROSÉ £4.99
Origin Rosé 2003 SPAIN

RED £3.99
Origin Malbec/Merlot 2003 ARGENTINA

RED £2.99
Terra Zano Rosso NV ITALY

WHITE £6.49
Talus Chardonnay 2002 USA

RED £11.99
Wolf Blass Gold Label Coonawarra AUSTRALIA
Cabernet Sauvignon 2003

WAITROSE

Head Office:
Doncaster Road,
Southern Industrial Area,
Bracknell,
Berkshire RG12 8YA

Tel:(01344)424680

WAITROSE WINE DIRECT

Freepost SW1647,
Bracknell,
Berkshire RG12 8HX

Tel:(0800)188881
Fax:(0800)188888

Email: customerservice@waitrose.co.uk
Website: www.waitrose.com

For Waitrose wines 14 points and under visit
www.superplonk.com.

18.5

WHITE £20.00

Virgilius Viognier 2002   AUSTRALIA

Canary Wharf and Kingston selection. One of the
greatest Viogniers made. Even has tannin to back up
the genteel lemony apricot. Condrieu, eat your heart
out – at half the price. (Condrieu is the expensive
Rhône white wine which pioneered the Viognier
grape but has since, one or two exceptions apart, lost
its way.)

17.5

FORTIFIED £10.99

Lusteau East India Rich Oloroso Sherry NV   SPAIN

Superb burned molasses richness without cloying
sweetness. This suits blue cheese best, or TV and a
chocolate bar.

17.5

WHITE £9.99

Rustenberg Chardonnay 2002   SOUTH AFRICA

One of the most complete Chardonnays under a
tenner, and it puts to shame many a Meursault. It has
superb creamy vegetality.

17

RED £32.99

Allegrini Amarone della Valpolicella DOC 1999   ITALY

Canary Wharf and Kingston selection. The essence of
what sweet dried grapes can achieve.

17

FORTIFIED (50cl) £8.99

Blandy's Alvada 5 Year Old Rich Madeira NV   PORTUGAL

A magnificent evening tipple. Offers prunes,
chestnuts, calamine lotion and off-dry molasses.

17

WHITE £5.99
Basedow Barossa Valley Sémillon 2001   AUSTRALIA
What a splendidly firm case it makes for this grape.
Lovely tangy lemon, pear and apricot with vegetal
pineapple.

17

RED £9.99
Bodegas Rejadorada Crianza 2001   SPAIN
Canary Wharf and Kingston selection. Superb
richness and unguent unguency from the tannins.

17

RED £9.99
Bonterra Merlot 2001   USA
What a wonderful blend of 77% Merlot, 15% Cabernet
Sauvignon, 8% Syrah. Superb berries and energy
from the tannins.

17

WHITE £15.95
Chardonnay Calera 2000   USA
Wonderful texture to add to the gentility of cream,
melon and a touch of peach.

17

RED £7.99
Château Ségonzac, Premières Côtes de Blaye 2002   FRANCE
Screwcap. Superb tobacco richness and soft tannins.
Real persistency and class here.

17

RED £8.99
Chianti Classico Borgo Salcetino 2001   ITALY
Lovely hearth-place aroma, ashes and roast game. Big
berries, touch sun-burned but very charming, and

hints of chocolate to the tannins, which also exhibit a
suggestion of creamy cherry.

17

RED £12.99

Gigondas Cuvée Les Tentrelles Les Espalines 2001   FRANCE
One of those wonderful Côtes-du-Rhônes which offers
teasing, aromatic glimpses of les garrigues, the
hedgerow, the coal mine and the cherry orchard. The
tannins are perfectly soft yet crunchy

17

RED £8.99

Les Vieilles Vignes de Château Maris,   FRANCE
La Lavinière, Minervois 2002
Superb! Strikes a fine complex line between rich
tannic finesse and soft berries with a chocolate
coating.

I appear to have had a sex change. Not only that. I have become
something of another wine critic altogether. According to the
Bordeaux wine manufacturer, Yvon Mau, I am Jilly Gluck. This is
how they address me in sending me their publicity magazine
Découvreur de Bordeaux, and the discovery of this has had the
amazing effect of holding up the instant jettisoning of the
magazine into the waste bin. I wonder how the Mau company
confused me with Miss Goolden? Could it be the vigour of my
golden curls? My wand-like waist perhaps? Could it be the way I
enunciate French with a high-pitched squeak? (Since pointing this
out in my *Guardian* column, the Mau company sent me an
apology and their bumff now arrives with my name correctly
spelled. Their magazine, alas, is not half as amusing as a result.)

17

WHITE £5.99
ITALY

Lugana Villa Flora 2003
It has so many twists of citrus, orange-peel texture
and fruit flavours, one luxuriates in the sheer class of
the liquid.

17

RED £11.99
CHILE

Montes Alpha Syrah 2002
Highly perfumed, chewy, deep, rich, exuberant and
exciting.

17

RED £14.99
SPAIN

**Marqués de Griñon Dominio de Valdepusa
Syrah 2001**
A real treat. Unites soft, ripe, spicy grapes with
vivacious tannins with great aplomb.

17

RED £6.99
SPAIN

**Viña Alta Mar Cabernet Sauvignon/
Merlot 2002**
Wonderful tobacco, cocoa, prunes, berries and licorice.

17

RED £14.99
NEW ZEALAND

**Villa Maria Reserve Cabernet Sauvignon/
Merlot 2001**
The sheer perfection of the smooth berries and tannins.

17

WHITE £6.02
NEW ZEALAND

Villa Maria Private Bin Chardonnay 2002
Screwcap. Has such beautiful footwork as it dances on
the tongue with subtlety, leafy melon and lemon. So
calm, so insouciant, so classy.
Also at Asda, Oddbins.

17 · WHITE £9.99
Catena Chardonnay 2002 ARGENTINA
A superbly smooth yet complex, characterful
Chardonnay with decisive 'Burgundian' undertones
yet firmly expressive classiness. It has mildly burned
hay, smoke, melon, lemon and cream (all subtle, to be
searched for), in highly civilised union. Great texture
to the liquid.
Also at Oddbins, The Wine Society.

16.5 · RED £11.99
Carneros Pinot Noir, La Crema 2001 USA
Superb, gamier than Sonoma, and has more tannic
oomph.

16.5 · RED £14.99
Cillar de Silos Crianza, Ribera del Duero 2001 SPAIN
Canary Wharf and Kingston selection. Expensive
Christmas treat. Wonderful with festive game dishes.

16.5 · RED £5.49
Château Villepreux, Bordeaux Supérieur 2002 FRANCE
Perhaps the best under-six-quid claret in the UK,
could pass for a £30 second growth.

16.5 · WHITE £11.95
**Château Haut-Gardère Pessac-Léognan,
Bordeaux 2001** FRANCE
Undeniably a treat of complexity and concentration.
Truly fine texture, multi-layered and very, very elegant.

16.5
WHITE £4.99

**Concha y Toro Casillero del Diablo
Chardonnay 2002**
Simply superb.
CHILE

16.5
RED £8.99

**Les Vieilles Vignes de Château Maris,
La Livinière, Minervois 2001**
FRANCE

A 100% Carignan red of uninhibited chocolate and
roasted berries. Fine hints of herbs and the tannins
balance the alcohol (14%) well. A brilliant casserole
red.

16.5
RED £20.00

**Craggy Range Block 14 Syrah,
Gimblett Gravels 2002**
NEW ZEALAND

A fine Rhône-meets-Barolo Syrah of style,
concentration and complexity. Very fine tannins.

16.5
RED £6.99

Ironstone Vineyards Cabernet Franc 2000
USA

Superbly at its peak now with its unguent gamey
tannins.

16.5
RED £4.99

**La Chasse du Pape Syrah,
Côtes du Rhône 2003**
FRANCE

Very firm rich vintage, surprisingly calm considering
the heat of 2003. Delicious tannins and classy berries.

16.5

**Montgras Limited Edition Cabernet
Sauvignon 2001**

Extra layers of chewy tannins to the berried bustle.

16.5

Mas Collet Celler Capcanes Montsant 2001

A blend of Garnacha, Tempranillo, Carinena and
Cabernet Sauvignon which gushes with flavour and
depth, juicily edgy, without berries being OTT. Fine
tannins to the finish. Richly unguent and gripping.
Richly unguent and gripping. Offers real excitement
and complex concentration.
Also at Booths.

16.5

Norton Malbec Reserve 2002

Has vivacity yet elegance, richness yet graciousness,
and complexity yet impressive quaffability.

16.5

**Petit Chablis, Cave des Vignerons
de Chablis 2003**

Screwcap. Oh! wonder of wonder! A terrific Chablis
which will stay fresh and finely textured thanks to its
screwcap.

16.5

**Schloss Gobelsburg Grüner Veltliner,
Lamm 2002**

Canary Wharf and Kingston selection. It
demonstrates rather as Mozart does, that supreme

complexity can emerge from Austria with an utter
silence.

16.5
WHITE £4.99

Soave Classico Vigneto Colombara, Zenato 2003 ITALY
Simply superb class in a glass: melon, lemon, pear.

16.5
FORTIFIED £9.99

Taylor's Chip Dry White Port NV PORTUGAL
A superbly different fortified white wine of depth and
richness. Brilliant with nuts and cold meats.

16.5
WHITE £7.99

Warwick Estate Chardonnay 2003 SOUTH AFRICA
Chewy edge of cream and citrus undertones, subtly
rich melon and young oak character. Cellar for up to
18 months for 18 points.

16
RED £13.99

Amarone della Valpolicella Classico 2000 ITALY
Prunes, licorice, plums and fine tannins. A real treat.

16
WHITE £9.99

Shaw & Smith Sauvignon Blanc 2003 AUSTRALIA
Screwcap. Very finely textured lemon fruit. Classily
complete.

16
WHITE SPARKLING £3.49

Arione Moscato Spumante NV ITALY
A simply delicious floral-scented, Muscat-grapey
aperitif for hot weather and back gardens.

16

WHITE DESSERT (half bottle) £5.99

Brown Brothers Late Harvested AUSTRALIA
Orange and Muscat Flora 2002

Lovely tangy fruit now. But will rate 18 by 2008.

16

WHITE £7.99

Brauneberger Juffer Riesling Kabinett, GERMANY
Willi Haag, Mosel-Saar-Ruwer 2002

19 points in 5-7 years. Wonderful dry honey,
grapefruit, lime and pear with mineral acids.

16

RED £7.99

Carmen Nativa Cabernet Sauvignon 2000 CHILE

Has three clichéd elements – acid, fruit, tannins – but
gives us a new overall highly integrated twist:
freshness and flavour with a hint of orange peel on
the tannic finish.

16

RED £2.99

Cuvée Chasseur, Vin de Pays de FRANCE
l'Hérault 2003

A wonderful bargain of richness, tannic presence, and
vivid berries of class and clout.

16

WHITE £9.99

Cottage Block Sauvignon Blanc, AUSTRALIA
Old Renwick Vineyard 2002

Stunningly exotic Thai food wine. Offers artichokes,
asparagus, peaches, lime and cream. Weird,
wonderful, whacky.

16

RED £4.59
FRANCE

Cahors Malbec 2002
Sheer rustic civility and panache.

16

RED £7.49
FRANCE

Château de Targe, Saumur-Champigny 2001
A bright, charred-prune red of elegance yet bite.

16

RED £4.99
CHILE

Cono Sur Pinot Noir 2003
Wonderful for under a fiver. There are ungainly
Beaunes at five times this price which have less
endeavour and wit.
Also at Budgens, Majestic, Morrison's, Somerfield,
Tesco.

16

WHITE DESSERT (half bottle) £9.79
FRANCE

Château Liot, Sauternes 2001
20 in 2012. Wonderful waxy ripeness and honied
sensuality.

16

WHITE £12.99
NEW ZEALAND

**Cottage Block Marlborough
Sauvignon Blanc 2002**
A wonderfully delicate Sauvignon of subtle tanginess
and under-ripe gooseberry and citrus. Very fine.

16

WHITE £5.99
FRANCE

Cheverny Le Vieux Clos, Delaille 2003
Delicious tangy gooseberry and under-ripe gooseberry
richness.

16   RED   £4.49

Concha y Toro Merlot 2003   CHILE
Very aromatic, clinging, extended berries.

16   RED   £6.99

Diemersfontein Pinotage 2003   SOUTH AFRICA
Unusually delicious, tobacco-edged Pinotage of
brilliant utility with game dishes.

16   WHITE   £4.99

Etchart Privado Torrontes 2003   ARGENTINA
The spice, the lychee/orange-peel fruit, the texture – it
has them all.

16   RED   £5.99

Errazuriz Syrah 2001   CHILE
Delicious combination of sweet plums and dry, dry
berries.
Also at Budgens, Threshers.

16   WHITE   £4.99

Finca Las Higueras Pinot Gris 2003   ARGENTINA
Wonderful firm apricot and citrus with a suggestion
of spiced pear. Touches of Alsace but finishes in fine
tango style.

16   RED   £5.25

LA Cetto Petite Sirah 2001   MEXICO
What opulence and richness here. The palate is
drenched, and the senses inflamed.

16

WHITE £4.99

La Baume Viognier, Vin de Pays d'Oc 2003 FRANCE
Delightfully insouciant yet committed. Dry apricot
and citrus.

16

WHITE £6.99

Leasingham Bin 7 Clare Valley Riesling 2003 AUSTRALIA
18 in 3–5 years.

16

WHITE £6.99

Les Fleurs Chardonnay/Sauvignon, FRANCE
Vin de Pays de Côtes de Gascogne 2003
Very full bodied, rippingly ripe yet dry and incisive to
finish.

16

RED £6.49

Mont Gras Carmenere Reserva 2001 CHILE
Lively plums and cherries.

16

RED £5.99

Mendoza Malbec Anubis 2002 ARGENTINA
Gritty softness – a paradox? Certainly a delight.

16

RED £45.99

Pinot Noir Bouchard Finlayson, SOUTH AFRICA
Tête du Cuvée Galpin Peak 2001
Outstanding, perhaps the most complete Pinot I've
tasted from the Cape. Beautiful tannins and high-class
fruit.
Also at Small Merchants (Hedley Wright, SWIG).

16

WHITE SPARKLING £24.99
Pol Roger Brut Réserve Non Vintage FRANCE
Champagne
A superb champagne where flavour, finesse and real
wit coalesce with great fervour.

16

RED £4.99
Graham Beck Wines Railroad Red 2003 SOUTH AFRICA
Very delicious adult jam, with the pips. So it's dry and
classy on the finish.

16

WHITE £5.99
Riesling Marlborough 2003 NEW ZEALAND
Very finely balanced lovely tangy richness. Will cellar
well 2–3 years.

16

RED £9.99
Reserve Pinot Noir 2002 NEW ZEALAND
Superb! Those tannins again! Soft talking but
eloquent.

16

WHITE £9.49
Sancerre, Domaine Naudet 2003 FRANCE
One of the most attractive of this breed I've tasted in
some while. Real class, clout, concentration and regal
gooseberry fruit.

16

WHITE £7.99
Springfield Special Cuvée SOUTH AFRICA
Sauvignon Blanc 2003
Wonderful grapefruit/citrus richness.

16

RED £8.49

Seigneurs d'Aiguilhe, Côtes de Castillon 2001   FRANCE

It's the succulence, yet dry richness and complexity of the
tannins which make it so good.

16

WHITE £5.49

Torres Viña Esmeralda 2003   SPAIN

Delightfully subtle yet emphatically complex, bold and
spicy-fish-dish friendly.
Also at Oddbins, Thresher.

16

RED £9.99

Viña La Rosa Don Reca Merlot 2002   CHILE

Hearty, rich yet delicate, almost autumnal in its
sombre fruity colouring, but delicious.

16

WHITE £5.99

Villa Montes Sauvignon Blanc 2003   CHILE

Real tanginess and class here.

16

WHITE £6.99

Villa Maria Private Bin Riesling 2003   NEW ZEALAND

Screwcap. Superb level of fruit, melon and a hint of
gooseberry, with fine citrus.19 points in 3-10 years.
Also at Budgens.

16

RED £14.99

Villa Maria Reserve Pinot Noir 2002   NEW ZEALAND

Real gamey ripeness with very fine tannins. Cellar it
2–3 years to achieve 18 points and wholly decant 3–4
hours.

16   RED   £6.99

Vigna Ottieri Molise Rosso 2001   ITALY
Delicious grilled plums with slightly earthy, burned
berries. Wonderful Italian food wine.

16   RED   £4.49

Waitrose Cabernet Sauvignon/Merlot 2002   CHILE
Very soft jammy ripeness.

16   RED   £24.50

Yering Station Reserve Pinot Noir 2000   AUSTRALIA
Canary Wharf and Kingston stores ony. One of Oz's
most convincingly crunchily gamey Pinots. Needs to
be drunk on a warm sunny day; decant 3–4 hours
before drinking as otherwise it can disappoint (on first
opening it is very shy).

On corks and corkscrews (No. 13)

The answer to the problem of corked wine is simple. Every wine maker in the world knows what it is. But, until the last few years, they hesitated to seize the chance to solve the problem once and for all. In spite of knowing that between 5 and 10 per cent of his or her wines will be tainted, and that many of the rest do not taste exactly as they should when they are opened by their ultimate consumers, the wine maker was reluctant to take the resolute, final and utterly foolproof step which will end corked wine at a stroke (or I should say, a twist). The answer is to use screwcaps. The cork should be given the elbow and this guaranteed faultless seal used instead.

16

WHITE £6.99

Yalumba South Australia Viognier 2003   AUSTRALIA

Very dry leafy apricot, will age to 17 points and
perhaps beyond by 2005/6.

16

WHITE £13.99

Zind 1 Domaine Zind Humbrecht, Alsace NV   FRANCE

A non-vintage blend of 50% Auxerrois, 15% Pinot Blanc
and 35% Chardonnay which has beguilingly casual
class, from one of Alsace's greatest wine makers.

16

RED £6.99

Ravenswood Vintners Blend Zinfandel 2001   USA

Chunky berries with cool tannins, a hint of spice, a
touch of savourily grilled plum.
Also at Asda, Booths, Majestic, Somerfield.

16

WHITE £5.99

Porcupine Ridge Sauvignon Blanc 2003   SOUTH AFRICA

Screwcap. Delicious gooseberry and citrus. Ripe but
delicate.
Also at Asda, Somerfield.

16

RED £13.99

Wither Hills Pinot Noir 2002   NEW ZEALAND

Screwcap. One of the most convincing Kiwi Pinots.
Has a gaminess, feral berried richness and aromatic
intensity, and finishes well.
Also at Booths, Oddbins, Small Merchants
(Jeroboams, Thos Peatling, Ballantynes of Cowbridge),
The Wine Society.

16

WHITE £7.99

Nepenthe Sauvignon Blanc 2003   AUSTRALIA
Screwcap. Has an edge of ripe gooseberry to vague
lemon and surprising chalky undertone, magnificent
news for shellfish.
Also at Oddbins.

16

RED £6.29

Neethlingshof Lord Neethling   SOUTH AFRICA
Pinotage 2001
Superb energy from the tannins which have complex
layers offering chocolate on the finish.
Also at Safeway.

OTHER WINES 15.5 AND UNDER

15.5

WHITE £9.99

Old Renwick Vineyard   NEW ZEALAND
Sauvignon Blanc 2003
Screwcap.

RED £4.99

Duque de Viseu Vinhos Sogrape 2001   PORTUGAL

RED £6.99

Brampton OVR 2002   SOUTH AFRICA

WHITE £7.99

Brampton Viognier 2003   SOUTH AFRICA

WHITE £8.99

Bonterra Chardonnay 2002   USA

WHITE £8.99

Carmen Winemaker's Reserve Chardonnay 2003   CHILE

ROSÉ £6.99

Château de Caraguilhes Rosé, Corbières 2003   FRANCE

RED £10.99

Costers del Gravet, Cellar de Capcanes,   SPAIN
Montsant 2000
Canary Wharf and Kingston selection.

RED £9.95

Dehesa de Rubiales Prieto Picudo Crianza,   SPAIN
Vino de la Tierra, Castilla y Leon 2001
Canary Wharf and Kingston selection.

ROSÉ £4.99

Domaine de Pellehaut, Vin de Pays des   FRANCE
Côtes de Gascogne 2003
Screwcap.

WHITE £4.99

Gavi La Luciana 2003   ITALY

RED £6.15

Gran Fendo Navarra Reserva 1998   SPAIN

WHITE £4.99

La Chasse du Pape Chardonnay/Viognier,   FRANCE
Vin de Pays d'Oc 2002

RED   £4.99

Inycon Shiraz 2002   ITALY

RED   £4.99

La Colombe, Côtes du Rhône 2003   FRANCE

WHITE   £3.99

La Boca Torrontes/Chardonnay 2003   ARGENTINA

RED   £6.99

Mont Gras Cabernet Sauvignon/   CHILE
Syrah Reserva 2002

RED   £4.99

Norton Barbera 2003   ARGENTINA

RED   £8.99

SMV Fairview 2002   SOUTH AFRICA

RED   £3.99

San Andres Carmenere/Cabernet   CHILE
Sauvignon 2003

RED   £4.99

Tatachilla Growers Grenache/Mourvèdre/   AUSTRALIA
Shiraz 2003
Screwcap.

WHITE   £4.99

Tatachilla Growers   AUSTRALIA
Sémillon/Sauvignon Blanc/Chenin Blanc 2003
Screwcap.

RED £5.29

Waitrose Special Reserve Claret,
Bordeaux Supérieur 2002   FRANCE

WHITE £4.99

Wild Cat Catarratto, Sicilia 2003   ITALY

WHITE £3.99

Riverview Gewürztraminer,   HUNGARY
Akos Kamocsay 2003
Also at Asda, Safeway, Sainsbury's.

RED £6.99

Deakin Estate Merlot 2002   AUSTRALIA
Also at Oddbins.

RED £7.89

Stellenzicht Golden Triangle   SOUTH AFRICA
Pinotage 2001
Also at Safeway.

15

RED £5.99

Anubis Malbec 2003   ARGENTINA

RED £7.99

D'Arenberg The Footbolt Shiraz 2001   AUSTRALIA
Also at The Wine Society.

WHITE £6.99 — SOUTH AFRICA
Bellingham The Maverick Chenin Blanc 2003

RED £18.00 — SPAIN
Barbara Fores Coma d'en Pou 2000
Canary Wharf and Kingston selection.

RED £6.99 — FRANCE
Château Cazal-Viel, Cuvée des Fées, St-Chinian 2002

RED (3 litre box) £14.99 — SPAIN
Eden Collection Tempranillo, Co-op Jesús del Perdon 2003

RED £3.99 — FRANCE
Fruits of France Grenache, Vin de Pays d'Oc 2002
Screwcap.

RED £7.25 — SPAIN
Finca Sobreno Crianza 1999

RED £4.49 — FRANCE
Les Nivières, Saumur 2002

WHITE £12.50 — AUSTRALIA
Leenwin Estate Art Series Riesling 2002
18 points in 2008.

WHITE £8.99
Montagny 1er Cru Montcuchot,   FRANCE
Cave de Buxy 2002

WHITE SPARKLING £8.99
Montana Lindauer   NEW ZEALAND
Special Reserve Brut NV

RED £7.99
Oyster Bay Merlot 2002   NEW ZEALAND
Screwcap.

WHITE £5.49
Palacio de Bornos Verdejo 2003   SPAIN

RED £6.99
Nepenthe Tryst Red 2003   AUSTRALIA
Screwcap. Also at Asda, Oddbins.

RED £15.99
Reserve Pinot Noir 2001   AUSTRALIA

WHITE £3.99
San Andrés Chardonnay 2003   CHILE

WHITE £5.99
Terrazas Alto Chardonnay 2003   ARGENTINA

RED £4.99
Traidcraft Los Robles Carmenere 2003   CHILE

WHITE £7.49

Wente Chardonnay, Livermore Valley 2001   USA

FORTIFIED (50cl) £9.99

Warre's Otima 10 Year Old Tawny Port NV   PORTUGAL

WHITE £4.49

Waitrose Touraine Sauvignon Blanc 2003   FRANCE

RED £4.99

Eden Collection Organic Merlot,   FRANCE
Jacques Frélin 2002
Also at Booths.

RED £4.99

Da Luca Primitivo/Merlot 2002   ITALY
Also at Budgens.

RED £8.99

Nederburg Private Bin Pinotage 2001   SOUTH AFRICA
Also at Safeway.

14.5

RED £5.99

Corallo Primitivo di Puglia 2001   ITALY

RED £15.99

Cloudy Bay Pinot Noir 2002   NEW ZEALAND
16 points in 18 months.

WHITE £3.99
SOUTH AFRICA

Cape Grace Sauvignon Blanc/
Chenin Blanc 2003

WHITE £4.99
FRANCE

French Connection Marsanne/Roussanne,
Vin de Pays d'Oc 2002

ROSÉ £4.99
FRANCE

La Baume Syrah Rosé, Vin de Pays d'Oc 2003
Screwcap.

RED £18.00
NEW ZEALAND

Mount Difficulty Pinot Noir 2001
Canary Wharf and Kingston selection.

WHITE £9.99
AUSTRALIA

Nepenthe Sémillon 2001

RED £16.99
SOUTH AFRICA

Pinot Noir Bouchard
Finlayson Galpin Peak 2001

WHITE £4.69
FRANCE

Saint-Pourcain Réserve Spéciale,
Cave de St-Pourcain 2003

RED £8.25
PORTUGAL

Villa Santa, J.P. Ramos, Alentejo 2001

WHITE £4.99
SOUTH AFRICA

Waterside White, Graham Beck 2003

WHITE £5.99
USA

Woodbridge Chardonnay 2002
Rich, very forward melon richness.

14

RED £13.99

Allegrini La Grola Veronese 2000   ITALY
Canary Wharf and Kingston selection.

RED £37.99

Allegrini La Poja Monotivigno   ITALY
Corvina Veronese 1999
Canary Wharf and Kingston selection.

RED £12.99

Barolo, Terra da Vino 1999   ITALY

RED £17.49

Château Laroque, St-Emilion Grand Cru 1999   FRANCE

WHITE £12.99

Château Gaudrelle Réserve   FRANCE
Spéciale Monmousseau, Vouvray 2002

WHITE DESSERT £14.99

Chivite Coleccion 125,   SPAIN
Vendimia Tardiva 2000

WHITE £3.49

Cuvée Pêcheur, Vin de Pays du Comte   FRANCE
Tolosan 2003

ROSÉ £3.49

Cuvée Fleur, Vin de Pays de l'Hérault 2003   FRANCE

WHITE £9.99
Craggy Range Sauvignon Blanc,   NEW ZEALAND
Gimblettt Gravels 2003

RED £55.00
Château La Fleur-Pétrus, Pomerol 1999   FRANCE

RED £5.49
Domaine La Colombette Grenache/Syrah,   FRANCE
Vin de Pays des Coteaux du Libron 2002

RED £5.99
Domaine de la Thebaide, Minervois 2001   FRANCE

WHITE (50cl) £8.99
Domaine des Forges,   FRANCE
Coteaux du Layon Chaume 2002

WHITE £4.99
Excelsior Estate Sauvignon Blanc 2003   SOUTH AFRICA

RED £7.99
Ermitage du Pic Saint-Loup,   FRANCE
Coteaux du Languedoc 2002

WHITE £4.99
Fief Muscadet,   FRANCE
Côtes de Grandlieu sur Lie, Guérin 2003

RED £6.99
Fetzer Valley Oaks Cabernet Sauvignon 2000   USA

RED £19.99
Gevrey-Chambertin Vieilles Vignes,   FRANCE
Domaine Heresztyn 2001

WHITE £12.99

Kunstler Kirchensbuk Riesling Spätlese 2002 GERMANY
17 points in 2010.

WHITE £35.00

Leenwin Estate Art Series AUSTRALIA
Chardonnay 2000

RED £16.49

Muga Reserva Selección Especial Rioja 1998 SPAIN

RED £4.49

Montepulciano d'Abruzzo, ITALY
Umani Ronchi 2002

WHITE £18.99

Meursault, Louis Jadot 2000 FRANCE

WHITE £5.99

Piedra Feliz Pinot Noir 2001 CHILE

RED £9.29

Penfolds Organic Cabernet/Merlot/ AUSTRALIA
Shiraz 2002

RED £9.99

Pujalet, Vin de Pays du Gers 2003 FRANCE
Screwcap.

WHITE £5.49

Quinta de Simaens Vinho Verde 2003 PORTUGAL

WHITE £4.29

Verdicchio dei Castelli di Jesi Classico 2003 ITALY
Screwcap.

RED £36.00

FRANCE

Vosne Romanée 1er Cru,
Clos des Réas, Domaine Michel 1999

RED £3.99

FRANCE

Waitrose Côtes du Rhône 2003

WHITE £5.99

GERMANY

Dr Wagner Ockfener Bockstein Riesling,
Mosel-Saar-Ruwer 2002

RED £6.99

ARGENTINA

Weinert Carrascal 2001

THE WINE SOCIETY

Members' Shop and HQ:
Gunnels Wood Road,
Stevenage,
Hertfordshire SG1 2BG

Tel enquiries: (01438) 741177

E-mail: memberservice@thewinesociety.com.
Website: www.thewinesociety.com

For Wine Society wines 15.5 points and under visit
www.superplonk.com.

THE WINE SOCIETY

17.5   WHITE £7.95

Wither Hills Sauvignon Blanc 2003   NEW ZEALAND
Screwcap. Unusual complexities here offering lime,
pear, pineapple and a hint of spice. More perfume,
friskier minerals and chewiness of texture. Simply one
of the Kiwis' sassiest Sauvignons.
Also at Booths, Oddbins.

17   RED £8.50

D'Arenberg D'Arry's Original Shiraz/   AUSTRALIA
Grenache 2001
Superb level of couth juiciness with soft yet firm tannins.
Also at Oddbins.

17   WHITE £9.99

Catena Chardonnay 2002   ARGENTINA
One of those rare treats where the much-travelled
Chardonnay becomes dreamily creamy and reminisces
about its days of being misunderstood in Burgundy.
Also in Oddbins, Waitrose.

17   WHITE £6.25

Gewürztraminer Turckheim d'Alsace 2002   FRANCE
A superb white wine of complex twists and turns as it
reveals spicy apricot, mango and lychee – but it never
gets too familiar or noisy.

17   RED £7.99

The Footbolt Shiraz 2001   AUSTRALIA
Hint of licorice to the ripe berries and fine tannins.
Also at Waitrose.

16.5
RED £8.95

Coyam 2001 CHILE

A very classy organic blend of Merlot, Syrah, Cabernet
Sauvignon and Mourvèdre. Thick, chocolate-coated
berries, very dryly roasted. A very elegant though
characterful red wine with cleft-chinned tannins.
Also at Asda.

16.5
WHITE £7.25

Macon-Farges, Domaine Paul Talmard 2003 FRANCE

A thrilling modern Macon with the calm vegetality
almost swamped by dry (hint of tannin) melon and
pear.

There are several reasons why a bottle of wine is an individual
experience for each drinker of it, and we can all understand how
this is connected with different levels of smell and taste
perception, differences in partiality to or intolerance towards acids,
alkalis, sugars and so on, and the way our individual appetites
have developed. But there is another factor, one not usually
thought about or considered so mightily individual: saliva.
No wine enters the gut of any drinker without being blended with
saliva. If each of us has such an individual recipe for this liquid
(which is made up not only of an enzyme to aid food breakdown
but proteins and mineral salts) then each of us brings to each
glass of wine we drink a different blending agent. The acids and
tannins, the sheer level of fruit and all the natural glucoid by-
products in a wine, combine to create, via our saliva, a unique
experience for each us.

16.5   RED £12.35

The Twentyeight Road Mourvèdre 2001   AUSTRALIA
Blackberry jam with attitude.

16.5   WHITE £11.99

Te Muna Road Vineyard   NEW ZEALAND
Sauvignon Blanc 2003
Screwcap. Very elegant and strikingly well textured.
Also at E-tailers (Virgin Wines).

16.5   RED £8.50

The Custodian Grenache 2000   AUSTRALIA
Strawberries and blackberries, hint of prune. Firm
tannins, hint of earthiness.
Also at Booths.

16   WHITE £8.99

Langenlois Kamptal Riesling Loimer 2003   AUSTRIA
Softer, richer, more citrussy than the excellent 2002.
Can be cellared 5–6 years (and opened and decanted
anything up to 10 hours beforehand). Hint of spice
gives it good food-matching qualities.

16   RED £5.50

The Society's Chilean Merlot 2003   CHILE
A very subtle red of restrained charm which food of
every robust nature blunts. Its plummy delicacy is
appreciated for up to 40 seconds after swallowing,
and anything rumbustious food-wise negates this
pleasure as the fruit dries out in the throat to reveal
chocolate and roasted nuts.

16

WHITE £6.50
AUSTRALIA

**Plantagenet Hazard Hill Sémillon/
Sauvignon Blanc 2003**

Lovely blend of opulence and citrussy undertonality.
Good balance of pear to the apricot. Brilliant with
gently spicy fish dishes.

16

WHITE £4.95
SOUTH AFRICA

Villiera Chenin Blanc 2003

A modern Sauvignon (Sancerre aficionados will not
recognise the grape as the same) of thickly textured
gooseberry and pear. A very enlightening glug.

16

RED £10.95

Warwick Three Cape Ladies Pinotage 2001 SOUTH AFRICA

Cabernet 41%, Pinotage 30%, Merlot 29%. Chewy,
proud, relaxed, cassis, cherry fruited, fine discrete
tannins.

16

RED £13.99
NEW ZEALAND

Wither Hills Pinot Noir 2002

Screwcap. One of the most convincing Kiwi Pinots.
Has a gaminess, feral berried richness and aromatic
intensity, and finishes well.
Also at Booths, Oddbins, Small Merchants
(Jeroboams, Thos Peatling, Ballantynes of Cowbridge),
Waitrose.

YAPP BROTHERS

Mere,
Wiltshire BA12 6oY

Tel: (01747) 860 423
Fax: (01747) 860 929

Email: sales@yapp.co.uk.
Website: www.yapp.co.uk.

For Yapp wines 14 points and under visit
www.superplonk.com

17

RED £20.00

Côte-Rôtie 'La Viallière', Joel Champet 1999 FRANCE

Has an amazing, almost casual richness, with herby
berries (thyme, sage) and black olive, lovely. Brusque,
rustic, wonderful.

16.5

RED £15.95

Bandol, Château de la Rouvière 2000 FRANCE

Superb rippling tannins with crunchy berries. An
impactful red of class, clout and great cohesion.

16.5

WHITE £11.95

Cassis, Clos Sainte Magdaleine 2002 FRANCE

One of the South of France's great white wines. Dry
apricot and citrus, all covered with sludge (oil). Superb
food wine. Can handle complex fish dishes, like kippers
with gooseberry marmalade, without turning a hair.

16.5

RED £8.25

Côtes du Roussillon 'Tradition', FRANCE
Ferrer-Ribière 2001

Manages to achieve rusticity with finesse. Has a
plummy ripeness, herbs and black olive, with tannins
of no little tenacity and unguence.

16.5

WHITE £9.25

Quincy Vin Noble, Denis et Nicole Jaumier 2003 FRANCE

Sauvignon Blanc as only Quincy can do it (and the
Jaumiers), redefines what dryness is in a wine. Has a
lanolin undertone to very under-ripe gooseberry.

16.5

Vouvray Sec, Daniel Jarry 2001
The unique, the glorious, the superb Chenin Blanc
Sec. Classic touches of gentle wet wool, peach,
gooseberry and citrus, it has a steeliness yet grapiness.
Very pure in feel and tone.

16

RED £11.50
FRANCE

Collioure La Tour Vieille, La Pinède 2002
Chewy, chocolate, herbs, gently roasted, insistently
delicious berries with gripping tannins.

16

RED £21.00
FRANCE

Cornas, Cuvée Renaissance 2001
This is what many a Shiraz producer, in the New
World, seeks in the holy grail of such things: utter
resplendent rusticality with polished richness.

16

RED £7.50
FRANCE

**Côtes du Ventoux, Château Valcombe,
Cuvée Signature 2001**
What a genteel if rustic liquid. Offers hints of many
things arboreal and flighty, but stays smooth and soft.

16

WHITE £8.25
FRANCE

**Côtes du Rhône-Villages 'Sablet',
Domaine St-Gayan 2002**
A blend of Viognier, Grenache Blanc, Clairette and
Bourbelenc of great élan and confidence. Teases with
its peachy dryness and lemon. Finishes with finesse
yet flavour. Class act.

16

RED £8.75
FRANCE

Côtes du Rhône-Villages,
Domaine de Durban 2001
Good lively tannins and fine sweet berries.

16

WHITE £5.25

Côtes de Gascogne, Domaine de Millet 2003   FRANCE
Has deliciously immediate tangy richness and grapey
freshness. Subdued spice and pear (with a peachiness
on the finish).

16

WHITE £6.00

Domaine de la Tour Signy, Cépage Sauvignon 2003 FRANCE
Better than many a Sancerre, this crisp gooseberry
wine! Lovely textured, chewy. Old-fashioned yet
modern.

On corks and corkscrews (No. 14)

The downside to screwcaps? Well, there is no doubt that certain
wines made to age for donkeys' years acquire some character
through the incredibly tiny entrance of air, via the cork, into the
wine. But this, in my experience, means that Riesling, often a
grape variety which takes a long time to age, ages differently and
better under screwcap rather than cork not in the short-term but
certainly in the medium and hugely certainly in the long. With reds
– and Cabernet-dominated reds from Bordeaux spring to mind –
corks have allowed the tannins to soften. How will they develop
with no air to aid them? I reckon better. It will be up to the drinker
to artificially age the wine by decanting it – and it will be a perfect
wine being so decanted, not one marred by its cork.

16
WHITE DESSERT (half bottle) £5.95
Domaine Bellegard, Jurançon Moelleux 2002 FRANCE
Also available in full bottles. Still young (needs
another 4–5 years to appear sublime). Has honied
richness yet not overt sweetness (so it's excellent with
foie gras).

16
WHITE £6.75
Muscadet, Domaine de la Mortaine 2003 FRANCE
One of the most agreeable Muscadets of this vintage
I've tasted. Restrained opulence, citrussy with subtle
apricot.

16
RED £9.25
Neagles Rock Grenache/Shiraz 2001 AUSTRALIA
Red-lip-smackingly rich and has that classic Clare
attribute of ruggedness with civility. Truly delicious,
lightly roasted berries of great class and quaffability.

16
WHITE £9.75
Riesling d'Alsace, FRANCE
Charles Schleret Cuvée Reserve 2000
Severe, strait-laced and very elegant (i.e. understated,
demure, smooth). Needs whole decantation 3–8 hours
beforehand.

16
WHITE £8.95
Neagles Rock Riesling 2002 AUSTRALIA
Screwcaps at Yapp! Vive la révolution! Already has
petrol developed and fine citrus. Will age well in 3–6
years to 17.5 points.

16

RED £6.50

Saumur, Vignerons de Saumur 2002   FRANCE
'Excites more comment than any other label we have,'
says Jason Yapp. The liquid is no less arousing. The
nose is tickled by spicy, almost charred cherry, and the
palate is provided with fresh grilled damsons.

16

WHITE £6.95

Thouarsais, Francois Gigon 2002   FRANCE
100% Chenin Blanc of principled perkiness and
lemony ripeness. Has a faint saline undertone
(minerals) of real class. Individual but not quirky.

16

RED £8.50

Vin de Pays Catalan,   FRANCE
Domaine Ferrer Ribière, Cépage Carignan 2002
Vigorously juicy and rich but enticingly herby,
raspberry jammy, yet rich in herbs and tannins.

OTHER WINES 15.5 AND UNDER

15.5

ROSÉ £6.95

Château des Gavelles, Coteaux d'Aix 2002   FRANCE

15

RED £8.25

Côtes du Rhône-Villages, St-Gayan Rasteau 2001   FRANCE

WHITE £8.85

Enpreinte du Temps, Vin de Pays Catalan,   FRANCE
Domaine Ferrer-Ribière, Cépage Grenache 2001

RED £9.25
Neagles Rock Cabernet Sauvignon 2001 AUSTRALIA

RED £5.25
Vin de Pays Vaucluse 'Petit Caboche' 2003 FRANCE

14.5 RED £9.75
Vacqueyras Pascal Frères, FRANCE
Côtes du Rhône-Villages 1999

14 RED £12.95
Brezeme, Grand Chêne 2001 FRANCE

WHITE £7.95
Domaine de l'Idylle, Vieilles Vignes Cruet 2002 FRANCE

RED £12.75
Domaine de Richaume, Cuvée Tradition 2002 FRANCE

RED £12.50
Mas de la Rouvière Bandol 2000 FRANCE

RED £10.25
Neagles Rock Shiraz 2001 AUSTRALIA

INDEX OF WINE NAMES

D

Da Chardonnay, Limoux 2002, **15.5**, *Asda*, white, 27

Da Luca Primitivo Merlot 2002, **15**, *Budgens, Waitrose*, red, 64, 325

Danie de Wet Barrel Fermented Chardonnay 2002, **16.5**, *Somerfield*, white, 233

Danie de Wet Chardonnay 2002, **16**, *Asda*, white, 20

Danie de Wet Chardonnay 2003, **15.5**, *Asda*, white, 27

Danie de Wet Chardonnay Sur Lie 2004, **16**, *Somerfield*, white, 238

Danie de Wet Limestone Hill Chardonnay 2002, **16**, *Somerfield*, white, 238

D'Arenberg D'Arry's Original Shiraz/Grenache 2001, **17**, *Oddbins, Wine Society*, red, 146, 333

D'Arenberg Hermit Crab Marsanne/Viognier 2002, **17**, *Booths, Magnum*, white, 42, 216

D'Arenberg Hermit Crab Marsanne/Viognier 2003, **17**, *Booths, Oddbins*, white, 42, 142

D'Arenberg High Trellis Cabernet Sauvignon 2001, **16**, *Booths, Oddbins*, red, 48,155

D'Arenberg Last Ditch Viognier 2003, **17.5**, *Oddbins*, white, 141

D'Arenberg Money Spider Roussanne 2003, **17**, *Bibendum, Oddbins*, white, 146, 216

D'Arenberg Olive Grove Chardonnay 2003, **16**, *Oddbins*, white, 155

D'Arenberg The Bonsai Vine 2001, **16.5**, *Oddbins*, red, 148

D'Arenberg The Coppermine Road Cabernet Sauvignon 2001, **14**, *Oddbins*, red, 170

D'Arenberg The Footbolt Shiraz 2001, **15**, *Waitrose*, red, 322

D'Arenberg The Sticks and Stones 2002, **14.5**, *Oddbins*, red, 168

Darting Estate Pinot Noir 2003, **15.5**, *Marks & Spencer*, red, 121

Darting Estate Riesling Durkheimer Michelsberg 2003, **16.5**, *Marks & Spencer*, white, 114

Dashwood Sauvignon Blanc 2003, **16.5**, *Oddbins*, white, 149

De Brégille Champagne NV, **15**, *Morrison's*, white sparkling, 136

De Martino Legado Chardonnay Reserva 2002, **14**, *Virgin Wines*, white, 84

De Martino Legado Sauvignon Blanc Reserva 2003, **14.5**, *Virgin Wines*, white, 83

De Martino Single Vineyard Pinot Noir 2002, **14**, *Virgin Wines*, red, 84

De Saint Gall Blanc de Blancs NV, **15.5**, *Marks & Spencer*, white sparkling, 122

De Toren V 2001, **14**, *Oddbins*, red, 170

De Trafford Straw Wine 2002, **17**, *Bibendum, SWIG*, white dessert, 215

De Wetshof Estate Lesca Chardonnay 2003, **16.5**, *Majestic*, white, 95

De Wetshof Limestone Hill Chardonnay 2002, **16**, *Thresher*, white, 290

De Wetshof Limestone Hill Chardonnay, Danie de Wet 2003, **15.5**, *Majestic*, white, 106

Deakin Estate Colombard/Chardonnay 2002, **16**, *Oddbins*, white, 155

Deakin Estate Colombard/Chardonnay 2004, **14**, *Oddbins*, white, 170

Deakin Estate Merlot 2002, **15.5**, *Oddbins, Waitrose*, red, 164, 322

Deakin Estate Sauvignon Blanc 2003, **14**, *Budgens*, white, 65

Deakin Estate Sauvignon Blanc 2004, **15**, *Oddbins*, white, 165

Deakin Estate Shiraz 2002, **14**, *Budgens*, red, 65

Dehesa de Rubiales Prieto Picudo Crianza, Vino de la Tierra, Castilla y Leon 2001, **15.5**, *Waitrose*, red, 320

Delbeck Brut Heritage NV Champagne, **16**, *Oddbins*, white sparkling, 159

Delegat's Wine Estate Oyster Bay Pinot Noir 2002, **14**, *Majestic*, red, 110

Delicato Shiraz 2002, **15**, *Somerfield*, red, 245

Denis Marchais Vouvray 2003, **14.5**, *Asda*, white dessert, 34

The Derelict Vineyard Grenache 2002, **18**, *Bibendum*, red, 211

Devil's Rock Riesling 2002, **14**, *Somerfield*, white, 249

DFJ Touriga Nacional/Touriga Franca 2001, **16**, *Safeway, Tesco*, red, 179, 265

Di Notte Valpolicella Valpantena 2002, **15.5**, *Tesco*, red, 266

Fleurie Georges Duboeuf 2002, **14.5**,
 Thresher, red, 298
The Footbolt Shiraz 2001, **17**, *Wine Society*,
 red, 333
Forresters Petit Chenin 2003, **16.5**, *Asda*,
 white, 12
Forresters Petit Pinotage 2003, **15**, *Asda*,
 red, 29
Fouassier Sancerre Les Grand Groux 2003,
 16.5, *Somerfield*, white, 234
The Foundry Double Barrel 2001, **16**,
 Sainsbury's, red, 192
Franz Reh Auslese 2002, **16**, *Morrison's*,
 white, 130
French Connection Chardonnay/Viognier
 2001, **16**, *Thresher*, white, 291
French Connection Classic Côtes du Rhône
 Blanc, Vignobles du Peloux 2003, **16**,
 Tesco, white, 258–9
French Connection Classic Côtes du Rhône
 Rouge, Vignobles du Peloux 2003, **14.5**,
 Tesco, red, 274
French Connection Côtes du Rhône White
 2003, **14**, *Tesco*, white, 277
French Connection Marsanne/Roussanne,
 Vin de Pays d'Oc 2002, **14.5**, *Waitrose*,
 white, 326
Friuli Sauvignon 2003, **14.5**, *Marks &
 Spencer*, white, 124
Frostline Riesling 2003, **16**, *Oddbins*, white,
 156
Fruits of France Grenache, Vin de Pays
 d'Oc 2002, **15**, *Waitrose*, red, 323
The Futures Shiraz Peter Lehmann 2001,
 16.5, *Booths*, red, 45

G

Gaia Estate Notios, Peleponnese 2003, **15**,
 Oddbins, white, 165
Gaia Notios, Peleponnese 2003, **14**,
 Oddbins, red, 170
Gallo Coastal Cabernet Sauvignon 2001,
 16, *Asda*, red, 21
The Galvo Garage 2001, **16**, *Bibendum*,
 Magnum, red, 228
Garganega Terre in Fiore 2003, **16**,
 Morrison's, white, 131
Gaston de Veau Chardonnay, Vin de Pays
 d'Oc NV, **15.5**, *Marks & Spencer*, white, 122
Gaston de Veau Merlot, Vin de Pays d'Oc
 NV, **15.5**, *Marks & Spencer*, red, 122

Gaston d'Orléans Vouvray Demi Sec 2002,
 15.5, *Tesco*, white, 266
Gavi di Gavi Raccolto Tardivo, Villa Lanata
 2002, **16**, *Majestic*, white, 100
Gavi di Gavi Raccolto Tardivo, Villa Lanata
 2003, **16**, *Majestic*, white, 100
Gavi La Luciana 2003, **15.5**, *Waitrose*, white,
 320
Gerard Bertrand Coteaux du Languedoc,
 Les Terrasses Quartenaires 2001, **16**,
 Asda, red, 21
Gevrey-Chambertin Vieilles Vignes,
 Domaine Heresztyn 2001, **14**, *Waitrose*,
 red, 328
Gewürztztraminer Tradition Preiss Zimmer
 d'Alsace 2002, **15**, *Morrison's*, white, 137
Gewürztraminer Grand Cru, Sonnenglanz,
 Bott-Geyl 2001, **17**, *Majestic*, white, 92
Gewürztraminer Turckheim d'Alsace 2002,
 17, *Wine Society*, white, 333
Gigondas Cuvée Les Tentrelles Les
 Espalines 2001, **17**, *Waitrose*, red, 305
Glen Carlou Pinot Noir 2002, **14**, *Oddbins*,
 red, 170
Glen Ellen Chardonnay 2002, **15**, *Tesco*,
 white, 269
Glen Ellen Merlot 2002, **14**, *Tesco*, red, 277
Goats do Roam in Villages 2002, **16.5**,
 Majestic, Somerfield, Tesco, red, 95, 235,
 254
Goats do Roam in Villages 2003, **16.5**,
 Majestic, white, 95
Goats do Roam White 2003, **16**, *Somerfield*,
 white, 238
Goiya Glaan 2003, **14.5**, *Tesco*, red, 274
Goiya Kgeisje Sauvignon/Chardonnay
 2003, **15**, *Tesco*, white, 270
Gold Label Chardonnay, Domaine Virginie,
 Vin de Pays d'Oc 2003, **15.5**, *Marks &
 Spencer*, white, 122
Gold Label Reserve Cabernet Merlot,
 Domaine Virginie, Vin de Pays d'Oc
 2001, **16.5**, *Marks & Spencer*, red, 114
Gold Label Sauvignon Blanc, Domaine
 Virginie 2003, **16**, *Marks & Spencer*,
 white, 117
Goldwater Estate Wood's Hill Cabernet
 Sauvignon/Merlot 2000, **15**, *Everywine*,
 red, 83
Goldwater Estate Zell Chardonnay 2002,
 16.5, *Harrods*, white, 88

Heartland Limestone Coast Shiraz 2001, **14**, *Oddbins*, red, 170

Heartland Limestone Coast Shiraz 2002, **16.5**, *Oddbins*, red, 149

Hearty Red NV, **14**, *Asda*, red, 36

Heidsieck Dry Monopole NV, **14.5**, *Tesco*, white sparkling, 274

Henri Harlin Champagne Brut NV, **14**, *Oddbins*, white sparkling, 171

The Hermit Crab Marsanne/Viognier 2002, **17**, *Booths, Magnum*, white, 42, 216

Herrick Syrah, Vin de Pays d'Oc 2002, **14.5**, *Budgens*, red, 65

High Altitude Chardonnay/Viognier 2002, **15**, *Tesco*, white, 270

High Altitude Malbec/Shiraz 2002, **14.5**, *Tesco*, red, 274

Hill & Dale Chardonnay 2003, **16**, *Morrison's*, white, 131

Hogue Gewürztraminer 2003, **14**, *Asda*, white, 37

Hogue Pinot Grigio 2003, **14**, *Asda*, white, 36

Houdamond Pinotage 2000, **16**, *Marks & Spencer*, red, 118

Houghton HWB Dry White 2002, **14**, *Thresher*, white, 299

Hugel Riesling, Alsace 2001, **16**, *Oddbins*, white, 157

Hungarian Pinot Grigio 2003, **16**, *Marks & Spencer*, white, 118

I

Il Padrino Syrah 2002, **14**, *Somerfield*, red, 249

Ile La Forge Cabernet Sauvignon, Vin de Pays d'Oc 2003, **16.5**, *Aldi*, red, 3

Ile La Forge Merlot, Vin de Pays d'Oc 2003, **16**, *Aldi*, red, 4

Ile La Forge Syrah, Vin de Pays d'Oc 2003, **16.5**, *Aldi*, red, 3

Inti Fresh White 2003, **14**, *Thresher*, white, 299

Inti Soft Fruity Red 2003, **14**, *Thresher*, red, 299

Inurrieta Tinto Norte, Bodega Inurreta Navarra 2002, **14**, *Booths*, red, 55

Inycon Cabernet Sauvignon Rosé 2003, **16**, *Morrison's*, rosé, 132

Inycon Chardonnay 2002, **16.5**, *Morrison's*, *Tesco*, white, 129, 255

Inycon Chardonnay 2003, **16.5**, *Somerfield*, white, 234

Inycon Fiano Bianco di Sicilia 2003, **17**, *Booths*, white, 41

Inycon Merlot 2002, **16.5**, *Morrison's*, *Tesco*, red, 129, 254

Inycon Sangiovese 2002, **16**, *Thresher*, red, 291

Inycon Shiraz 2002, **15.5**, *Waitrose*, red, 321

Iona Sauvignon Blanc 2003, **16**, *Booths*, white, 48

Ironstone Vineyards Cabernet Franc 2000, **16.5**, *Waitrose*, red, 308

Ironstone Vineyards Petite Sirah 2002, **15**, *Asda*, red, 29

Irsai Oliver, Akos Kamocsay 2003, **16.5**, *Safeway*, white, 176

Isla Negra Cabernet Sauvignon 2003, **16.5**, *Tesco*, red, 255

J

J. & K. 'The Outsider' Shiraz 2002, **14**, *Oddbins*, red, 170

Jackson Estate Sauvignon Blanc 2003, **15.5**, *Booths*, white, 52

Jacob's Creek Cabernet Sauvignon 2001, **14.5**, *Tesco*, red, 274

Jacob's Creek Cabernet/Merlot 2002, **14.5**, *Sainsbury's*, red, 199

Jacob's Creek Chardonnay 2003, **14**, *Tesco*, white, 277

Jacob's Creek Chardonnay/Pinot Noir NV, **14**, *Asda*, white sparkling, 37

Jacob's Creek Dry Riesling 2002, **15.5**, *Asda*, *Tesco*, white, 27, 267

Jacob's Creek Grenache/Shiraz 2003, **14**, *Tesco*, red, 277

Jacob's Creek Merlot 2002, **15**, *Asda*, *Tesco*, red, 30, 273

Jacob's Creek Reserve Chardonnay 2002, **15**, *Asda*, white, 30

Jacob's Creek Reserve Shiraz 2001, **15**, *Asda*, red, 30

Jacob's Creek Sémillon Blanc 2003, **15**, *Tesco*, white, 270

Jacob's Creek Sémillon/Sauvignon/Chardonnay 2003, **15.5**, *Tesco*, white, 267

Jacob's Creek Shiraz 2001, **14**, *Tesco*, red, 277

Jacob's Creek Shiraz 2002, **14**, *Asda*, red, 37

Lusteau East India Rich Oloroso Sherry NV, **17.5**, *Waitrose*, fortified, 303

Lyeth Chardonnay 1997, **15.5**, *Majestic*, white, 106

M

'M3 Vineyard' Adelaide Hills Chardonnay, Shaw & Smith 2002, **16.5**, *Tesco*, white, 255

McLaren Vale/Padthaway Shiraz 2000, **16.5**, *Oddbins*, red, 150

Macon Villages 2003, **14**, *Marks & Spencer*, white, 125

Macon-Bussières 'Le Clos' Verget 2002, **15**, *Oddbins*, white, 166

Macon-Farges, Domaine Paul Talmard 2003, **16.5**, *Wine Society*, white, 334

McWilliams Hanwood Estate Chardonnay 2002, **16**, *Tesco*, white, 260

McWilliams Hanwood Estate Shiraz 2002, **14**, *Tesco*, red, 277

Mainzer Domherr Spätlese 2002, **14**, *Somerfield*, white, 250

Malambo Chenin Blanc/Chardonnay 2003, **15**, *Somerfield*, white, 246

Malambo VR Chardonnay/Chenin 2003, **16**, *Somerfield*, white, 240

Mandorla Syrah MGM, Mondol del Vino 2003, **16**, *Marks & Spencer*, red, 119

Mantrana Vivanco Crianza Rioja, Telma Rodrigues 2002, **15**, *Marks & Spencer*, red, 123

Manzanilla Sherry NV, **14**, *Marks & Spencer*, fortified, 126

Marabee Point Hunter Valley Chardonnay 2001, **14**, *Marks & Spencer*, white, 125

Marc Ducournau, Vin de Pays des Côtes de Gascogne 2003, **14**, *Majestic*, white, 110

Margaret River Chardonnay, Cullen Wines 2001, **16.5**, *Oddbins*, white, 151

Margaret River Sauvignon Blanc/Sémillon, Cullen Wines 2002, **16.5**, *Oddbins*, white, 151

Marqués de Casa Concha Chardonnay 2002, **16**, *Thresher*, white, 292

Marqués de Casa Concha Merlot 2002, **16.5**, *Sainsbury's*, red, 187

Marqués de Griñon Dominio de Valdepusa Syrah 2001, **17**, *Waitrose*, red, 306

Marqués de Griñon Reserva Rioja 1999, **16**, *Budgens, Tesco*, red, 63, 260

Marqués de Griñon Rioja 2001, **15.5**, *Tesco*, red, 267

Marqués de Griñon Rioja 2002, **16**, *Morrison's, Thresher*, red, 132, 292

Marquises Réserve Merlot/Grenache, Vin de Pays d'Oc 2003, **14**, *Sainsbury's*, red, 201

Marselan, Vin de Pays de l'Hérault, Domaine Coudoulet 2003, **16.5**, *Lay & Wheeler*, red, 219

Martin Estate Riesling 2003, **16**, *Marks & Spencer*, white, 118

Mas Collet Celler Capcanes Montsant 2001, **16.5**, *Booths, Waitrose*, red, 44, 309

Mas de Daumas Gassac Blanc 2003, **14**, *Booths*, white, 55

Mas de la Rouvière Bandol 2000, **14**, *Yapp Brothers*, red, 344

Masterpeace Cabernet/Shiraz/Grenache 2003, **15**, *Thresher*, red, 298

Masterpeace Rosé 2003, **14.5**, *Co-op*, rosé, 75

Matua Valley Malbec/Merlot 2002, **16**, *Thresher*, red, 292

Matua Valley North Island Chardonnay 2003, **15.5**, *Tesco*, white, 267

Matua Valley North Island Red 2002, **15**, *Tesco*, red, 270

Matua Valley Paretai Sauvignon Blanc 2003, **16**, *Asda*, white, 22

Matua Valley Sauvignon Blanc 2004, **14**, *Asda*, white, 37

Matua Valley Wines 'Innovator' Syrah 2002, **16**, *Sainsbury's*, red, 189

Maturana Blanco Viña Ijalba Rioja 2002, **16**, *Vintage Roots*, white, 81

Mayrah Estates Cabernet Sauvignon NV, **14-5**, *Aldi*, red, 7

Mayrah Estates Chardonnay NV, **15**, *Aldi*, white, 7

Mendoza Malbec Anubis 2002, **16**, *Waitrose*, red, 314

Menetou-Salon, Domaine Henry Pelle 2003, **15**, *Majestic*, white, 108

Mercier Champagne NV, **16**, *Tesco*, white sparkling, 259

Merloblu Castello di Luzzano, Vino da Tavola 2002, **15**, *Booths*, red, 53

Merlot 2003 (25cl), **14**, *Aldi*, red, 8

Merlot 2003, **17**, *Tesco*, red, 253

Merlot No. 2, Vin de Pays d'Oc 2002, **16**, *Somerfield*, red, 239

INDEX OF WINE NAMES

INDEX OF WINE NAMES

INDEX OF WINE NAMES

T

INDEX OF WINE NAMES

V

Vergelegen Chardonnay 2003, **17.5**, *Oddbins*, white, 141
Vidal Estate Chardonnay 2003, **15.5**, *Everywine*, white, 82
Vidal Estate Sauvignon Blanc 2003, **16**, *Thresher*, white, 295
Vidal Estate Syrah 2002, **16**, *Thresher*, red, 295
Vigna Ottieri Molise Rosso 2001, **16**, *Waitrose*, red, 317
Villa Jolanda Moscato d'Asti DOCG NV, **15**, *Tesco*, white sparkling, 272
Villa Malea Oaked Viura 2002, **15.5**, *Sainsbury's*, white, 196
Villa Maria Cellar Selection Chardonnay 2002, **16**, *Oddbins*, white, 161
Villa Maria Cellar Selection Merlot/Cabernet Sauvignon 2002, **16.5**, *Safeway*, red, 178
Villa Maria Cellar Selection Riesling 2002, **16**, *Oddbins*, white, 161
Villa Maria Cellar Selection Sauvignon Blanc 2003, **16**, *Oddbins*, white, 162
Villa Maria Cellar Selection Syrah 2002, **17**, *Oddbins*, red, 144
Villa Maria Clifford Bay Sauvignon Blanc 2003, **16.5**, *Oddbins*, white, 152
Villa Maria Keltern Vineyard Chardonnay 2002, **17**, *Oddbins*, white, 145
Villa Maria Pinot Noir 2002, **16.5**, *Thresher*, red, 288
Villa Maria Private Bin Chardonnay 2002, **17**, *Asda, Oddbins, Waitrose*, white, 11, 145, 306
Villa Maria Private Bin Chardonnay 2003, **17**, *Unwins*, white, 216
Villa Maria Private Bin Gewürztraminer 2003, **17**, *Asda*, white, 11
Villa Maria Private Bin Merlot/Cabernet Sauvignon 2002, **17**, *Oddbins*, red, 145
Villa Maria Private Bin Riesling 2003, **16**, *Budgens, Waitrose*, white, 63, 316
Villa Maria Private Bin Sauvignon Blanc 2003, **17**, *Oddbins, Somerfield, Tesco*, white, 145, 233, 253
Villa Maria Reserve Cabernet Sauvignon/ Merlot 2001, **17**, *Waitrose*, red, 306
Villa Maria Reserve Pinot Noir 2002, **16**, *Waitrose*, red, 316
Villa Maria Reserve Sauvignon Blanc 2003, **17**, *Sainsbury's, Thresher*, white, 185, 286
Villa Maria Riesling 2002, **16**, *Thresher*, white, 294

Villa Maria Sauvignon Blanc 2003, **16**, *Asda*, white, 24
Villa Maria Waikahu Vineyard Chardonnay 2002, **17**, *Oddbins*, white, 145
Villa Montes Sauvignon Blanc 2003, **16**, *Waitrose*, white, 316
Villa Montes Sauvignon Blanc Reserve 2003, **16**, *Sainsbury's*, white, 192
Villa Regia Douro 2000, **14**, *Asda*, red, 38
Villa Santa, J.P. Ramos, Alentejo 2001, **14.5**, *Waitrose*, red, 326
Villalta Amarone della Valpolicella DOCG 1998, **17**, *Marks & Spencer*, red, 113
Villiera Chenin Blanc 2003, **16**, *Wine Society*, white, 336
Vin de Pays Catalan, Domaine Ferrer Ribière, Cépage Carignan 2002, **16**, *Yapp Brothers*, red, 343
Vin de Pays des Côtes Catalanes, Vignerons Catalans NV, **14**, *Sainsbury's*, red, 202
Vin de Pays des Portes de la Mediterranée Chardonnay/Vermentino 2003, **15.5**, *Marks & Spencer*, white, 123
Vin de Pays des Portes de la Mediterranée Niellucciu Merlot, Corsica 2003, **14**, *Marks & Spencer*, red, 126
Vin de Pays du Gers, Plaimont 2003, **15**, *Marks & Spencer*, white, 124
Vin de Pays Vaucluse 'Petit Caboche' 2003, **15**, *Yapp Brothers*, red, 344
Vin Five Collection Sémillon/Sauvignon 2002, **16**, *Thresher*, white, 294
Vin Five Next Generation Cabernet/Merlot 2003, **15.5**, *Thresher*, red, 297
Vin Five Next Generation Chardonnay/ Sémillon 2003, **14.5**, *Thresher*, white, 299
Vin Five The Collection Cabernet Sauvignon 2001, **15.5**, *Thresher*, red, 297
Viña Albali Cabernet Sauvignon Reserva 1998, **15**, *Asda*, red, 31
Viña Albali Gran Reserva 1997, **16**, *Morrison's*, red, 135
Viña Albali Reserva, Bodegas Feliz Solis 1999, **15.5**, *Sainsbury's*, red, 196
Viña Alta Mar Cabernet Sauvignon/Merlot 2002, **17**, *Waitrose*, red, 306
Viña Casablanca Pinot Noir 2003, **16**, *Marks & Spencer*, red, 121
Viña Casablanca Sauvignon Blanc 2003, **16**, *Somerfield*, white, 242

INDEX OF WINE NAMES

Viña Herminia Excelsus Rioja 2001, **15.5**, *Oddbins*, red, 164

Viña La Rosa Don Reca Merlot 2002, **16**, *Waitrose*, red, 316

Viña Morande Merlot 2003, **16**, *Safeway*, red, 180

Viña Sardasol Merlot, Bodega Virgen Blanca 2002, **16**, *Booths*, red, 50

Vinedos Organicos Emiliana 'Novas' Cabernet Sauvignon/Merlot 2002, **16**, red, 82

Vinedos Organicos Emiliana 'Novas' Chardonnay 2003, **15**, *Vintage Roots*, white, 83

Viognier Fairview 2003, **17**, *Bennets Fine Wines, Hedley Wright Wine Merchants, Liberty Wines, Noel Young Wines*, white, 216–17

Vire Clesse 'La Verchère', Christopher Cordier 2003, **14.5**, *Majestic*, white, 109

Virgilius Viognier 2002, **18.5**, *Waitrose*, white, 303

Volnay Le Meurger 2000, **14.5**, *Morrison's*, red, 137

Vosne Romanée 1er Cru, Clos des Réas, Domaine Michel 1999, **14**, *Waitrose*, red, 330

Vouvray Domaine de la Pouvraie 2003, **14**, *Marks & Spencer*, white, 126

Vouvray Sec, Daniel Jarry 2001, **16.5**, *Yapp Brothers*, white, 340

Voyager Estate Chardonnay 2002, **14**, *Oddbins*, white, 172

Voyager Estate Shiraz 2002, **15**, *Oddbins*, red, 167

W

Waimea Estate Pinot Noir 2002, **14**, *Majestic*, red, 110

Waimea Estate Sauvignon Blanc 2003, **16**, *Majestic*, white, 104

Waipara West Chardonnay 2000, **15.5**, *Oddbins*, white, 164

Waitrose Cabernet Sauvignon/Merlot 2002, **16**, *Waitrose*, red, 317

Waitrose Côtes du Rhône 2003, **14**, *Waitrose*, red, 330

Waitrose Special Reserve Claret, Bordeaux Supérieur 2002, **15.5**, *Waitrose*, red, 322

Waitrose Touraine Sauvignon Blanc 2003, **15**, *Waitrose*, white, 325

Wakefield Gewürztraminer 2003, **14**, *Oddbins*, white, 172

Wakefield Promised Land Unwooded Chardonnay 2003, **15**, *Oddbins*, white, 167

Wakefield Riesling 2003, **14.5**, *Oddbins*, white, 169

Walkers Pass Cabernet Sauvignon 2002, **16**, *Oddbins*, red, 162

Walkers Pass Chardonnay 2001, **16**, *Oddbins*, white, 162

Warre's Bottle Matured LBV 1992, **16**, *Asda*, fortified, 24–5

Warre's Otima 10 Year Old Tawny Port NV, **15**, *Waitrose*, fortified, 325

Warwick Estate Chardonnay 2003, **16.5**, *Waitrose*, white, 310

Warwick Three Cape Ladies Pinotage 2001, **16**, *Wine Society*, red, 336

Weandre Stream Shiraz 2002, **14**, *Marks & Spencer*, red, 126

Weinert Carrascal 2001, **14**, *Waitrose*, red, 330

Wente Chardonnay, Livermore Valley 2001, **15**, *Waitrose*, white, 325

Western Australia Sauvignon Blanc 2003, **16**, *Somerfield*, white, 242

Western Australia Shiraz 2001, **16**, *Somerfield*, red, 242

Western Australia Unoaked Chardonnay 2003, **16**, *Somerfield*, white, 242

Wild Cat Catarratto, Sicilia 2003, **15.5**, *Waitrose*, white, 322

The William Wine 2000, **17.5**, *Bibendum*, red, 213

The Willows Sémillon 1996, **17.5**, *Thresher*, white, 283

Winemakers Series Sauvignon Blanc 2003, **16**, *Thresher*, white, 289

Winter Hill Red, Vin de Pays d'Oc 2003, **14**, *Somerfield*, red, 250

Winter Hill White, Vin de Pays d'Oc 2003, **14**, *Somerfield*, white, 250

Wirra Wirra Church Block Cabernet Sauvignon/Shiraz/Merlot 2002, **16**, *Sainsbury's*, red, 192

Wirra Wirra 'Mrs Wigley' Rosé 2003, **14**, *Oddbins, Sainsbury's*, rosé, 172, 200

Wirra Wirra Sexton's Acre Shiraz 2002, **15.5**, *Sainsbury's*, red, 196

Wither Hills Chardonnay 2001, **17.5**, *Oddbins*, white, 141–2

Wither Hills Pinot Noir 2002, **16**, *Ballantynes of Cowbridge, Booths,*